ENTANGLEMENTS

ENTANGLEMENTS
Weaving Our Futures

Simon Western

KARNAC
firing the mind

First published in 2026 by
Karnac Books Limited
62 Bucknell Road
Bicester
Oxfordshire OX26 2DS

British Library Cataloguing in Publication Data

A C.I.P. for this book is available from the British Library

ISBN: 978-1-80013-454-6 (paperback)
ISBN: 978-1-80013-456-0 (e-book)
ISBN: 978-1-80013-455-3 (PDF)

Typeset by vPrompt eServices Pvt Ltd, India

www.firingthemind.com

MIX
Paper | Supporting responsible forestry
FSC® C007915

Karnac Books is committed to a sustainable future for our business, our readers, and our planet. This book is made from Forest Stewardship Council® certified paper.

To Lily and Albert

Weaving beautiful futures

With gratitude

to Megan and Martyna for their work to produce this book

to Agata for sharing a beautiful journey with me

to colleagues & friends of the Eco-Leadership Institute
for the soul-work we do together

Contents

Part II
Rising tides

Part III
Weaving our futures

About the author

Dr Simon Western is Founder and CEO of the Eco-Leadership Institute, a global think tank advancing innovative leadership practices through action research, development programmes, and cultural change work. He works with diverse organisations including humanitarian NGOs, global manufacturing, finance and global technology companies. Simon's work integrates theory and practice, drawing on psychoanalysis, critical and anarchist theory, theology, and social movement perspectives. His work transcends the university, and is grounded in extensive lived experience (see Chapter 1). He is the author of influential books including *Leadership: A Critical Text* (SAGE, 3rd edn) and *Coaching and Mentoring: A Critical Text*. Formerly, Simon led the Masters in Organisational Consultancy at the Tavistock Clinic and was Director of Coaching at Lancaster University Management School. A past President of the International Society for the Psychoanalytic Study of Organizations (ISPSO), he has trained over 600 coaches worldwide in his research-based Eco-Leadership Coaching System. He writes regularly on Substack and hosts the popular Edgy Ideas podcast, both focusing on what it means to live a good life and to create the good society.

Introduction

Messy entanglements are at the heart of human relationships, and our social and cultural lives are entangled with our non-human companions on this planet. There is an interdependence that has long been ignored or marginalised. This book aims to explore these entanglements, not with the aim to untangle or simplify, but to add something not previously considered, to provoke thinking that lies outside our normal way of seeing a situation. We live in a moment in time where we share a broad societal predicament. Our challenge is how to transition away from a twentieth-century modernist way of being, where a good society is perceived as being ordered, stable, hierarchical, and boundaried. The modernist way of being is underpinned by a faith in science, rationality, and hierarchy alongside excessive individualism and constant 'progress' driven by growth that is based on extractive economics. This has led to the environmental crisis and societal inequities that undermine social solidarity.

We have entered a new era, the Precarious-Interdependent Age (P-I Age).[1] The P-I Age reflects that polycrisis and precariousness have become the norm. Our interdependences on each other, on our multispecies companions, and on planet Earth itself have become unsettlingly obvious. The P-I Age undoes the status quo, and our task now is to learn how to live well in a world of environmental, technological, and social disruption. How do we live well in an unstable and increasingly entangled, fluid, interconnected society? Modern mindsets extract humans from the environment, creating a social imaginary that separates culture and nature. Nature became an object to exploit, a resource to use for power and pleasure.

To make the transition from modernity to the P-I Age means to relate differently to our lived-in worlds. Humans belong to a dynamic and fragile ecosystem, a web of life made up of people, technology, and the natural environment. There are no separate parts, only interconnections and interdependencies. This transition ignites tensions between those who recognise our independencies, who press for a collaborative engagement, and those in retreat, building walls in our minds based on fear.

The purpose of the book is to support the transition towards a dynamic and collaborative existence. One that embraces our entangled, lived-in worlds and discovers a richness within them. Drawing on psychoanalysis, social critique, and personal experience, the book observes what moves beneath the surface. The aim is to glimpse insights beyond the obvious, which may open us to engage with our entangled lives in more creative and dynamic ways.

The book weaves together social threads harvested from a series of short essays written over the past seven years. These stand-alone essays were written to search for diverse meanings, to take ethical stances, to identify unconscious dynamics lurking within our social imaginations, and to make connections between deep personal experience and the political and social worlds. Each essay was written at the time a particular event or cultural theme took place, bringing the book immediacy and aliveness.

Each event and theme is explored through the lens of looking awry. As a movie director moves and changes the angle of filming to reveal a new reality, we too change our gaze, using a critical and curious lens in order to see something fresh that adds a new dimension to our understanding. This work is done with a psychoanalytic sensibility to gain access to the unconscious and emotional content of social events and themes. I take a meta-position, to gain insights into how events and themes have symbolic and signifying meanings that get lost in day-to-day responses. I also bring a micro-position, a personal and subjective perspective. In my work as a coach and therapist, I work with the concept of the 'self-as-an-instrument', where my clients and I use our emotions, thoughts, and body experiences as data that tells us something about the wider system we are part of. Bringing our deepest human experience to the work of building a good society is at the heart of this book. There are three parts:

Part I: Dislocating events. These chapters address powerful events that have had a dislocating impact on society. I begin with the Covid pandemic that shook the world and move to the invasion of Ukraine and the conflict in Israel and Palestine. These two wars provoked me to question where do I/we stand and what can I/we say in the face of such horror and violence. I then reflect on the death of Queen Elizabeth II, which marked a significant moment and raised questions about institutions and power. This theme continues in a different way, exploring the rise of populism through the lens of Brexit and Donald Trump's first presidency.

Part II: Rising tides. The chapters in Part II are not about specific events but about social themes that have gained prominence and reveal the shifting sands of our cultural landscapes. Taken-for-granted norms are challenged, such as how therapy culture and positive thinking have become pervasive in westernised culture. They address dominant social themes that spoke directly to my experience. The themes I have chosen are those that left me troubled, because of the way they polarise, entrap, and influence us. The environmental emergency, political culture wars, diversity, therapy culture, the positivity trap, and the digital age all create rising tides of emotions and tensions. I finish this section with three chapters on re-enchantment. These focus on making personal soul connections with everyday living and creating a link to Part III.

Part III: Weaving our futures. This section finishes the book with two chapters: one offering a meta-view of the new paradigm we face, which I call the Precarious-Interdependent Age. The final chapter weaves together some of the themes that occur throughout the book and presents thoughts on our futures.

This book was born from the entanglements that emerged when these singular essays were first looked at as a collective. Written as stand-alone polemic commentaries on particular events as they happened, a retrospective overview reading them collectively revealed interconnected and entangled threads. These threads, when woven together, create patterns that offer insights into how we might weave together better futures.

CHAPTER 1

What authored the author?

We are all formed by our experience, and every book is autobiographical in some way. This first chapter takes a meandering look at my work story, making connections between a lived experience and the thinking behind the writing. By making transparent the entanglements that inform our thinking, helps the reader locate themselves in relation to the events and themes discussed.

'We work in organisations, organisations work in us'

This chapter reflects on the long, diverse, and enriching work journey that I have travelled. However, it is more than a work biography; it is an emotional experience shared. Work is a huge part of our lives, and yet the organisations, sectors, places, and experiences we have at work are rarely reflected from a perspective of how they impact and influence us. How does belonging to a certain organisation and taking a particular role influence your thinking and being?

There are many stories we can tell of ourselves, and I have told my own story many times over, both in writing and in person to diverse groups. More than other aspects of my teaching, this story stirs something powerful in people, which surprised me at first, but now I realise this is the point. It's not about me, this story is like a mirror, it reflects something back to the reader. What it triggers, stirs, and sparks in you is important, it asks you the question, 'What authored you'?

You can't step into the same river twice—Heraclitus

Each time I tell this story to a live audience, I am surprised as the story changes, the saying 'You can't step into the same river twice' captures my experience. My unconscious speaks through me, and I forget something and leave it out, or I emphasise something strongly that I don't usually pay attention to, or I might get emotional at a particular part that awakens me. This story has its own way of telling itself, and as I reread it, the story plays games with me, teaching me something new about my past life and also about my current self. I notice new things, I feel powerful emotions, I make new connections between past and present and what has shaped my thinking.

My story

This short biographical narrative is my personal experience of 'locating myself' to make connections between my experience of work, myself, and wider society.

I was born on a council estate (public housing) in Bristol, UK. My upwardly mobile parents bought their own house, my mother was a teacher, my father a postman, and I was the third child of four boys. My beautiful brother Steven died of leukaemia aged seven; I was five years old. I attended a tough all-boys working-class school that offered little education, and a lot of sport. I loved rugby but the rest of school seemed like a survival programme. I left school with few qualifications and began work at the age of seventeen as an office boy in a paper-bag-making factory. This was a difficult transition, from being a playful schoolboy, a child, into a very harsh adult work environment. In the factory, I witnessed Taylor's 'scientific management' techniques on production lines. Unionised labour, clocking in and out, women spending all day packing paper bags which tumbled off loud, clattering machines, men labouring to keep the machines going twenty-four hours a day, feeding them with heavy rolls of paper and ink: this mundane work (now exported to Asia) was brutalising. I remember hardened men and women drawing on fierce humour to cope. The office boy before me had left, terrorised by the women who teased us mercilessly. Factory work was manual labour; the employer bought the labourer's time and body. Emotions and thinking were to be left at home. You came to work to earn money, not to be passionate or to develop yourself. We were human cogs in the organisational machine.

The factory had a lasting impact on me and how I regard people at work. In my writings, consultancy, and teaching, I critique human resources and management techniques that instrumentalise employees to become 'working machines'. We are human beings, not objects or resources. In today's digital world, I see the dangers where algorithmic management rules our lives. Workers are under constant surveillance; their performance is digitally measured, we are asked to measure every service we receive and to wear 'superego technologies' that tell us we have to move, count every step, and monitor our sleep. We are in danger of internalising the dystopian factory ideology into our workplace cultures and into our bodies and minds.

Encouraged by a friend who I played rugby with to apply for nursing, I left the factory at the age of eighteen to train as a general nurse. I hadn't ever considered nursing as a career but was happy to leave the factory, and 'working with people' seemed like a good idea. It also surprised my friends; for a start, men aren't nurses … are they?

Embodied work

Nurses work intimately with the physical body, probably more so than any other profession. Touching and cleaning, injecting, lifting and turning, administering drugs, dressing wounds, and evacuating bowels. The nurse works with the inside and outside of the body, and with the living and the dying body. 'Laying a patient out' is the phrase used in nursing to clean and dress a patient who has died. I found this process deeply moving, especially when I had nursed the patient with care, and formed an attachment to them and their family.

Compassionate and loving caring of a dead body seemed to me to be a continuation of the nursing care and what the patient and the relatives deserved. I noticed that at some stage in the 'laying out' work, I could almost physically witness the soul leaving the body. I was an atheist at this time, so this experience surprised me and also comforted me. Retrospectively, I see the link between the loss of my brother Steven and my work as a nurse. I had no conscious plan to be a nurse, but I believe my unconscious guided me into nursing as a way of reparation, to try to make good the loss I had experienced, and to make sense of death, which had been with me since childhood.

Working with the injured, sick, and dying made me acutely aware of the existential issues of mortality and also how our emotions, thinking, and identities are embodied. I saw and experienced many things unusual for an eighteen to twenty-one year old. I worked in the emergency department, encountering broken bodies and young men dying in front of me after a motorcycle accident. I spent time in surgery, witnessing amputations and brain surgery, and was intrigued by the rituals, rhythm, and discipline of the surgical process. My favourite work was nursing the elderly, dying, and stroke patients because it enabled me to make deeper connections and relationships with my patients.

I worked long nursing shifts, experiencing the primitive human emotions of fear and anxiety when facing mortal threats. Later, when I worked in offices and universities, I reflected on how the body is largely ignored.

The hospital leadership context was a rigid matriarchal nursing system that had echoes of the military—a commander in chief (the matron) with uniforms denoting rank, strict authority, and no first names on the ward. The hospital organisation was structured as a social defence against facing the emotional pain of working with illness and death.[2] Nurses weren't encouraged to talk about their feelings, and many patients were cared for physically but not emotionally. After working with a traumatic death, no counselling was offered, just an early coffee break and gallows humour in the bar after work.

Space invaders

I loved the work, made great friends, and learned huge amounts about life and myself, but I struggled in this constraining institutional culture. Nursing leadership was predominantly female, from ward sister to hospital matron, in opposition to the medical leadership, which was predominantly male. This dual leadership created a symbolic structure replicating a 'hetero-normative' parental structure—the father leading with technical expertise and the mother being the carer.[3] This raised my awareness of gender issues, power, responsibility, and pay disparity. I was a male on the female team; there were two males in a class of thirty nurses.

Often in life, I have found myself in the position of experiencing being 'othered' by class or gender, and it has really helped me empathise with others who are marginalised through ethnicity, age, class, gender, or disability. At times, I was just one of the gang, feeling accepted and a great sense of belonging. At other times, I was fetishised and objectified as 'an exotic and sought-after object' on the one hand and as a displaced object who was a 'space invader'[4] on the other. I was treated as a lifting machine, as a strong male. I was called to lift heavy patients across the hospital. I was not allowed to work on women's wards, and was once sexually harassed by a ward sister who asked me to sit on her knee when giving me my student report. I refused, got a negative report, and nearly left the profession.

Dependency cultures

Within this archetypal parental leadership model, Daddy Doctor and Mummy Nurse, the patients were symbolically childlike in their dependency. When a patient is facing major surgery or death, the contemporary rhetorics of individual choice and our desire to be in control are confronted by Freud's 'reality principle'. Sometimes, we have to accept our dependency on others. For some patients, the dependency culture was wholly appropriate, enabling them to give up their autonomy to enable the surgeon's knife to be wielded and to be bed-bathed, toileted, and cared for like an infant. For others in rehabilitation, the dependency culture was completely wrong and hindered their attempts to regain autonomy and make decisions about their treatment and care.

Dependency cultures have a place. In education, for example, learning requires us to enter a state of 'not knowing', for if we already know, we cannot learn something new, and therefore a level of dependency is required in order to learn.[5] In the hospital, this dependency culture unfortunately affected the staff as well as patients and became very damaging, undermining innovation and decision making. Since this time, I have been alert and sensitive when I experience too much hierarchy, dependency, and a lack of autonomy in the workplace.

During this period, I was a talented rugby player, playing at a senior level and the captain of my local club, experiencing leadership at an early age. Rugby provided me with the opportunity to learn motivational skills and self-discipline and to experience teamwork. The rugby club was probably the most honest and egalitarian community I have ever participated in. Our club consisted of lawyers, entrepreneurs, business leaders, the unemployed, and ex-convicts, and all were treated with respect. Anybody pulling ego or rank over another was teased mercilessly; it was a levelling experience. We ran the club as a social enterprise, and the ethos was interdependency. Leadership, teamwork, having the courage to have a go, and being able to laugh at myself were lessons I took from leading the rugby club.

While doing general nursing, I became fascinated by the human condition. After my student training, I went travelling and returned to work in a geriatric hospital, where I was in charge of an acute female ward for a year. This was quite a responsibility for a twenty-one year old, managing a feisty team of diverse nurses and assistants, dealing with relatives often facing the loss of their parents and loved ones, and with patients and their very varied mental and physical conditions. I loved this leadership role and learnt buckets. Working with the aged was also a privilege and enlightening: the humour, wisdom, and resilience I witnessed was moving. I have a real concern about the age apartheid happening in our society, where young and old rarely meet, and the role of our elders is diminished in a society that yearns to be forever young.

The asylum

I left to train as a psychiatric nurse and found freedom in a more relaxed, uniform-free setting, and I became totally engaged in human psychology, discovering a lifelong passion for psychotherapy and the 'talking cure'. I worked with the severely mentally ill, obsessive, neurotic, depressed, bipolar, schizophrenic, and psychotic patients in one of the Victorian-built asylums set on the outskirts of cities, which Goffman described as a 'Total Institution'.[6] The asylum, or mental hospital, was a huge grey building, set in large grounds behind intimidating walls, which separated the sane world from the mad world. This hard boundary between sanity and madness was, of course, a false boundary and served only to hide distress in the community, to stigmatise, and, at times, to imprison vulnerable people for life.

I witnessed electro-convulsive therapy and worked on wards where seventy men slept in long dormitories without curtains or any privacy. Behaviourist approaches such as 'token economy' were used with the institutionalised patients. Patients received tokens that were exchanged for cigarettes to reinforce good behaviours, for example, for getting out of bed, and they had tokens taken away for 'bad behaviour'. Institutionalisation had an impact on both staff and patients: it undermines humanity and autonomy, creating conformist behaviour and thinking. This experience of the asylum and the totalising institution has stayed with me. I am very sensitive to conformist cultures in the workplace or in fundamentalist churches for example, where I get a physical anxiety reaction when I confront institutionalisation.

The asylum had two aspects; first, for some, it did provide 'asylum', that is, a container, a safe and caring space, a refuge from the terrors of the world for those suffering severe mental trauma. There were suffering aspects to the asylum, but there was also kindness, warmth, and humour shared by patients and the whole mix of staff that became a community, particularly in some wards where compassionate leadership was quite moving. In one ward, the charge nurse created an allotment and had chickens on the grounds, and the long-term patients found great joy in being responsible for their upkeep. On the other hand, it was an oppressive and totalising space, and, in certain wards, a dehumanising space.

When working in corporations and large public sector organisations I am often reminded of the asylum, seeing a refined version of the token economy and institutional culture control take place but in a more benign, hidden form. Human beings are not human resources, and yet HR teams flourish. Managers and trainers use transactional leadership, 'carrot and stick' to change behaviour, measure behavioural change, and reward performance goals, and I wonder about the humanity of their methods. Transformational leaders draw on culture control to create peer and self-surveillance where we police each other and ourselves, working long hours, never free from mobile technologies that chain us to the workplace.

Later, when an organisational consultant working in a global bank, I witnessed institutionalisation in a different way. Conformist employees, all wearing dark-suited uniforms, sitting in rows upon rows in vast open-plan glass offices, staring at screens, eating again in rows in the canteen. And I experienced a different version of a modern-day asylum. Conformist language and thinking prevailed, and although the rhetoric promoted diversity, in reality, peer and self-surveillance and culture control meant that any real difference was eliminated.

My body will never forget this formative experience in the asylum, which alerted me to ethics and the power of institutionalisation. The humanising of organisations has become one of my passions, and I ask myself when working, 'Does this leadership stance enhance or diminish humanity?' Another important lesson from psychiatric nursing was to discover how thin and blurred the line is between madness and sanity, and this has helped me work with the undiagnosed pathology that occurs in all workplaces. I also realised that insanity and madness are both biological and social phenomena. At different times in history and in different cultures, madness is defined differently, particularly for disempowered groups; for example, I met a woman who had suffered from postnatal depression in the 1950s and had never left the asylum.

I also learned counselling skills, group facilitation skills, and, most importantly, how to manage my own and others' anxiety when facing dangerous and psychotic disturbances and distress. Containing my own anxiety and managing to contain the anxiety of others has been a great transferable lesson for me and is a very important and underrated leadership capability.

Therapeutic community

At the age of twenty-three, I worked in a regional residential facility for emotionally disturbed adolescents. This was run as a therapeutic community with the philosophy to devolve leadership for running the community as much as possible to the young people themselves, empowering them to find their voices and talents, to be really valued, and to learn how to take responsibility for themselves and others in a safe environment. Within a year, I was promoted to charge nurse, often running the community, which was a huge amount of responsibility at a young age, working with young people who had serious emotional and psychological problems such as anorexia, who were suicidal, and who had been abused.

Working closely with the staff team, we radicalised the centre to make it more self-reliant. After a long battle with the hospital authorities, we cancelled the daily meal delivery and received a budget to become fully self-catering. Planning and preparing meals became a central learning feature of the centre, and the joys of sharing communal meals prepared with love was the best therapy in the world! The medical input was marginalised, removing the dependency culture and the stigma of being given a medical diagnosis and treated as a sick patient. This was the most therapeutic environment I have experienced, and I learnt two key lessons here. First, my anarchic idealism that if you remove leadership, rules, and status, then power will disappear, and a pure egalitarian democracy will flourish; this idea was crushed. Power and status always exist, however much you democratise. The most important lesson was to make power and status more transparent in order to mediate and negotiate more fairly. In today's organisations, the fad of creating self-managed or leaderless teams can learn a lot from this reflection. Second, devolving power and decision making responsibly and enabling leadership potential to emerge within safe boundaries works wonderfully. Our so-called 'disturbed' young people were able to run the centre, making important decisions together while working on their emotional selves at the same time. They helped us to interview and appoint new staff, took control of their budget, the cooking, and their own destinies, and supported their peers with great skill and empathy.

This experimental community, set in the NHS, marginalised the medical model and gave power back to the client group. I am indebted to this intense learning experience and to Mike Broughton (now deceased), an excellent leader and the first workplace leader to see my leadership potential beyond my own realisation. He trusted me and promoted me to a leadership position against the wishes of the hierarchy above him, who considered me too young and inexperienced. At this community, I also trained in group psychotherapy and drama and art therapy: working with these creative therapies opened up new worlds for us all.

Single parent

In my mid-twenties, I spent nearly four years as a single parent (co-parenting my son Fynn with his mother, who lived separately and worked). I lived on welfare payments and again found myself challenging gender stereotypes, wandering into mother and toddler groups and struggling with the responses I received. Sometimes, I was mothered (which I rejected), and other times, I was considered a space invader and a threat to the group norm, an external male body to be ejected. However, I loved the freedom of being a home parent, each day being thrown back to my own resources to make ends meet and creating each day with my beautiful and delightful son, Fynn. I was living on the margins in terms of money and found that living without the identity and social respect work brings to be a real challenge. 'What do you do?' This familiar question made me realise the importance society gives to work identities and how devalued home parents and unemployed people are made to feel.

I was nevertheless immensely happy as a father, making fires, stories, and pancakes; this was a time of poverty in financial terms, but of wealth in time and adventures!

Family therapy

On returning to work, I spent ten years training and working as a family therapist and psychotherapist with the urban underclass in Liverpool, a post-industrial city that was economically impoverished. I was a clinical manager of a community-based, multi-professional healthcare team. I loved family therapy and took the opportunity to be very creative in therapy sessions. In family therapy, you quickly discover (a) that power is not where you (or the family) think it is, (b) how systems impact individuals, and (c) how relational patterns can completely entrap us, even if we really want to change. This learning has had a huge influence on my leadership and coaching work and has helped me to understand team dynamics. Today, I work with teams and coach leaders, always remembering that the presenting challenge is often not the challenge to solve but a symptom of a more systemic issue.

In my thirties, I returned to education and studied for a master's in counselling and psychotherapy at Keele University. It was my first time at university, and I felt exposed and overwhelmed by the academic language, rituals, and culture, which made me feel inadequate and like an imposter (not having A-levels or a bachelor's degree). I adjusted over the year, found great joy in learning, and excelled in my studies, gaining a distinction. My thesis was written on 'Puppets, masks, and psychotherapy', relating to my interest in how 'therapy' has storytelling and cross-cultural roots.

Later, I studied for another master's degree in psychoanalytic approaches to organisational consultancy at the internationally renowned Tavistock Centre. My interest was to understand why organisational change was so resisted and to learn how to promote collaborative working across health, education, and social services in order to better serve families. Developing an understanding of the unconscious processes that underpin organisational culture was a huge learning experience for me, which I have applied in my work ever since.

I finally left the NHS, feeling 'burnt out' from the pressure of working with disturbed families and suicidal teenagers in an under-resourced provision. I was frustrated by a leadership dominated by medical power, which allowed little room for constructive dissent and change, particularly if it came from a nurse. This hierarchical medical model provided the wrong leadership, wrong culture, and wrong treatment for these young people and their families. For the most part, my clients were not ill but suffered from the emotional and social strains of living in a post-industrial society undermined by poverty, drugs, crime, and unemployment. They required therapeutic and emotional support, more resources, and structural-political change rather than a medical diagnosis, labels, and medicines. My attempts with talented and committed colleagues to make changes were partly successful, and more collaborative work now takes place. However, the NHS has an institutional leadership culture that allows little room for innovation or creativity, and it was time for me to break out of this constraint.

Led by the spirit: Quakers and social movements

Another experience which has informed my understanding of leadership and organisational culture is my religious affiliation. I became a Quaker (Religious Society of Friends) in my mid-thirties, which contrasted with the secular society all around me. Quakers have an unusual organisational structure without formal leadership. They do not appoint church ministers but believe in a 'priesthood of all believers', abolishing *not* the idea of priests but abolishing the laity. The business meetings are run (as they have been for 350 years) by spiritual consensus. Local, regional, and national gatherings, which can mean up to 1,000 Quakers, decide on Quaker 'policy' (www.quaker.org.uk). Quakers don't vote but wait in silence until spiritual consensus is agreed, which means individuals often have to balance personal convictions with the collective. This decentres the ego and places the spiritual collective above individual desire. Quaker meetings are structured around the idea of equality. Sitting in a circle, in silence, anyone moved to speak can 'minister' to those present. The Quaker history was an important part of my PhD research, leading me to examine how their informal leadership and organisation has accommodated social change over the centuries, while still holding onto the core culture and structures.

More recently, I joined the Church of Ireland and have dual membership of Quaker and Anglican communities, appreciating both traditions and their very different leadership and organisational structures.

My experience of leadership has been further informed by engaging with social movements and friends who are activists in trade unions, feminist, anarchist, and green movements. This informed my research on autonomist leadership[7] and my thinking about eco-leadership.[8] I work with the idea that the human spirit is important in leadership and organisations, whether you have a defined faith or not.

In the past few years, I have worked with Church of England leaders and visited Rome to support a Jesuit-led leadership programme, delivered across the Catholic church. The aim is to support Pope Francis's initiative of a synodal Church, that is, a Church that changes from the bottom up and engages with the marginalised, youth, Indigenous, and women to have a greater role in leading the Church. Engaging with the spirit and soul at work has become important for me, and I recognise the disenchantment and search for meaning and purpose in the secular world of work. In September 2024 I led the Eco-Leadership Institute's first 'Soul at Work' event in a convent in Spain. This brought an international group of seekers together, to reflect on what it means to bring our souls to work, and develop soulful workplaces.

Academia

Frustrated and burnt out by the intense therapeutic work and the bureaucratic institutionalisation of the NHS, I decided to seek new pastures. I wanted to deepen my understanding of leadership and organisations and also look beyond the public sector and experience the private sector to see what I could learn. I was accepted to undertake a PhD in leadership at Lancaster University Management School and quickly found full-time employment at the university working in executive education. Academia is underpinned by a dependency culture that replicates educational models of 'teacher–student' dynamics and tends towards bureaucratic managerialism. These days, the university also embraces market capitalism and is financially driven, to the dismay of many on the faculty. Lancaster was a leading research university with some brilliant faculty members that took me to new levels of learning. What was very impressive was the cross-disciplinary learning, and I found myself studying sociology, theology, environmentalism, and critical organisational studies underpinned by philosophy.

I worked in the senior leadership department and suddenly found myself working internationally with senior corporate leaders, designing experiential leadership development and coaching interventions. The cultural difference and the language of the corporate world was a huge learning curve for me. A big adjustment took place from working with the poor, disempowered, and disturbed to working with the rich, successful, and powerful. My saving grace was the capacity I had developed to 'think in the face of anxiety', drawing on my past experiences, which enabled me to work in depth with these powerful executives.

I was later appointed director of coaching at Lancaster, where I established a critical approach to coaching, drawing heavily on psychoanalytic and systems thinking. I designed and ran a new postgraduate coaching course. After ten years of executive education, I left the university to work as an organisational consultant and became director of the Tavistock Clinic's master's degree in organisational consultancy (where I was previously a student) for a short period.

I left the Tavistock following a personal family tragedy and later chose to work independently, setting up a new coaching and consulting company specialising in eco-leadership.

Entrepreneur

I founded the Eco-Leadership Institute to develop eco-leadership theories and to develop eco-leadership as a practice. The institute runs coaching and leadership training courses, consulting programmes with organisations, and offers eco-leadership development. The institute is also home to a dynamic community of practice and a think tank that continually researches, develops, and publishes ideas. Our purpose is to support leaders to act in good faith to create the good society, adapting to the climate crisis and the technological and social disruptions in our Precarious-Interdependent world.

Being an entrepreneur is interesting. The shift from being a sole trader to a start-up company and thinking about marketing, branding, and building a team is fascinating and creative. My work continues to draw on the past experiences I have shared (and many more I have not shared). I remain intrigued by psychoanalysis and the unconscious at work, and, in 2017, I was elected president of ISPSO, the International Society for the Psychoanalytic Study of Organizations. Additionally, the Eco-Leadership Institute partnered with Save the Children and the Humanitarian Leadership Academy for two years to support new leadership in the humanitarian sector. This work takes me full circle in many ways, bringing a life's work with people back to the fundamentals of how to create a more humane and compassionate world.

Reflections

I host a podcast called Edgy Ideas, which explores 'what it means to live a good life and create a good society', which I guess is a nice summary of the purpose of my life's work.

A journey: Body, mind, individual, small group, organisation, society, environment

My journey highlights a movement from working with the body in the factory and as a general nurse to working with the mind as a psychiatric nurse and therapist. Working deeply with individuals has always been central to my work, particularly with patients in nursing and later in coaching and therapy. Family therapy and taking a clinical team leadership role moved my work into small groups; whether working with a family or work team, small groups are a vital part of our social, emotional, and psychological lives, which are always relational. From small group work, I moved to study organisational systems and institutions in my PhD and as an organisational consultant and in executive education working with leadership development and organisational culture change. Institutions and organisations have a big influence on the individual and wider society and, like small groups, are important nodes in the web of life we weave. Currently, I write and host a podcast on psychosocial and critical perspectives on wider society, and the Eco-Leadership Institute is engaged in environmental concerns.

Our lives are intersections and entanglements across all these dimensions: the body, mind, individual, team, organisation, social, and environmental; yet so often, these are separated and categorised. My journey of work tells a story of integration and holism, a journey that has been so very rich and continues to feed my imagination.

Part I

Dislocating events

Original artwork, hand-drawn by Martyna Adamska

Introduction to Part I

Part I presents a series of chapters written about events that have been dislocating for many of us. Unexpected war in Europe, a global pandemic, Trump as president of the USA, Brexit, the death of the longest-serving monarch, and the catastrophe of the Israel–Palestine conflict have shaken all sense of post-war stability and optimism previously held. We find ourselves dislocated, shaken, and wondering what will come next. These essays bring a particular lens to each situation. They do not attempt to offer any solutions but offer fragments of insights, hoping to promote fresh thinking. They are divided into four subsections: Covid entanglements, war, monarchy, and populist politics.

The first two chapters offer different perspectives on the worldwide pandemic caused by Covid-19. The first is a micro-perspective, where profound personal insights are gained from my experience of lockdown. The second is a meta-perspective reflecting on how Covid-19 revealed new truths and announced a new Precarious-Interdependent Age.

The next section engages with two wars that have had a huge impact on those suffering within them and on wider geopolitical dynamics. At the time of writing, both are ongoing with no sign of an end. These chapters explore what our moral and ethical stance should be in the face of such violence. My family hosted two young Ukrainian women (sisters) during the first year of the war, and we witnessed the anxiety and fear and how families are separated first hand. My work with Save the Children UK and the Humanitarian Leadership Academy took me to Poland to work with Ukrainian and Polish non-governmental organisation (NGO) leaders, supporting their work. Being close to the Ukrainian war, then seeing the pain of Jewish colleagues and friends after the Hamas attack, and having personal relationships with humanitarian colleagues struggling to help those in Gaza suffering terrible violence, brings these 'distant' traumas to life.

The 'meaning of monarchy' chapter, written soon after the death of Queen Elizabeth II, explores the relationship between monarchy and establishment, what it means to be a citizen and/or a subject and between dependency and interdependency. Part I finishes with two chapters, one on Brexit and the other on the 'meaning of Trump': they explore the rise of populism in politics, which is having a profound sociopolitical impact across the globe.

CHAPTER 2

Lockdown: In praise of the thermos flask

This essay was written at the height of government lockdowns that were taking place across Europe and the world. These unprecedented restrictions impacted our liberty to travel, to leave the house, go to school and work, meet others, and to shop, which had major consequences. Yet these limitations also opened up new possibilities that are shared in this chapter.

Introduction

The pandemic unleashed many unforeseen consequences. Perhaps the biggest were the lockdowns that took place at an unprecedented scale. In April 2020, half of humanity was locked down in more than ninety countries.[9] Lockdowns were legal requirements by the state ordering its citizens to either stay at home or travel very limited distances with the intention of reducing the spread of the virus. Lockdowns were contentious for some, but the fear of death and severe illness meant that most people agreed with their government's attempts to 'flatten the curve' to reduce the spreading of the Covid virus, although some lockdowns were more extreme than others. Lockdowns had other impacts alongside the effects of the pandemic. There were positive impacts in relation to lowering crime figures and reducing air pollution, and negative impacts on businesses, the economy, children's education, and the mental well-being of many.

I live in Galway, Ireland, where we had some of the longest and most restrictive lockdowns in Europe. A five-kilometre limit on travel was established and meeting people indoors was banned.[10] My social and work life was disrupted. My trips to the café for socialisation were banned, and I found myself returning to an old friend for comfort, 'the thermos flask', which then triggered a stream of associations captured below.

Lockdown: In praise of the thermos flask

Wrapping small cold fingers around a hot cup filled with home-made vegetable soup is my earliest recollection of the thermos flask. My family visited Blackpool each October on our half-term break to visit my grandmother. Sat with my family huddled together on a windswept beach, the sweet aroma escaped from the large green flask as the soup was served with home-made brown bread and butter.

Back home in the kitchen, a different thermos flask was used as my mother's yoghurt maker, following the centuries-old method. Boiled milk was left to cool until body temperature; a finger dipped in the milk was the test. A spoonful of yoghurt was stirred into the warm milk from the previous batch, the flask was filled, the lid screwed on and eight hours later the magic had happened. If Jesus did water to wine, then Mum did milk to yoghurt. As a child, this small miracle produced a family delight we relished. Chilled yoghurt served with a large sprinkle of demerara sugar that glistened and then dissolved into a watery syrup. The brown sugary liquid made patterns on the white yoghurt and the sweet taste contrasted beautifully with the sharp tangy live yoghurt. From the flask, goodness flowed.

In my teenage life, the flask had different associations. It accompanied me on fishing trips with my older brother or with my friends. I suffered from little patience which made me a poor fisherman, but I loved being free from parental control and being in nature with mates fooling around. There was a very particular and unforgettable smell when fishing: a blend of maggots, sandwiches, and hot flask tea combined with the musty smell of a freshwater river or lake.

Quickly bored, I would devour all my sandwiches in the first hour, having usually lost my fishing tackle in the weeds, then go off exploring and tree climbing, returning to finish my hot tea and admire my brother's catch.

Later, the flask became a transitional object, bridging the gap between home and my travel destinations. It provided the wake-up coffee on my weekly train journey from Chester to London where I studied for a master's degree. My garden was next to the railway and Fynn, my young son, would stand on a chair looking over the hedge, waving and hoping to spot me as the train sped past. I would lean out of the train window waving back madly and catching his grin, before sitting back in my seat, opening the flask, and smelling the hot coffee that accompanied the cheese and chutney sandwiches I pulled from my bag.

The flask became the connection that would nourish me between the home I left and the bustling, dynamic city that greeted me at Euston Station. It also became my walking companion, as I ventured into the mountains of the Lake District and Wales, and on our epic journey across the length of the United Kingdom, from John o' Groats to Land's End. Our lunch breaks and coffee breaks took place in beautiful landscapes, whether in bright sunshine or huddled against the wind and rain, where the flask was at the heart of the action, in a similar way that a fireplace is the warming hearth of a home.

In my younger adult life, coffee, sandwiches, and cakes bought from cafés and train buffet bars were an exception, an expense beyond my budget. Aside from the economics, the flask also became an object of micro-resistance to the onslaught of the consumerist world that was devouring everything in its way and, in the process, transforming our desires and our lives.

The rise of the 'cappuccino cult'

The flask as a travel companion slowly became redundant as it was replaced by paper cups of tea and coffee bought at the railway station before a trip, in the train buffet during it, and in cafés on arrival. As my career progressed, I could now afford to buy coffee on the go, and social norms meant the flask dissolved as a commonplace object and necessary travel companion for me and others.

Meanwhile, I was taking adventures abroad, and I delighted in the café societies I discovered throughout the world. I lounged in the grand cafés of Krakow, Budapest, Vienna, Paris, and Mexico City. I hung out with my son, meeting travellers and bohemians in the street cafés of Turkey, Beijing, and Kathmandu, or taking in the sun with friends in the outdoor plaza cafés in Italy, Cuba, and Spain, or writing postcards home in the dark romantic writers' cafés such as Bewley's Oriental Café in Dublin.

Back home, café society in the UK expanded, breaking out from the binary café choice we grew up with. There was the posh tea house serving loose-leaf tea in China cups, triangular sandwiches, scones with jam and cream, and Victoria sponge or Dundee fruit cake. Or the working class 'greasy spoon' cafés serving builder's breakfasts, egg and chips with white bread, and mugs of strong sugared tea (still a favourite). New family-owned niche cafés emerged, borrowing from our European neighbours, serving espressos and Italian-style cappuccinos. In London and other major cities, continental-owned cafés were already familiar, but these new places were different, they aimed their slick coffee products at a new laptop-carrying, digital generation. I delighted in finding these cool cafés to read papers, socialise, and write in.

Then came the mass expansion of café culture, driven by the gentrified hipster café cultures born in cities like San Francisco, Seattle, and Melbourne. The 'cappuccino cult' spread rapidly across the Western world, escalating from niche coffee houses into global corporate brands such as Starbucks. Starbucks had a mono-culture business model: the aim was to flood a chosen area with Starbucks, killing off all the small local cafés that provided diverse aesthetic spaces with delightful home-produced food. Big brands became dominant, pushing local and niche cafés to the margins. They inflicted their conformist decor and cheap-tasting coffee with high-sugar and low-quality food on their new mass market.

As in many other commercial areas, consumers identified more with the brand than with the quality of the product or service. To join this new elite cappuccino cult meant learning the new hip, latte language: 'Skinny latte, two shots with hazel please.' I watched a friend order his coffee and respond to the question 'What kind of coffee?' he answered 'Normal coffee with milk' and was looked at with derision by the barista.

While avoiding the chains as much as possible, like millions of others I became seduced by the coffee craze. A good, strong, creamy flat white coffee is a pleasure for sure, yet my consumption went beyond pleasure and became a habit. The cappuccino cult had become a mainstream norm, an addictive social ritual for myself and millions of others.

The demise of the flask

The old-school coffee flask disappeared in the new world of cool coffee culture. The flask couldn't produce the frothy coffee or the heart-shaped chocolate topping, and it certainly couldn't help you identify with the new brands that produced a tribe of 'cool' coffee aficionados. If Coke was the 'real thing' in the 1970s, cappuccino culture had won the day in the new millennium. Branded takeaway coffees with fancy names and prices to match, pre-made supermarket meals, and the mass uptake of home-delivery food created a momentum that changed how people ate and drank. The instant gratification of consuming fast foods and takeaway drinks replaced the delayed gratification of slow foods created with love and care at home.

The thermos flask was an iconic symbol of the slow-food way of life, and its demise signified an important social change and a significant loss. The flask was eliminated both as an object of desire and as an object of economic necessity for a growing middle class.

The thermos flask was relegated to a few mountain walkers and perhaps a few pensioners who kept the faith. A partial flask comeback happened with the designer water bottle and the personalised coffee mug (a flask by another name), which also became a part of the new hipster look. The side pouch of a computer bag needed a designer water bottle to keep up with the cool fad, which, to its credit, was more sustainable than buying plastic bottles of water, but to its discredit, it also belongs to consumer culture.

The demise of the flask mirrored how the ethic of autonomy and self-sufficiency was lost to the ethic of dependency on consumption. The flask as a transitional object connecting home and the external world had been replaced by the alienating experience of standing in a queue and returning a smile to the tired barista who performs a thousand smiles a day as part of the emotional labour in their work contract.

The corporate beast produces its milky comfort food, the breast milk for adults, and personalises the cup, stroking our fragile and needy egos. I have always thought there was something infantilising about supping warm flavoured milk from the plastic 'lid-teat' of a coffee cup.

Covid-19 and the 'return of the repressed'

The thermos flask had become a repressed memory, a forgotten object that occasionally surfaced on a mountainside or when it popped up in an old photo or movie. That is until Covid-19 struck, lockdown took hold, and coffee outlets and cafés shut. An initial common response from friends was how they would cope without their morning latte fix. Daily routines and addictive habits were broken by Covid.

When not travelling for work and grabbing multiple coffees on the go, my pre-Covid routine was to work at the home office, and then take a late morning break to move my body and socialise a little. This meant cycling along the coastal path into Galway City to meet a friend for coffee. I would then continue working in the 'coffice', a family-owned café that became my office for an hour or so each day. Now what was I to do? Staying at home all day would drive me insane. How would I meet my friend and have a coffee when all cafés were shut? Then a 'return of the repressed' moment occurred. The flask danced back into my mind and I invited my friend to meet me on Furbo Hill, each of us with a flask of coffee and a sandwich.

Furbo Hill is the highest point on the beautiful wild peat boglands seven kilometres outside Galway City, and a good short workout on the bike to get there. When on the hill, a 360-degree view greets you. On one side, looking across the peat bog, is Galway Bay, and beyond the glistening water is the limestone landscape of the Burren in County Clare, reflecting the sunlight and creating a canvas that the cloud shadows dance across. On a clear day, looking out to the Atlantic, the three Aran Islands, Inis Mór, Inis Meáin, and Inis Oírr can be seen gently rising out of the water in the far distance. Turning in the other direction, granite grey boulders sit on the brown-green expanse of wet bogland with wind turbines whirling in the distance.

Sat on Furbo Hill with hot coffee, home-made bread and jelly made from the blackberries, sloes, or rose hips we picked last year with the children revitalised my spirits in this extraordinary time. The simple joy of home-made food, accompanied by hot drinks, fresh air, and beautiful views, made me so much more content than the previous routine of sitting in a café in town, drinking more coffee than was good for me.

The flask was resurrected, and since that first visit to Furbo Hill, I now take a flask and sandwich whenever I go walking, canoeing, picnicking, or cycling. Previously, I would stop at a garage or café for takeaway coffee and a sugary, fatty muffin when on my road bike. Now, I find sheltered spots to rest, read a book or paper, and drink tea or coffee with home-made bread and an apple. My favourite spots are a small derelict schoolhouse built in 1958, which sits on top of the bog, or the old church and graveyard overlooking the beautiful Spiddal Harbour in Connemara.

Flask-time is liberation time

I realised that a 'consumerist addiction' had crept up on me. A social injunction demanded I reward myself with milky caffeine and a biscuit or cake that I didn't really want, need, or enjoy. Being liberated from this ritual is not only a relief but has also recovered an old pleasure that I call flask-time.

Flask-time transcends 'ordinary time'. In the Christian Church, 'ordinary time' is the time between special spiritual seasons, for example, Advent, Easter, and Christmas. Flask-time is also a special time that, in a different way, also sits outside 'ordinary time'. When I take our two children on our cargo bike to their favourite playground, and I sit on fishing nets leaning against the lobster pots on the beautiful Claddagh overlooking Galway harbour, I enter flask-time. A time of peace, a time of reflection, and a time of deep pleasure.

Flask-time merges past, present, and future

Past

Flask-time reconnects me to the past that lives within me, to my childhood memories of being with my family on holidays. As two brothers and both parents have now passed, this evocation is both subtle and powerful. Flask-time also connects me to the picnics I shared with my son Fynn when I was a home parent, taking our sandwiches to Chester Cathedral gardens or sitting on a canal path together. I lost Fynn more than ten years ago and flask-time often evokes his delight when picnicking or his smile when waving as my train sped past.

Present

Flask-time in the present day means sharing the delights of eating and resting outdoors with a close friend, or with my wife and children on our family picnics, on a canoe expedition together, or on the secret limestone pavement we found hidden away near Menlo village, with its marvellous water-formed rock shapes and magical plant life. Flask-time when alone brings me a special peace, a space to listen to nature, to the sea washing up on the beach pebbles or the grasses rustling in the wind, and also to listen to what my internal nature is communicating to me.

Future

Flask-time connects me to the future as my children will internalise the same experience I did as a child, recalling our picnics and simple yet transcendent pleasures. They help me make my own bread and jams and turn these into the sandwiches we share with our hot and cold drinks in outdoor spaces. They will take flask-time into their futures in their own particular ways. Quiet moments on my own, reconnecting to nature and listening to the children play on the swings as I watch cormorants fish for their dinner in the harbour also connect me to the future. It opens a space for drifting, allowing my unconscious to speak, my imagination and creativity to manifest, and in doing so provides new ideas for future writing, work, and life plans to emerge.

The paradox: Lockdown and liberation

Lockdown has freed me in so many ways. It has liberated me from the challenging travel schedules my work demands, but more than that, it has freed me from patterns of behaviour and brought to my realisation the joys of flask-time.

Flask-time reconnects me to living 'the good life'. A re-enchanting experience that goes beyond the stimulus of noise, busyness, and instant gratification. When on a monastic retreat at the Camaldolese Benedictine hermitage in Big Sur, California, a monk told me that I had a strong 'monk-within' and that I should make time to nurture it. Flask-time has become a time I nurture my monk-within, taking me into a deep peaceful experience that guides my soul.

Flask-time is an act of resistance, bypassing the consumer experience that always demands excess from us—whether another coffee, cake, or buying a designer water bottle. It liberates me so that I now freely choose to have a flat white and visit one of my favourite cafés because I really want to, not because of an addictive habit or an injunction that demands I follow the social norm. Freed from the compulsion of excess coffee consumption, the pleasure of the occasional special coffee is renewed. Freed from being sat indoors or tied to being within walking distance of a coffee shop, I can now drink coffee wherever my bike and soul take me.

Writing 'In praise of the thermos flask' has been a way of revisiting what is important in life and of asking myself what really matters. What rituals, patterns, and social norms have I drifted into, that disrupt what helps me to live a 'good life'?

The flask symbolises autonomy and self-sufficiency, breaking free from the dependency-consumerist culture that entraps us all. It is one of the small steps towards building a 'good society', free from the disabling consumerist habits of constantly chasing surplus enjoyment and instant gratification.

Flask-time produces special moments, it is a time of re-enchantment that allows us to stand outside ordinary time and commune with our souls, with nature and to experience the sublime.

Flask-time is a symbolic time of emancipation, one that lockdown has unlocked.

CHAPTER 3

The Covid event: Revealing new truths

The Covid-19 viral pandemic unleashed global disruption, economic impact, fear, illness, and death beyond anything most of us have experienced in our lifetimes. This essay was written in response to a 'lack'. In psychoanalysis, lack points to the real, and in this case, what was missing (lack) in the many commentaries about Covid was a meta-view of what Covid signified to us. There were many discussions about the virus, and much language used as if we were being invaded by an alien culture and had to defend ourselves. What was missing was a recognition that we were all entangled in the production of this pandemic. This essay explores this entanglement.

Introduction

The Covid-19 pandemic reveals a new paradigm of precarity and interdependence and perhaps signifies the final nail in the coffin of modernity. Modernity is a way of being that emerged from the Enlightenment, industrialisation, and urbanisation in the West. It has dominated how we in the Global North (and beyond) think and how we relate to the world we live in. This modernity mindset determines how we organise our economy, our sociopolitical affairs, and our relationships. Modernity aspires to apply science and reason to our world, with the belief that economic improvement and social progress will be the outcome. Modernity favours individuality, purity, and, above all else, human control over nature.

Nature as a divine intervention

In pre-modern times, big events such as natural or human-made disasters were interpreted as communication from the Gods; a natural disaster would be linked to human failure and interpreted as a divine judgement. In secular times, we 'moderns' buffered ourselves from the pre-modern world, which was alive and enchanted by spirits.[11] Modernity applied reason and science to the world, enabling humans to take greater control over their destinies, which included trying to control nature. Humans became the central actors in the global theatre. Wildness was to be tamed; nature was a resource for human consumption and domination. While this gave humans more omnipotence and autonomy, this separation also removed us from a holistic and interconnected understanding of humans' relationship with the natural environment. We became omnipotent and lived 'as if' we humans were outside nature and that we could extract from nature as an unlimited resource.

I am not advocating that we interpret the Covid pandemic as a divine judgement on humanity. However, I am suggesting that we try to interpret the pandemic through a systemic and holistic lens that acknowledges our inescapable entanglement with the environment. This means reading the Covid pandemic differently and challenging the mainstream interpretation that Covid was either an unfortunate viral outbreak that happens once a century, that is, it was nature breaking out, or it was a human laboratory error.

Covid as an event

This global pandemic should be read as an Event or (*événement*) to use the philosophical term from Alain Badiou.[12]

> An Event succeeds in representing a part which is previously unrepresented. This unfolding of new representations from an Event produces Truths, Subjects, and new social systems.[13] (McLaverty-Robinson, 2014)

This essay explores how the Covid Event has produced a truth about our human interdependencies with each other and with the non-human world. In doing this, Covid unleashes a new awareness about our human subjectivity. It reveals to us who we are in relation to other humans, to our non-human companions, and to the environment. This awareness can open a space that enables us to create new social systems that can adapt to the new paradigm we are entering. Or, we can turn a blind eye and continue as if modernity will save us.

Covid signifies interdependence

J.-A. Miller writes that 'Capitalism and science have combined to make nature disappear.'[14] This Covid Event undoes our twentieth-century fantasy that science and mankind have conquered nature, that we have overcome nature. Nature has been speaking to us for a while, and the environmental movement has been listening, but most of us have not. Even when we acknowledge an environmental crisis, we continue to turn a blind eye to its implications. What we find most difficult is to reassess our relationship with our non-human companions on this planet. We maintain the modern mindset that turns nature into a commodity that we extract from for economic use and pleasure. Turning nature into a commodity makes nature disappear as a web of life we are dependent on. We imagine we can exist without it and live outside it.

Covid is an amplification of what nature has been telling us for a while. The natural environment has been reappearing and breaking through our 'buffered worlds' in traumatic ways. The climate crisis brings heatwaves, desertification, water shortages, floods, and wildfires with social consequences of migration, increased poverty, and political conflict. These macro-environmental emergencies are increasingly imposing themselves upon us, and Covid has imposed its micro-biological viral network upon us, unleashing a contagion that is shaking the world.

The Covid Event is interpreted by mainstream commentators as untamed nature inflicting trauma upon humanity. The reaction is either denial or a further application of 'capitalism-science' to try to tame nature again. We try to strengthen our walls of defence, to increase our separation. There is nothing wrong with the rush to protect the economy and invest billions in vaccination research, but we should also learn the real lessons. The environmental catastrophes and this Covid pandemic are not nature acting as an external force, but they are 'nature-humanity-technology' acting together as a complex ecosystem.

The Covid-19 ecosystem

> Covid-19 is an ecosystem consisting of animals and humans, viruses and marketplaces, urban density and social etiquettes, political decisions and actions, economic practices, globalised trade, mass travel, digital information networks and emotional and affective networks. Collectively, these and other actants became a stable enough network, which enabled the pandemic to occur. Socialised human activity forms the contagious networks in which the new virus thrives.[15]

The false division between humans and nature has been exposed by this Covid Event. Nature can no longer be seen as an external resource to be tamed, utilised, and consumed by humans. Nor is it a preordained natural order imposed by the law of nature or by God or some other divine force.

The Covid Event reveals to us: 'There is no longer an outside called nature, humans are nature'.

Our world is a hybrid ecosystem consisting of 'nature-humanity-technology'.

This hybrid ecosystem is producing new traumatic events. The natural world is entangled with human influence—some call this the Anthropocene. The human world is entangled by nature's influence. Increasingly powerful technologies are entangled and influence both our social and natural worlds.

A master signifier of contagion

Covid-19 is a master signifier of contagion. A master signifier unleashes a chain of signifiers; the master signifier contagion unleashes fear, death, panic, connectivity, interdependence, and no escape. Contagion is not limited to the infectious virus; many other things become contagious. People are contagious; emotions go viral, economic fear of collapse goes viral, political and social anxieties go viral, facts and fiction go viral, and conspiracy theories, narratives, and stories go viral. The coronavirus is not a singular thing but an entanglement.

Unleashing a truth of the P-I Age

Covid-19 is not unleashing a new truth; it is unearthing a preknown truth, but one that has become repressed. *Precarious-Interdependence* is the truth enunciated by the signifier Covid-19. This truth of precarity and interdependency is reviled and repressed because acknowledging it undoes the omnipotent fantasies of twentieth-century modernity. Our life-worlds have always been interconnected and interdependent, but a great acceleration of connectivity has taken place in recent years. A triple disruption has occurred in our ecosystems:

> *Technological disruption:* the internet, mobile communications, AI, and quantum computing are unleashing unprecedented change in political, social, and economic realms.
>
> *Environmental disruption:* climate warming and biodiversity loss are creating polycrisis.
>
> *Social disruption:* technological and environmental disruptions impact us in profound ways—both in macroeconomics and trade and also in politics and society, including how we relate to each other.

These three disruptive forces, together, have created precarity and undermined any stable future that modernity promised. The digital financial interdependencies led to the financial crisis in 2008, and climate change continues to unleash local and global environmental crises. Covid-19 is the final awakening; no longer can we deny the precarious times we live in, nor can we pretend we are not living interdependently with each other and with nature.

The awakening

Covid-19 is an example of a traumatic event, breaking through a collective unconscious fantasy that we 'can just carry on carrying on'. We ignore what the environment, what our bodies and our psyches, are telling us at our peril. Covid reveals not only a virus, but it amplifies our inequities and our fragile states of well-being. Similar ecosystem events will keep intruding on our life-worlds in traumatic ways until we engage with the truth that Covid shares with us. Repressions and repetitions lead us to invest more in capitalism-science as if techno-utopianism can provide the answer. Industrial mindsets cannot solve ecosystemic challenges; new mindsets and new ways of living are urgently needed.

The problem is not a Covid-19 virus; this is merely a symptom of a greater problem which is our way-of-being-in-the-world.

What is to be done?

An urgent demand requires an urgent response. Covid-19 is hopefully a tipping point, which will connect us to other traumas we face, such as climate change, and to our potential for resilience and adaptation. This will hopefully lead to a change of worldview, allowing as Gramsci puts it, a new 'collective will' to mobilise us to action.[16] This collective will is more inclusive than the human collective will that Gramsci was referring to. The challenge is to find a collective will to belong to the whole and make good with those around us, our human and non-human companions, who share this fragile planet with us.

CHAPTER 4

Taking a stance on the Ukrainian war

This essay was written four days after Russia's unwarranted, unnecessary, and brutal invasion of Ukraine, which shook me to the core. Once the war had started, the fears from the last two wars in Europe resurfaced, and I knew immediately that the invasion would lead to horrors that would be very difficult to end. This essay was posted on social media and received a powerful response, mostly supporting the call for all to stand against the tyranny of an authoritarian regime imposing its will with pure violence. It was also written as a response to a minority of professionals in my field, who believed that systems thinking meant they should take a neutral stance on the invasion.

Drawing from my background in psychoanalytic and systems thinking, critical theory, and Group Relations Conferences (GRC) insights, I would like to challenge some of the perspectives I have heard from a minority of colleagues in my field about the current war. A number of psychosocially informed colleagues have made a link between their systemic-psychodynamic approach and being neutral and not taking a stance on the Russia–Ukraine war. Their argument usually goes like this: 'We mustn't fall into the trap of binaries and blame.' 'We mustn't take a paranoid–schizoid position.' 'If we take a systems-psychodynamic perspective, we see that there are no clear rights and wrongs, that we are all implicated.' 'Deeper and more systemic insights are needed to understand this war, don't just blame Russia.' 'It's too easy to create Putin as a bad object and position Ukrainians as the good object.'

My response is that this is a poor use of systemic, psychodynamic, and group relations thinking that brings our field into disrepute. I would add that this approach lacks a critical theory approach that focuses on structural power imbalances and emancipatory politics. I believe that coaches, consultants, therapists, psychologists, and others who make up our field and are informed by psychodynamic and systemic thinking should take a stance against this aggression and war. I set out in this short essay why it's problematic to not take a stance and end by stating why taking a stance is the ethical position to take.

Why not taking a stance is problematic

1. Yes, the war, and the cause of war, is systemic

Everything is systemic, but using this term doesn't alleviate us from the responsibility of taking an ethical stance. Apartheid was systemic, but it was brutal and wrong. Nazi Germany was systemic, but it was also a terrible and evil regime. Saying this war is systemic is fine, but using systemic thinking should help us make better judgements by taking a wider perspective. Systemic thinking does not mean seeing everything from all sides, and therefore, we can't take a stance or make a clear judgement. Sometimes, in a system, there is an aggressive protagonist that needs managing. Working as a systemic family therapist, when an abusive parent was exposed, we had to make difficult decisions like removing parents or children from families because understanding why the parent was abusive wasn't enough. Likewise, in larger systems, trying to understand from diverse perspectives is important, especially to prevent a breakdown. However, that doesn't mean not taking an ethical stance that supports decisive action to prevent further harm.

2. Taking a psychodynamic and systemic stance—a privileged position or a misuse of power?

It feels like claiming to be systemic/psychodynamic is like claiming a special power. 'We take a meta-position ... we have a depth understanding.' There has always been an elitism, perhaps even a grandiosity in the psychoanalytic, systems, and group relations world. 'Our meta-position means we see the bigger/deeper picture.' Perhaps our training does give us some insights that can help, and perhaps we should also be a little humble. Our insights do not always help us collaborate with each other or the rest of the world (the schisms in psychoanalytic organisations tell their own story). Taking a particular identity can unwittingly become a misuse of power; drawing on Foucault it can become a 'power–knowledge' play. Yes, these perspectives can be useful, but only if they are put to good use.

3. *Applying psychodynamic and systemic thinking brings some insights, but they are always limited and partial*

I notice how in our field, we repeat mantras to cover a lack of real thinking. The mantra, 'it's systemic' followed by an absence of ideas, policy, or actions is an empty slogan. Saying it is 'splitting' or it is 'fight-flight' rarely enlightens a complex situation.

4. *Not taking a stance is taking a stance*

As Joan Lurie, a systemic thinker, recently shared on a LinkedIn post,

> Building on the axiom of Paul Watzlawick that 'you cannot not communicate'. In a system of interrelations everything we do is a communication. Silence is a behaviour. Absence is a behaviour. No decision is a behaviour. Inaction is action. There is no non-behaviour.

Being neutral, and not standing up against an act of unwarranted terror, aggression, and war is clearly taking a stance. Non-action is action, it is a green light for the aggressor. The neutral stance of not condemning what is clearly wrong goes beyond abandoning the Ukrainians who face terror and a future of repression (as do many Russians). Not taking a stance is a systemic intervention that has widespread consequences. It undermines the brave protesters in Russia and Belarus, and those in neighbouring states fearing Russian aggression. It also undermines Russian citizens who will reap the fruits of an increasingly repressive and authoritarian regime. The Putin regime will relish those who are blind to his aggression and violence. Sometimes 'a cigar is just a cigar' as Freud said, and sometimes 'an oppressor is just an oppressor'. Rationalise it any way you like, but this is an unwarranted war against a people who do not deserve this dreadful violation against their families, communities, and their country's future.

Why we should take a stance against aggression and against the war

Taking a psychodynamic view, we need to look beyond rational thinking and look at the emotional attachments and desires behind this invasion. Viewing the situation through psychodynamic ideas of desire and utilising a critical theory analysis of power, we can see that the Putin regime does not desire a rational dialogue or peaceful solution. They desire to tighten their power hold domestically and to re-establish as much of the Soviet empire as possible. I hypothesise that this desire is to cement Putin's legacy as a great Russian leader. Another desire seems to be to send a message to Georgia, Belarus, and other neighbouring countries that open democratic societies are not welcome on the Russian border. Open democracies threaten Putin's power base much more than NATO, which is his fig leaf excuse for attacking. His support of the brutal dictatorship in Belarus and his open silencing of any strong opposition in Russia reveal his anxiety about democratic movements and his desire to prevent them. Hitting Ukraine hard is a communication to the wider system. To deepen our understanding means to look at the data and learn from experience. The true desire behind this war is for the Putin regime to maintain power at any cost; a war gives permission for the clampdowns his regime needs.

Tireless attempts by President Macron and many others to open dialogue and find peaceful solutions were made when the Putin regime had already planned war. They unleashed violence—the systemic position now is to take a stance that will have the greatest impact to stop further bloodshed. This means to support the Ukrainians with humanitarian and defence aid and to try to end the war as quickly as possible. That doesn't mean to stop trying to understand or look for peace dialogues or to deepen our understanding of the pressures and psycho-systemic impacts of choices now being made on all sides. Taking a stance means supporting difficult choices, making difficult decisions, drawing red lines, and creating economic sanctions to bring internal systemic pressures on this regime that is intent on war and oppression. Other practical choices are to support the suffering Ukrainian refugees fleeing terror and to support those at home fearing for their lives and their future.

Taking a systemic perspective reveals this war is a symptom of an increasingly authoritarian regime that was anxious to cement the leadership position. It has succeeded already by further repressing free speech and opposition at home. The Putin regime attacked what it considered an easy target in order to further its own power base and aims. The invasion is having systemic impacts around the world, and to help stop those impacts from becoming ever more dangerous and traumatic, we all need to take a stance against this unnecessary and terrible war.

CHAPTER 5

What canst thou say? Israel and Palestine

This essay was written a few weeks after the brutal and shocking Hamas attack on innocent Israeli citizens, killing 1,400 and kidnapping 250. The Israeli Defence Force had begun to raze Gaza to the ground, killing and maiming innocent citizens, many of whom were children. Much, much worse was to come after the essay was written.

Introduction

This chapter reflects on the war and conflict between Israel and Hamas in Gaza. It begins by drawing on George Fox and the Quakers who invite us to look inwardly at our spiritual and moral selves in order to find our voices to speak out when facing this traumatic and very disturbing conflict/war.

George Fox, the founder of the Quakers, asked 'What canst thou say?' to those he ministered to in the 1650s.

'You will say Christ saith this, and the apostles say this, but what canst thou say?'[17]

Fox was confronting the religious orthodoxy of the time. He and fellow Quakers believed that each person should be guided by their individual experience of the 'light within' them. The Quakers were radicals, they shunned the institutional Church and challenged the powerful priests who interpreted the Bible on the peoples' behalf, telling them what to believe and think. They created an egalitarian, pacifist Church led by a 'priesthood of all believers' where any person attending their Quaker worship meetings (men or women) could stand and minister to the gathering if they felt led by the spirit. The Quakers continue today as 'The Religious Society of Friends' and won the Nobel Peace Prize in 1947 for their social justice and peace activism. The question 'What canst thou say?' is an important starting point when we reflect on the Israel–Palestine crisis, as it makes us think beyond the abstract and answer directly from our own conscience, values, and beliefs.

So 'What canst thou say' about the Israeli–Palestinian conflict?

What does your inner light lead you to say, to think, to do? We are all people of faith, whether this is expressed in religious or spiritual terms, or whether our faith is in humanism, the question remains the same: how does your spirit guide you and lead you to speak and act?

Different responses to the Israeli–Palestinian conflict

There are some who take polemic sides in this conflict, unable to condemn the terrible violence from one side and wholly blame the other side for the horrific violence and conflict.

There are some who are conditional in their condemnation of one side's terrible violence, claiming the context excuses or even produces it. For example, Palestinian supporters blame the Israelis, saying that Hamas's brutal violence is a product of Israeli occupation and the long-term persecutory policy against the Palestinian people who are in despair. Or Israeli supporters justify Israel's unleashing of terrible violence in Gaza that is killing and harming so many civilians because they are at war and Hamas threatens their very existence.

Another response is withdrawal and disengagement. Either due to being overwhelmed or through fear that any comment might be jumped on (and it does feel dangerous to speak about this conflict/war).

There are others, and I am one of them, who clearly and unequivocally condemn the shocking and brutal violence of both sides. The horror that Hamas unleashed on innocent Israeli citizens and the vicious killing of young people and aged Holocaust survivors, in my mind, can never be explained away and/or excused because of prior Palestinian suffering. The Israeli response to the Hamas attack, placing innocent civilians in a siege, stopping food, water, and fuel, and mass bombings of densely populated civilian areas and refugee camps is totally wrong. Killing innocent children cannot be explained or excused by the rationale that the Israelis have the right to lay siege to and attack civilians in Gaza in order to destroy Hamas.

What is our moral duty?

Being clear about disavowing brutal and inhuman violence, particularly on the innocent, is one part of our moral and spiritual duty.

Recognising the underlying issues and supporting peacemakers, who can show leadership, is another part of our moral and spiritual duty.

Holding open a space for dialogue with others and working against the polarisation this conflict/war brings is also our moral and spiritual duty. This conflict is spilling into the streets; antisemitism is on the rise, as is Islamophobia. The Israeli–Palestinian conflict adds to other societal and cultural wars and divisions that lie within our own communities. It takes ordinary citizens to prevent society from splitting into fragments and polarised sides, and there are many politicians and others with agendas who will take advantage of these splits.

What can I say?

I speak from my personal moral and spiritual place …

I totally and utterly condemn the terrible suffering caused by the awful attack by Hamas on Israeli citizens. I stand in solidarity with the Israeli and Jewish people to live in a safe state, and in safety wherever they are in the world.

I totally and utterly condemn the terrible suffering caused by the awful attacks by Israel on the innocent citizens of Gaza. I stand in solidarity with the Palestinian people to live in a safe state, and in safety wherever they are in the world.

The context does matter, but it doesn't give permission or excuse the violence

My personal responses do not, however, remove me or others from facing the context, the complexity, the history, and the challenges to secure peace in the region.

Acknowledging the Israeli/Jewish right to exist in a safe state, acknowledging the terrible and genocidal history of the Holocaust, the centuries of discrimination, massacres, and pogroms, and the anti-semitism that still exists across the world, there has to be a recognition that the recent Hamas attacks evoke more than the immediate dreadful shock and horror; they also evoke the deep trauma of past events.

Acknowledging the Nakba (the catastrophe when the Palestinians were forced from their land), acknowledging the 1.5 million Palestinians (some third generation) living in refugee camps; and the recent enforced movement of people from north Gaza, re-inscribes the Palestinian people with their past trauma.

The anguish of living in Gaza, one of the most densely populated places on earth, with mass unemployment, poverty, poor drinking water, surrounded by fences, with access in and out controlled by others, is deeply traumatising, causing daily humiliations including the ever-increasing illegal Israeli settlers and the wider occupation of their legal territory in Palestine. Being forced yet again to move from their homes evokes the Nakba and the deep trauma of past events.

The return of the repressed

These present traumas are producing repetitions and compulsions, where a return of the repressed takes place. There is a conscious knowledge of the past traumas experienced by individuals, families, and collective peoples. There is also an unconscious repression that is inevitable and necessary in order to alleviate the suffering, enough to continue to live day by day.

Present traumas reactivate these repressed feelings, which return with great force as an embodied physical and psychological response. This return of the repressed unleashes fear and trauma, making reflective thinking and communication challenging.

Another form of repression takes place when one community/people displaces or denies the trauma that their community/people have inflicted upon another people. Has Britain ever really faced the trauma it inflicted on others through slavery and colonisation? This is an example of a continuing deep collective repression. This mixture of disavowal of trauma which 'the other' suffered and the reactivation of one's own trauma can open up the very dangerous unleashing of violence. A fantasy is created that the violence will lead to more security or that the collective punishment of innocent people can be just.

President Biden's warning to Israel in October 2023 to not make the same mistakes as the USA did after 9/11, and 'not to become consumed by rage' was a salutary warning.

Adding petrol to the fire, the international community takes sides and feeds the antagonism. Whether the USA, Arab states, Iran, Europeans, Russians, or the Chinese, they mobilise their righteous anger when it aligns with their political ends, and they turn a blind eye to what they don't want to see or believe. There are, however, other institutional actors, humanitarians, political individuals, and countries working ceaselessly to reduce violence and open a space for peace.

Blessed are the peacemakers

We have many examples and patterns when faced with terror and violence. In Ireland, where I live, when the provisional IRA (Irish Republican Army) took up arms and fought a horrendous war against loyalist paramilitaries and the British army, with more than 3,000 deaths and so many innocents suffering, some stood their ground for peaceful solutions.

Pat and John Hume from the Catholic community stood firm against using violence, alongside many grassroots activists from all sides of the conflict who put their lives at risk for peace. Brendan Duddy was a 'secret peacemaker' who put his life at risk behind the scenes in Northern Ireland to find a pathway to early negotiations on the peace treaty. I invited Brendan to speak at a leadership and faith conference, and he told me how he was guided by his own spiritual truth, which he accessed on long walks in the mountains behind his fish and chip shop in Derry, a stronghold of the IRA and a place at the heart of the Troubles.

Today, in Gaza, committed humanitarians are risking their lives to help those in need. Organisations like Doctors Without Borders and Save the Children are unequivocally calling for an end to the inhumane violence against children and innocent civilians. They are calling for the restoration of basic humanity and the end of collective punishment in Gaza.

Some say there is no peace without justice, and I agree. However, no peace doesn't equate to a violent response that feeds the cycle of hatred. It means working ceaselessly for peaceful and just outcomes, to work against the structural and institutional violence of racism and all forms of oppression that sow the seeds of injustice and tensions. Peace will come slowly and only when all parties have security, safety, and a place to call home. This requires a politically just settlement, one that will not be perfect, not give everybody everything, but one that can be lived with by all.

In 1656 the early Quaker movement was being persecuted by the state. George Fox was imprisoned and he wrote from prison to his people:

> Be patterns, be examples in all countries, places, islands, nations, wherever you come, that your carriage and life may preach among all sorts of people, and to them; then you will come to walk cheerfully over the world, answering that of God in every one.[18]

It is a relevant message today, encouraging us to live by our values and beliefs, and to see all humans as 'children of God', in Quaker terms; or in humanistic terms, by each human life being valued and respected. This is a tough ask when violence continues and the trauma is raw, but anything less will feed the cycle of horror.

CHAPTER 6

The meaning of the monarchy

This essay was written shortly after the death of Queen Elizabeth II, which evoked a huge response in the media, both in the UK and globally. The majority of the commentary about Queen Elizabeth II was reverential in tone, admiring her long 'selfless' service given to the country and Commonwealth. The end of the second Elizabethan age perhaps marks something more than the death of the long-serving queen. It may be an event that signifies a moment of social transformation in Britain and beyond.

Introduction

Queen Elizabeth II was a symbol of stability over her seventy-year reign. Will her death amplify the slow meltdown of core institutions that claim to offer stability? Will it increase social fragmentation? Or, has her death and the huge response to it given the monarchy and other establishment institutions, such as the Church of England and Parliament, a new boost as we remember the importance of 'the establishment'? Is this a moment that reinforces deep emotional attachments to a monarchy that symbolises a social contract of hierarchy and power at the centre? Or does the queen's death reflect the passing of the old ways, and is it a catalyst of a 'centre that can no longer hold'?

The death of Queen Elizabeth II has impacted millions of people from all walks of life. There have been scenes of mourning and unprecedented coverage of her death by the mainstream media. Wall-to-wall reporting highlights the influence she had on the nation and Commonwealth and how her death impacted the emotional life of her subjects living in the UK and citizens beyond. So much has been said, and so much will be said about the death of Queen Elizabeth. This chapter shares my associations with the entanglements between the monarchy, the establishment, leadership, and transition.

Monarchy—what does it mean?

The monarchy has many meanings; these differ depending on each of our relationships to the monarchy and our position in wider society. If you are a hereditary peer, a traditionalist conservative, a supporter of the establishment more generally, and a committed royalist, then the meaning you attach to her death will be different than if you are an active republican, an anarchist, a radical leftist, or if you are anti-royal for other reasons. I asked a left-wing social activist friend of mine to share his response to the news of her death, and he replied promptly, 'Honestly, all I feel is relief that we might finally move out of the ossified, moribund societal state we have been trapped in.'

The monarchy means a lot to 'the establishment'. This is no surprise as the monarchy is the 'establishment body' at the heart of the United Kingdom and of the Commonwealth of Nations. In the establishment world, the monarchy has been at its core for her whole reign. She was a global symbolic figure courted and recognised by the wider establishment figures across the world, ranging from Saudi Arabian princes, African leaders, and presidents of the USA and the French Republic. What is striking is how republicans and others representing countries previously very anti-monarchic still want the kudos of being seen in the company of the great queen. Establishment and power clearly transcend political loyalty.

Pleasure in our displeasure

Watching the BBC offer its solemn commentary with presenters in black, they clearly delight in their role of being the voice of the nation, aligning the state broadcaster with the wider establishment, taking up their role with both gravitas and great skill; they really do it very well. The constant reporting of the length and waiting times of 'the queue' to walk past the coffin seemed to act as a justification of their wall-to-wall coverage, 'You see, the nation really is in mourning!' Yet, there is more than grief and mourning taking place.

Rob Johns, a political professor who surveyed 400 members of the queue said, 'It is less a case of royalists simply wanting to mourn the queen in person, and more a collective gathering that is as much about the queue as it is about reaching the end of all the queueing … It's not grief-stricken, it's not about weeping and wailing,' he added, 'Those queuing reported more positive than negative emotions. People are enjoying it … Not in a festival kind of way but in a kind of mutually satisfying way. Enjoying the collective, enjoying the gathering.'[19] A Church of England bishop spoke solemnly, saying the queue is like a pilgrimage, where the journey and the companionship on the way are as important as the endpoint. On the morning of the funeral, the BBC Radio 4 lead reporter said that 'Today was a mixture of a funeral, a military parade, and a Glastonbury festival for royalists.'

Psychoanalysis gives the insight that we gain 'pleasure in our displeasure',[20] and how we gain unconscious gratification even when we are consciously upset or troubled. Even when there is death and sadness, there can be a lot of pleasure within and beyond our sadness. As an Irish friend once said to me, 'I enjoy a good funeral much more than a wedding.'

The monarchy evokes many emotions, and it helps to create a libidinal bond between people and the state. We are socialised and conditioned to enjoy our tribal relationships, and humans have a deep longing to belong. The monarchy also offers the masses a distraction from worldly worries. There is much personal and collective pleasure gained from personal and collective identifications with the monarchy. Strong feelings are evoked of national pride and togetherness, connections with a nostalgic-imagined past, and for us subjects living in the United Kingdom, to be reconnected with our greatness!

An institutional container

Whether at a royal funeral, birth, wedding, or other major national events, the monarchy is present as both an emotional container and as a stimulus for our emotions, projections, identifications, and unconscious investments. Often, ambivalent feelings are present, there is sadness at the loss of 'our Queen', and many tears are shed, 'She was our country's grandmother', while, at the same time, there is pride and real enjoyment in the pageantry and communal gathering. Those who attend gain recognition from family and friends, from the self-importance and kudos gained from being present at such a historical event. A common refrain from those present when asked why they were there was, 'I wanted to be part of history.' This pleasure gained is not only for those physically present, the gathering takes place virtually, too. Friends and families gather around TVs and connect via social media. The coverage was so extensive that we were all present in some way. The monarchy institution has for years stimulated and contained the emotions that many in the nation feel; whether sadness, happiness, pride, or disdain—it provides a different space and a distraction from the daily routine and a focal point to express ourselves.

Political leaders rally to the call and compete to be the most articulate, straining to find their most mournful voices and solemn facial expressions alongside any genuine sadness felt. I feel a loss myself, even as an anti-monarchist. I acknowledge that the queen was a remarkable leader. My family gathered, like millions of families, for her visit to our family living room every Christmas Day at 3 pm for the Royal Christmas Broadcast. In Britain, where I grew up, the saturation of media coverage makes it feel like there is 'no outside' from the monarchy space, and yet research points to a power that has subsided. My grandparents and parents' generation had a much greater social and emotional bond to the monarchy than present generations, which opens the question of what comes next after Elizabeth.

State spectacle and performance of power

The British state performs the rituals led by the monarchy exceptionally well, with such pathos. Other countries have marvellous pomp and grandeur, but the only competing rituals with the power of Queen Elizabeth II's funeral that I can recall were the great Soviet communist state parades.[21] The huge pageantry, the involvement of the military, the emotions of the masses, and the absolute power on display stand out in both rituals. On display is the soft power revealed by the personal and collective identifications either with the queen as the 'mother of the nation' or with 'Father Stalin'.

The hard power follows, a huge military presence at both, and then the political institutions that lead the mourning: a hierarchy of prime ministers and presidents, the Parliament, the state religion, bishops and the Church of England, or the communist regime in the USSR. In both cases, the power and authority of the establishment speak through the great spectacle. Watching the funeral, one couldn't help but be struck by how the monarchy and military are completely entwined. The monarchy represents the establishment power of the nation, the military presence a signifying message communicating to us that 'establishment power will always be protected by force when required'. Over 500 heads of state from all over the world paid their homage to Queen Elizabeth II. They also came to align themselves with the meaning of the monarchy and to stand together, a living commitment to reaffirm the establishment status quo, in spite of political diversity.

The queen led such rituals and national events for seventy years, which is one of the many reasons she will be missed. These events are not neutral, they carry symbolic meaning, telling us loud and clear where real power lies.

The pictures and pageantry tell their own story which says to the masses, 'This is where power lies; yes with us, the establishment. Take a good look, we are good at this, we have been around a long time and we are not going anywhere. Know your place, for we know ours!'

The new establishment

The monarchy offers a living 'establishment body', symbolic of establishment figures everywhere. Global corporations with their mighty power are keen to muscle in, and show how they are not only economic players but have become part of a new establishment, a political powerhouse. Remarkably, Apple, the USA global giant, replaced its website's front page with a picture of Queen Elizabeth II on news of her death. This in a company founded by establishment disruptor Steve Jobs, in a country that fought a War of Independence to free itself from Britain's monarchy. Yet the subliminal message is clear: Apple is not just a profit-making business, it is part of the new world order, and is aligned with traditional establishment figures.

Empire, power, and glory

> Rule, Britannia! Britannia, rule the waves!
> Britons never, never, never shall be slaves.

These words ring out each year on the last night of the Proms, a UK classical music tradition in the Royal Albert Hall. The monarchy is entangled with empire, the Commonwealth, the hereditary principle, governance, the House of Lords, land and property ownership, wealth, class, and elite power. George VI called the royal family 'the firm', a name adopted fondly by the royals today. The firm is powerful and very wealthy, and it has one clear primary task, which is succession. As John Gapper in the *Financial Times* writes:

> It is a charismatic enterprise that works constantly towards a single target: succession. The monarchy is a selfish gene, working to pass itself down generations, with the sovereign body occupying the throne at any one moment part of that effort. We are watching a once in a generation product launch.[22]

It is the physical body of the living monarch that represents the wider royal family, the monarchy, the nation, and the Commonwealth (and previously the British Empire). That is a lot for one human body to hold together. The death of the queen leaves a space for a new body to hold the weight of the nation. There is no gap, 'The Queen is dead, long live the King', no time for slippage or doubt to creep in.

Continuity and stability

There is an undeniable argument that the institution of the monarchy enters the nation's psyche and offers emotional containment at times of national anxiety. It symbolises continuity, tradition, and social stability. I see this, I appreciate this. The establishment rallies around this position and millions of citizens find comfort in this position, and yet this containment and continuity comes at a heavy price.

Dependency and deference to power

The price is that of dependency and deference. Is it possible to have a slimmed-down and symbolic monarchy? Can symbolism, continuity, and stability be achieved without the privilege of immense wealth and the links to the established Church, to governance, and to power? Other countries, such as the Netherlands, show that great wealth and governance power do not have to be part of a symbolic monarchy. Defenders of the monarchy will say that the UK monarchy adds more impact. However, the monarchy is not just about continuity; it is about retaining elite privilege and raw power, which demands immense wealth, too.

The monarchy creates a dependency culture that reinforces class barriers and creates a 'know-your-place' ideology based on deference to those above us. I grew up in the UK and was indoctrinated into a culture of low expectations. As a youth, I was never told it was possible to transcend my class background, write a PhD, become an author, or run my own business. The careers advisor pointed to car mechanics, factory work, or the army in my all-boys comprehensive school. The worst thing is that these low expectations become internalised into our minds and beings, and we police ourselves and our peers. 'Do not rise above your station' is the hidden message. The musician Morrissey captures it nicely in his 1992 song, 'We hate it when our friends become successful', singing 'If we can destroy them, we bet your life we will destroy them.' In spite of transcending my lack of early education, I still hear my inner voice say, 'This is not your place' when giving a keynote speech or teaching as a professor at university. In spite of all the neoliberal rhetoric about personal freedom and achieving your dreams, the data shows that the status quo remains, the gap between rich and poor increases, and the hereditary principle of wealth is the dominant way wealth is retained by elites.[23] Thomas Piketty's research shows how the rate of return on capital outstrips the rate of growth; therefore, inherited wealth will always grow faster than earned wealth. Rich kids go from gap year to internship and job at their father's friend's bank/ministry/TV network, while poor kids sweat into their barista uniforms or deliver pizza. It is not an accident, it is the system working normally.

Service for what ends?

There is a paradox at the heart of the monarchy. The royal family make a great play of the service they give to the nation, and they hold the idea of service at the heart of their ethos, and yet they serve from a place of absolute privilege. Their service to the nation also serves to maintain the establishment's elite status at the expense of aspiration and social mobility.

The monarchy means many things, but let us not hide the fact that it means reproducing age-old dependency cultures. The hereditary wealth, elite status, and establishment power structures are so ingrained in the UK that the hypocrisy and paradoxes are missed. For example, the UK champions and fights wars for democratic principles, and yet a key part of the UK governance structure is monarchical and includes the House of Lords, an unelected second chamber at the heart of the governance system. It includes hereditary peers (the power to govern passed down through wealthy families), and it is a partial theocracy, with unelected bishops from the Church of England taking seats.

Containment without monarchy

The challenge for anti-monarchists and republicans is to find new ways that solidarity can be found without identifying with nationalism, militarism, and the monarchy. In times of increasing uncertainty new ways of finding collective containment without the baggage of dependency and deference are required. I recently became a citizen of Ireland, and I have witnessed three very impressive presidents who have commanded national and international respect: Mary Robinson, Mary McAleese, and Michael Higgins (all elected) who take up this symbolic role on behalf of the nation in the Irish Republic. They represent the country in a similar way to the monarchy, yet without the links to wealth and the hereditary/class principle. Admittedly, the great spectacle and pageantry of the monarchy is lacking, but perhaps a representation that is toned down in volume on national occasions is not such a bad thing. Perhaps, there is a greater unity and containment achieved when the containment is more self-authorised and comes from a more egalitarian and participatory ethos, rather than a top down subservient one.

Empire-in-our-minds

The monarchy is entangled with ideas of empire. 'Crowds gathered to witness the last roar of the vanished British Empire' was the *Irish Times* headline reporting on the queen's funeral. While the British Empire is no longer with us in a political sense, there exists an 'empire-in-our-minds' that is harder to shake off. David Armstrong wrote of the 'organisation-in-the-mind', saying how we carry imprints of the organisations we work in emotionally and unconsciously within us.[24] Likewise, my experience of growing up in England is that we carry a remnant of 'empire-in-our-minds'. It shows up mostly as an unconscious idea of the superiority of being British. This idea gets magnified and used by politicians, such as during the Brexit campaign. Monarchy cannot escape this relationship, and while the manoeuvre towards the Commonwealth of Nations was one of Queen Elizabeth's triumphs, the past stains and traumas of the empire remain unaddressed, and the contemporary 'empire-in-our-minds' thrives.

The crimes of the empire are dreadful, simply dreadful. Relatives of the Mau Mau rebels who were put into concentration camps and tortured in the early days of Queen Elizabeth II's reign will hold a different 'empire-in-the-mind' than the average British citizen. The 'empire-in-the-mind' I was conditioned to hold lacked the evils done in the name of empire. It heralded a great nation that benevolently ruled the waves, passing on traditions of democracy and economic infrastructure (civilising), with only a passing nod to the devastating trauma. The 'empire-in-the-minds' of the working and middle classes meant that while we were to know our place within the UK social and economic structures, we also knew that our place in the world was mighty indeed.

The nation state is a comparatively new phenomenon, whereas the idea of empire is much older, and I expect it will outlast the nation state. We see a revival of empire ideology today. The Chinese are expanding their influence and harking back to previous empires as inspiration and justification for their expansionist process. Russia lost its Soviet empire and the Putin regime harks back to the Tsar and the Orthodox Church to reimagine a new Greater Russia empire. As the Kremlin's first chief of staff, Sergey Kiriyenko says, they are now at war to recover liberated territories in Ukraine 'because they are part of our empire and our state'. It seems like the empires in our minds are never far from us. The monarchy keeps the link of empire in our minds strong and alive.

Leadership

I wrote a spontaneous LinkedIn post on hearing of the queen's death, praising her leadership, yet standing against the monarchy, copied below:

> Born and raised in England, I am not a monarchist, I am filled with ambivalence about the commonwealth and ashamed of the disgraceful aspects of Britain's colonial past and present, which is entangled with the monarchy. And yet I recognise and admire the truly great leadership Queen Elizabeth demonstrated in taking up a relentless role, showing dedication, dignity, and service over a whole lifetime. A unique contribution from a steadfast personality who inspired and offered comfort to so many. RIP Queen Elizabeth.

I received many responses and comments thanking me for expressing the conflicted feelings that others shared. To acknowledge and mourn the loss of a great leader, a symbolic figure who has been a stable presence throughout our whole lives, whether we like the monarchy or not, is an important thing to do. Carrying the weight of the Crown, and all it means and for so long, within one human body, is something to behold. Her death will mean different things to each of us, also triggering the other personal losses we each have.

Leadership and gender

The queen was a matriarchal leader and we have now moved to a patriarchal king. As mother of the nation, the queen attracted maternal projections, such as caring for us, looking after us, and loving us. Her reign mirrored the political ideas of the twentieth century that produced a maternal/caring welfare state, which is fast eroding in the twenty-first century.

Transition

The loss of the queen creates a transitional space. Practically, there is a transition between a matriarchal and patriarchal monarchy. King Charles III is perhaps a 'transitional object' who, at the age of seventy-three, needs to focus less on creating his own monarchic style, and more on keeping the show on the road and preparing the ground for his son. Perhaps more importantly, after seventy years, a space opens up where the possibility of greater transitions can take place. As Winnicott identified, a transitional space is a potential space.[25] To fulfil this potential will mean moving from dependency positions to engage in critical thinking and rediscovering our agency. The meaning of the monarchy requires deciphering, decoding, and rethinking. There is a desire for more stability and continuity in our fast-changing, uncertain, and precarious age. There is a greater need for adaptation in order to embrace the social and political change required to address the ever-growing chasm between rich and poor and from the brink of environmental catastrophe.

From dependency to interdependency

The greatest transition we need to make is from a dependency culture to an interdependency culture. This means shifting our perceptions that hierarchy and top-down control are the norm. We have to decentre ourselves as humans and see how we can only survive by recognising our interdependence with the natural environment.

This is a far cry from our existing cultural norms of accepting power at the centre, empire-in-the-mind, and monarchy. It requires radical new envisioning and liberating ourselves from being dependent subjects. It means letting go of the monarchy-establishment story that has dominated for so long. It is time for a new story.

CHAPTER 7

Brexit: The politics of enjoying displeasure

First published in 2019, this essay is a response to the political mayhem that occurred between the Brexit referendum in 2016 when people in the UK marginally voted to leave the European Union (EU) and the actual leaving in 2020. This short essay draws on specific leaders to represent universal challenges. If you are not familiar with the three politicians, think of them as symbolic representations of current leaders you encounter in different contexts.

Introduction

The media columns are filled with Brexit analysis: the blame game, the numbers, the lies, the tribes and factions, the apocalyptic future. But what unconscious dynamics are at play that fuel this coalition of chaos? By looking at three key political leaders of the moment, it becomes clear that they (and their supporters) share commonalities, which gives a fresh insight into why the UK is in this mess.

Theresa May, Jeremy Corbyn, and Jacob Rees-Mogg all signify how the political class has become invested in the politics of perverse pleasure that we see enacted in this Brexit political soap opera.

At the time of writing, the roles of these three protagonists are as follows:

- Theresa May is the UK prime minister and leader of the Conservative Party.
- Jeremy Corbin is the leader of the opposition and leader of the Labour Party.
- Jacob Rees-Mogg leads the ERG (European Research Group), a powerful hard right, euro-sceptic, and pro-Brexit group within the Conservative Party.

These leaders do not operate in a vacuum; they are symbolic representatives of wider systemic dynamics. They are mobilised by those they represent, enacting the shadow side and underlying fears, anxieties, and desires of the British people. These 'odd leaders' have been unconsciously mobilised by their collective supporters, they are not lone mavericks. The Brexit chaos embodies how the people of the UK have collectively and unconsciously retreated to phantasmatic politics. They are lost, taking great 'pleasure in displeasure',[26] enjoying the chaotic parliamentary performances and also enjoying complaining about them.

While each of these political leaders is very different in terms of personal presentation and political affiliation, they share two common themes that determine their political actions and their inability to work collaboratively.

Theme one is that they are all 'outsiders', which informs how they make sense of and engage with the world around them. Theme two is that each leads the politics of dissatisfaction. Each has a strong tendency towards the 'wounded-self',[27] leading others by mobilising fear and identifying as victims, enabling their supporters to gain 'satisfaction from their dissatisfaction'. Rational politics that work towards mature outcomes involving negotiations and compromise become secondary to the far more powerful unconscious and libidinal[28] dynamics that drive a more fight-flight process.

A perfect storm has occurred. Three political outsiders, chosen by a dissatisfied electorate, aim to satisfy their followers' dissatisfaction, not by overcoming it but by amplifying it. The conscious and authentic aim is to find political solutions, yet they have become leaders at this time precisely because of their personal capacity to mobilise the discontent of their followers. The idea that 'we get the leaders we deserve' needs a reframe here: 'we get the leaders we (unconsciously) desire'.

This political drama is played out while these politicians attempt to negotiate the nation's most challenging restructuring in decades. Europe looks on mostly with bewilderment and dismay at the UK's seemingly self-harming behaviour.

NOTE: The context of when this was written is that Theresa May as prime minister is negotiating Britain's exit from the EU. The deal she has agreed is not acceptable to more hard-line Brexiteers (led by Jacob Rees-Mogg) who say it gives Europe far too much power and control over Britain, that is, it's not the Brexit people voted for. May and the Europeans say that what the hard-line Brexiteers want is to have comprehensive trade agreements that favour the UK, but not be part of the European regulation structure, and this dual desire is not possible. There is a stalemate.

Theme one: Outsiders

Theresa May cuts a lonely figure, clearly struggling to relate to 'the other' in any meaningful way. Parodied as 'the Maybot', she embodies a robotic figure in interviews and discussions. May represents the alienated outsider, an individual set against the world, burdened with huge responsibilities but without personal authority or the ability to mobilise widespread support. At the same time, Theresa May has created chaos due to her ego attachment to being the lone heroine. She has displayed a narcissistic streak that puts herself at the centre of all things. She inverts the charismatic heroic ego-driven leader in a classic reverse move, identifying herself as a 'servant leader' and enjoying her victimhood.

Her body language portrays her 'wounded-self' as she performs the role of 'the lone heroine suffering for the true cause'. Servant leadership has always been a paradox to me. It invites leaders to let go of their egos and become saints, putting everyone else before them. At the same time, they revel in their servant leader role, portraying themselves as self-less servants of others, which paradoxically makes them greater than other 'ego' leaders. There is a place for servant leadership, and it belongs to those who live in faith communities and really give up everything.

May's upbringing as an Anglican vicar's daughter clearly had a big impact on her.

From the outset, Theresa May has ploughed a lone path as prime minister, not collaborating or building consensus within or across parties. Whatever the final outcome of Brexit, this isolated approach will lead to her demise. May's obsessive determination to face down all opposition has been packaged as resilience and determination by her spin doctors. Like a stuck record player, she repeats her mantra, 'my deal or no deal', which aims to slowly kill the desire of others. It is as if repeating this mantra is a substitute for collaborative dialogue, real negotiations, and true leadership. The hard-right Brexit supporters in the Conservative Party block May at each attempt she makes to vote through her agreement with Europe. She has blindly continued and sustained the heaviest parliamentary defeat of any British prime minister in the democratic era after MPs rejected her Brexit deal by a resounding majority of 230.

Jeremy Corbyn cuts another lonely figure at the top. During his long political career as a left-wing radical, he clearly enjoyed his outsider rebel-activist status. This figure from the edge now finds himself centre stage. After self-branding himself as an honest, authentic, and values-driven leader who works tirelessly for the poor and marginalised, Corbyn quickly gained grass-roots support, particularly with younger voters, gaining the party leadership in a shock to the political mainstream.

He played the left-populist card and hoovered up those discontented voters. This quietly spoken man initially portrayed a monk-like leader persona, modest and calm, in contrast to the classic, politically charismatic extrovert. Yet his ego was exposed when he clearly enjoyed his moment of stardom a little too much. Psychoanalysis teaches us to be aware of surplus enjoyment (*plus-de-jouir*) as it creates a distorted sense of reality. The real task (in Corbyn's case to deliver a socialist Britain) becomes displaced by the unconscious desire to enjoy too much. 'More enjoyment please!' demand our unconscious drives. For Corbyn and his followers, unconscious pleasure is gained from their identifying as the 'good' rebel activists, fighting against the bad capitalist other. This attachment to the pleasures of being an activist displaces the realpolitik task of collaborating with a wide group of stakeholders to build a more equitable future. The choice is between enjoying fighting the bad big Other, and actually changing society for the better.

The highlight of Corbyn's leadership came at the mighty Glastonbury Festival, which has a huge attendance and global TV following. Corbyn was invited onto the main stage, and the chant 'Ohhhh Jeremy Corbyn' was sung by thousands ringing out across the meadows. Corbyn bathed in his glory, giving a grandiose utopian speech that demanded world peace and an end to global poverty. He also referred to his recent electoral gains, claiming 'The elites had got it wrong.' In doing so, he pinned his political colours securely to the populist mast. Corbyn was now sharing the same political platforms with Trump, Le Pen, the Five Star movement, and others. Trump builds his walls between Mexico and the USA and between the elite and 'the people'. Corbyn builds walls between business and workers, capitalists and socialists, good and evil, and the elite and the people. These binary positions are amplified by right and left populists to appeal emotionally to the discontented. Yet they are a psychic retreat from addressing the huge challenges that demand more nuanced, mature, collaborative responses. While proclaiming a leftist message, his populist stance revealed his deep attachment to being the outsider-activist and a 'splittist politician'. The inevitable resignations from his party, the splits within it, and the antisemitism[29] problems are a predictable repetition of the politics of splitting.

After this brief period of messiah worship, including the JC Saviour T-shirts worn by his supporters, Corbyn has since appeared as a melancholic character. Depression usually follows mania. He looks like a lost sheep and presents as a being 'absent in his own presence'. At a time of political opportunity, when he should be wreaking havoc as opposition leader to the weakest and most chaotic government in living memory, Corbyn disappears into the shadows. His initial silence and lack of leadership over the antisemitism crisis, coupled with his sitting on the fence on Brexit votes, hoping the May government will self-immolate, reveals a man way out of his depth. As an idealist, Corbyn could comfortably sit on the outside throwing rocks at the establishment; and this is an important political role, we need diverse voices pushing boundaries on social justice. However, when confronted with the reality principle of power and governance, he portrays an outsider who is bewildered by the demands of party and national leadership.

Jacob Rees-Mogg leads the third force in this political landscape. He presents himself as an iconoclastic outsider. Rees-Mogg publicly performs as a 1930s aristocrat, signifying his social conservativism and a lost utopian past when Britain ruled the waves. Using social media, he announced on Instagram the birth of his sixth child named Sixtus Dominic Boniface Christopher Rees-Mogg. This entertaining stance raised his profile and popularity in the Conservative Party. The ageing demographic of the Conservatives identified with 'traditional values', and he soon became a new potential leader. When asked in an interview if he had ever changed a baby's nappy (diaper), he replied: 'No, I haven't. I don't think nanny would approve because I'm sure she'd think I wouldn't do it properly. … Bearing in mind this is the nanny that has worked for my family, in September, for fifty-two years—so she knows a thing or two about doing it properly.'[30] To some, he is a comic figure, and to others, a protector of true British/English values. Yet, his comic act covers a deep desire for power and those who saw him as a figure of fun are not laughing now. His politics could best be described as 'Trotskyite neo-Conservative'. This outsider leads a party within a party, a militant tendency striving for libertarian economics and conservative social values, and he hopes to radicalise the Conservative Party from within … very politely!

From outsider to power broker

These three outsiders all share the experience of finding themselves catapulted to the centre suddenly and unexpectedly. May became the party leader and prime minister when David Cameron suddenly resigned with little choice after the disastrous and unexpected referendum defeat on Brexit. She was selected as the safe pair of hands, the non-factional leader who could hold a divided party together. Corbyn became party leader after being put on the ballot for Labour leader as a nominal protest candidate with seemingly no chance of winning. Following populist leadership trends in the USA and Europe, he rode the train of discontentment that other populists have thrived on and won. Rees-Mogg saw his opportunity as his two right-wing political rivals, Michael Gove and Boris Johnson devoured each other in the Conservative leadership election contest. Gove bet on his chance of taking over the Tory leadership from May by being loyal to her, while Boris played on the edges, watching and waiting for his chance to challenge for leadership. Rees-Mogg meanwhile became leader of the hard-right Brexit faction and suddenly found himself centre stage as a key power broker.

Theme two: Politics of discontentment

The other theme these leaders have in common is that they all lead by mobilising the politics of discontentment. Each gains excess 'pleasure from their displeasure'. Psychoanalysis explains how we are doubly subjected, firstly to our conscious desires and secondly to our unconscious demands. Our unconscious often derives enjoyment from what we consciously complain about. Freud identified that pleasure and pain are closely aligned. These leaders have a personal unconscious attachment to enjoying their dissatisfaction, which enables them to see this trait in others, and which enables them to mobilise and amplify the discontentment in their followers.

Jeremy Corbyn and his followers gain surplus enjoyment from being the rebel activists fighting on behalf of the poor against the rich and elite big Other of capitalism. Unconsciously attached to their 'activist rebel identity', they defend their identity with their lives. They prioritise protecting this identity and, by doing so, undermine themselves when faced with the opportunity to lead real social change.

Corbyn and his tribal followers gain their unconscious enjoyment from two positions. First, they cannot function without an evil 'big Other', in other words the capitalist system represented by figures such as Thatcher or Trump. The Marxist left, like the hard right, has a long tradition of splitting and fragmentation. Each in-group delights in believing they hold the 'pure truth' and claiming 'the other' factions are betraying this truth. The 'narcissism of small differences' plays out as they delight in fighting over doctrine while the real fight for social justice passes them by. This infighting serves to bond the in-group together, reinforcing the pleasure they gain from being pure and righteous. Corbyn and his followers' rationale for existence depends on their particular unconscious essence that they repetitively circle around. This essence can be best summed up by the cry, 'It's unfair!'

Theresa May clearly gets off on the unconscious pleasure of being 'the suffering one'. The daughter of a vicar, she embodies the Christian ideal of personal suffering for the greater good. This serves as her martyr alter ego. A modern-day Joan of Arc, her embodied presence proclaims, 'I alone am the one who will save the nation.' Her supporters identify with the resolute woman standing alone against the terrible others who persecute her, the EU who bully her, the Rees-Mogg faction who make impossible demands, and Corbyn and the crazy left.

However, unlike some who really suffer altruistically for the benefit of others, May plays politics when it suits. To gain right-wing support, she created what she calls a 'hostile environment' for immigrants, betraying her claims to Christian morality by attacking the most vulnerable in society. May and her supporters identify as 'suffering martyrs', and the essence that they continually circle around can best be articulated with the cry, 'Alone against a persecuting world!'

Jacob Rees-Mogg and his followers gain their unconscious pleasure from a nostalgic attachment to a utopian past, blaming others for 'stealing their enjoyment'. Whether it's blaming immigrants for stealing jobs, multiculturalism for undermining their Christian culture, or EU bureaucrats for stealing their democracy, their identity depends on the notion of 'the other' stealing their enjoyment. Regaining this lost enjoyment can only happen if 'the other' is vanquished and a return to the Edenic past takes place. Their unconscious pleasure is derived from their identity as being protectors of Great Britain and the true (imperial and colonial) past. Like Corbyn and the leftists, they need a big Other to rail against. In their case, it's the elite outsiders who steal their pleasure. The essence that the Rees-Mogg supporters repetitively return to can be summed up with the cry, 'They have stolen our pleasure!'

Conclusion: Traversing the fantasy

These politicians are part of a wider trend across many parts of the globe, representing discontented and disenfranchised citizens. Populist, nationalist, and also liberal politicians are mobilising fears and anxieties and stirring up identity politics. Each creates binary splits between themselves and a persecuting big Other. Each has their particular essence, which they circle around again and again, which entraps them in a way of being. For citizens to overcome this entrapment, a new formulation for our identifications towards leaders is required.

These three outsider leaders who are attached to this way of being have had their fifteen minutes of fame. Brexit is not the biggest issue the UK is facing. Whatever the outcome, leave or remain, a soft or a hard Brexit, if this perverse form of political leadership continues, the UK will struggle. The biggest issue the UK, much of Europe, and the world face is rediscovering the capacity to identify with leaders who can work with a greater emotional maturity.

This doesn't mean giving up on a political vision. As citizens, it is time to traverse the fantasy that our troubles can be solved by amplifying our hatred, blame, and fears of an arbitrary bad other. Leaders who can contain emotions and fears rather than amplify them are urgently required!

CHAPTER 8

The meaning of Trump

This essay was written when Donald Trump first became the US president in 2017. As I write this preview, Donald Trump is again the US president. This essay resonates today, as to overcome the polarised and dangerous political environment, we must try to understand 'the meaning of Trump' and what he symbolically represents to the USA and wider society.

Introduction

This is not an attempt to give meaning to Donald Trump, the individual, for Trump himself is not a very compelling or interesting person. I regard him as a savvy opportunist and populist, prepared to go to any lengths to dominate media interest and delve to any depths to exploit political vulnerabilities without concern for individuals or groups beyond his own success.

What does interest me is to look at Trump as a social object which so many people have coalesced around. The aim is to ask what specific psychosocial and political dynamics produced this 'Trump object' that so many people identified with to enable him to win the presidency. I am not denigrating his personality or ability; as a scholar of leadership, I can see how it takes someone smart and with some charisma, however much we may dislike them or their politics, to pull this off. However, it is only when certain conditions are in play that any individual can harness and utilise the energy, anger, frustration, and cultural zeitgeist to take advantage of these conditions.

The myth that individual leaders create the conditions they utilise is a fantasy we keep propagating because the heroic narrative is comforting. We are conditioned to put our unconscious hopes in a messiah leader[31] who can save us and be in control of what feels out of control. Another way of deciphering the meaning of Trump is to think of him as a social symptom and to discern what Trump is a symptom of and what this social symptom signifies and reflects to wider society. Trump, in this sense, is like a mirror reflecting to us our 'civilisation and its discontents', to play with Freud's book title.

Taking Trump as a social object and a social symptom, I am exploring three possible meanings of Trump:

1. A new authoritarian settlement
2. Libidinal politics reign
3. The triumph of melancholia

A new authoritarian settlement

The election of a 'democratic authoritarian' to the White House, the high temple of Western democracy, signifies a rupture in the political system in the West.

The authoritarian settlement is more complex than the rise of Trump and the other right-wing populists and nationalists. These leaders are a symptom of a wider authoritarian settlement that mostly goes unrecognised. Trump's success is a product of two other strands of 'soft' authoritarianism that are hidden.

The first soft form is liberal-progressive authoritarianism, which operates through a cultural control that is most easily identified and seen in politically correct cultures. These are Hillary Clinton supporters who hid their authoritarian tendencies from themselves and others under the rhetoric of equality and diversity. There is a genuine need to fight for progressive politics, but this fight can and has become distorted. This creates a perverse situation whereby liberal progressives at one level fight for a fairer, more democratic, and inclusive society, yet at the same time, they impose an excessive level of cultural control on themselves and others and exclude those who don't fit into their tribe, looking down on them.

When Clinton called these excluded people 'the deplorables' it revealed her true feelings. Fighting for a better, more equal society is progressive; using discourse, language, and power to humiliate, bully, and oppress those who aren't in your 'tribe' is regressive and authoritarian. Free speech has become much more limited. You are only free to speak if you know the coded language of the politically correct elites who impose their authoritarian culture across college campuses and civic spaces.

The second form of soft authoritarianism is a totalising and hidden form that is imposed by neoliberalism and the excessive rise of corporate power. The Reagan-Thatcher political and economic project has finally come to a shuddering halt. It has failed miserably. Their promised land of economic and civic wealth, which they believed would arrive through 'free trade, deregulated markets, and flexible working', has finally been exposed as a failure. Global corporate power is authoritarian power; it imposes its neoliberal will on the masses without any accountability or regard for the communities it exploits. Flexible working and the loss of so many skilled jobs to automation means today's work is precarious work for the majority of people. This means that employees always feel insecure and vulnerable and are therefore compliant with the cultural control exerted by their companies. Catherine Casey describes these corporate employees as 'capitulated selves', unaware of their own subjugation.[32] Corporate authoritarianism is a soft form of power that impacts employees, rendering them as cogs in the corporate machine. It also influences and impacts citizens, turning them into passive consumers at every turn, stealing their autonomy and capturing their souls. Trump is a product of this authoritarian settlement, and he is a symptom playing back to society its malaise. In many ways, his form of angry authoritarianism is a way of making the hidden authoritarianism of the liberals and the corporations explicit.

One way of understanding the meaning of Trump is that he is the 'return of the repressed'. He is returning a harsh and explicit form of democratic authoritarianism to counter the hidden forms of authoritarianism that have oppressed so many for so long. Sadly, replacing soft implicit forms of authoritarianism with a harsher explicit form does nothing to improve things, and can be dangerous at many levels. The only hope is that there is a civic awakening when the authoritarianism becomes visible and divisive.

Libidinal politics reign

Trump is a product of libidinal politics triumphing over rational politics. Today's networked society is a disruptive society. Digitalisation and new technologies disrupt huge businesses, social media disrupted dictators in the Arab Spring, digital finance disrupted the whole finance system, leading to the 2008 crash, and new technologies are disrupting normative politics in the USA. When 40 per cent of Americans gain their news from Facebook, the rules of the game have changed. The huge financial advantage and mobilisation of activists in the Clinton machine couldn't overturn the power of social media and the algorithmic logic that favoured Trump's approach.

Trump is a product of libidinal politics. His campaign fed off the libidinal energy that flowed from those who loved him and from those who railed against him. Every time he pressed the libidinal button, he triggered responses in mainstream and new media. Love, admiration, aggression, anger, and hatred flowed to him and energised his campaign. Those who hated Trump and got angry, and at the same time took great pleasure in their hatred, rage, and self-righteousness. Lacan, the French psychoanalyst, theorises 'jouissance' is a particular form of unconscious enjoyment that derives pleasure from displeasure. *The Guardian* and *New York Times* delighted in expressing their displeasure of Trump, educated liberals enjoyed their highbrow stance looking down on the deplorables, and Trump fed off their libidinal energy just as much as he did off his admiring supporters. When people 'enjoy too much', they move to regressive positions and get distracted from the values they fight for.

The meaning of Trump in this context is that libidinal politics wins over rational politics in today's network society. This will change the political landscape for years to come. Tapping into emotions in politics is not new, but the network society changes the coordinates of how emotions go viral and how people feed each other's passions that bypass reason and 'truth politics'. Facebook became known as 'fakebook' as the algorithms entrapped people in ways of thinking that provided excessive pleasure to reinforce their mindsets. Hatred, greed, and fear hook people, and the algorithm's job is to hook people for longer, as that drives the profits. Trump was good at hatred, greed, and fear, and the algorithms obliged. Libidinal politics don't have to be regressive as used by Trump, but they cannot be ignored or pushed into second place. As the Democrats found out, the political rules have changed.

The triumph of melancholia

Freud's famous paper, 'Mourning and melancholia', shows how melancholia occurs when a lost object is not properly mourned. Freud writes, 'In mourning, time is needed for the command of reality-testing to be carried out in detail … when this work has been accomplished, the ego will have succeeded in freeing its libido from the lost object.'[33]

Without mourning, the ego cannot free itself from the lost object and continues to over-identify with it, leading to melancholia. Trump's identification with the lost object, 'the American Dream' and his constant references to MAGA, making America great again, was a classic melancholic response to the end of the empire. Freud goes on to observe the way melancholia has a manic side to it, which is another way to avoid facing the reality of the lost object. Trump's rallies are indeed filled with melancholic mania.

When a great nation is so divided internally, when it imprisons so many of its young black men, when whole regions are inflicted with unemployment and endemic drug abuse, when health care and basic welfare are severely limited or withdrawn, and when a nation has a military might that massively overpowers any other nation, yet it loses its recent conflicts in Iraq and Afghanistan, and Putin dominates the agenda in Syria and Ukraine, one can clearly point to the demise of empire. To renew and regenerate, the nation needs to face the reality principle and mourn the loss of the American Dream and the empire it had. Without this mourning, melancholia will dominate the political agenda. Democrats claim things are not so bad and there is a bright future, and Trump is claiming he can magically cure all ills and return the USA to a promised land. Together, they both create the imaginary fantasy that recovering what has been lost is possible. This undermines the potential of discovering something new and building a different way forward.

Trump's campaign was one of 'paranoid nostalgia', that is, paranoid about elites and immigrants stealing America's enjoyment and nostalgic about recreating a fantasy utopian past where industrial jobs can return en masse, globalisation can be reversed, and walls can be built to exclude the bad other (Mexicans and Muslims).

Conclusion

The meaning of Trump is that his election signifies that the world has radically changed. To draw on Lacan, Trump is a quilting point (*point-de-capiton*). Lacan said a quilting point fixes things just enough for action to be taken when all is in flux. Trump is a quilting point that held together a flux of discontented people in a turbulent world. He offered strong, simple narratives where he would return control to the people. When everything seemed in a mess, Trump promised to MAGA.

He parodied the soft authoritarianism of the liberal and corporate elites and offered surplus authority in their place. He championed melancholia and manically laughed in the face of mourning, refusing to face the loss of the American Dream and its empire. He offered the people a fantasy instead, and many liked it. He adapted quicker than those around him to the new reality that libidinal politics, powered by social media, win elections in the twenty-first century. The meaning of Trump is that he is a symptom of these social and political changes, he plays back to society it's excess. His politics are the politics of excess. He offers surplus authority, excessive libidinal energy, and surplus enjoyment (melancholic mania) in the face of the loss of an American Dream.

Part II

Rising tides

Introduction to Part II

The chapters in Part II are not about specific events but about rising tides, meaning the social themes that have gained prominence and reveal the shifting sands of our cultural landscapes. I have divided them into seven categories with brief introductions to each below.

- Environmental crisis
- The culture wars
- Therapy culture
- The positivity trap
- Diversity
- Navigating our digital age
- Re-enchanting our worlds

Environmental crisis

The environmental crisis has become a shadow that lurks behind everything. I explore some of the issues it raises by reflecting on 'the meaning of Greta Thunberg', the young activist who became the unlikely leading spokesperson for the environmental movement.

The culture wars

This section addresses a very powerful cultural shift in the past few decades. A cultural shift that has created huge political and social divisions. We begin with the environmental crisis that has been adopted in the culture wars, reflected through the powerful emotional projections that Greta Thunberg receives from devoted followers and also from those who react negatively to her persona. Emotional and unconscious attachments to increasingly polarised positions are central to these reflections. Chapter 10 addresses the rise of the term 'woke', tracing its origins and how it is mobilised by different political actors. Chapter 11 reveals how our response to dissonance has changed and how dissonance has become a political force.

Therapy culture

Therapy culture is pervasive; it is so embedded in Western society that we no longer notice it. Therapy moved from the clinic to wider society, and these three chapters take diverse perspectives to highlight key issues. Chapter 12 reviews the wounded and celebrated selves and how therapy culture divides us into two polemic identities. Chapter 13 reflects on the therapeutic question of what is our true desire, and Chapter 14 takes a look at how we like to think we are helping others but are often performing 'helpless helping'.

The positivity trap

My work takes me into very diverse organisations; I work within global corporations and in humanitarian not-for-profit organisations. In the past few years, I have worked with Ukrainian NGOs from a war zone, with Save the Children teams in Zimbabwe, and also with senior leaders in Silicon Valley hi-tech organisations, international banks, and global car manufacturers. What I have noticed when working across these geographical regions and diverse sectors is the ever-growing positivity trap. The corporate sector certainly has been influenced by US positive thinking ideologies with strong cultural behaviour codes that demand positivity. If you want to get on, you need to stay positive! In the NGO sector, this plays out differently, but there is a difficulty in sharing strong difficult emotions such as sadness, shame, guilt, or showing vulnerability. Chapters 15 and 16 reflect on the social demands that we should be happy and that the social injunctions that tell us we can achieve anything if we believe enough are not as helpful as they seem.

Diversity

Diversity issues are high on the polarised cultural agenda but rarely worked with well. I was moved to write two chapters in response to my own curiosity about diversity and the challenges it poses. Chapter 17 discusses staying with the trouble, and Chapter 18 discusses what it means to find your body is in the 'wrong' space.

Navigating our digital age

This section has four chapters beginning with Chapter 19, 'The network society is a disruptive society'. Chapter 20 takes a journey through our fast-changing relationships with borders and boundaries, and Chapter 21 explores how virtual and physical spaces create unusual experiences of presence and absence. Chapter 22 utilises the acronym NIPI (networks, identity, power, and influence), to help guide our work in organisations. The chapter discusses how we need to reimagine organisations as networks of desire.

Re-enchanting our worlds

This section is close to my heart. I believe it is our collective task to re-enchant our worlds. This is a necessary step before any real social change can take place. Modernity has delivered many positive things, and it has also delivered environmental catastrophe and, alongside this, a pervasive sense of disenchantment. I see this in workplaces, in my therapy and coaching sessions with individuals, and in the world around me. Re-enchanting our worlds is a process that we discover as we go. I finish Part II with three short chapters which are personal reflections on moments of grace when on a monastic retreat and how personal soul connections inspire and fulfil me when engaging in seemingly mundane tasks.

CHAPTER 9

The meaning of Greta

Original artwork, hand-drawn by Martyna Adamska

Introduction

The environmental crisis is a daily news item. Among all the noise and concern, one individual stands out: a young woman with no political or media experience breaks through the overload of information, and she makes people listen. This chapter was written after Greta made a huge impact when addressing world leaders at the United Nations (UN) in 2019. It explores the remarkable rise of a vulnerable schoolgirl who became the voice and face of the environmental movement.

Greta Thunberg dramatically rose in a very short space of time to become the face of environmentalism. This chapter explores the social meaning of Greta Thunberg and asks what she evokes in our social imaginary.[34] What conscious and unconscious identifications are projected onto Greta that have made her the unlikely famous person she is? This social reading of Greta is important to counter the seductive and reductive retreat into individualistic thinking. These questions are not about exploring her individual psychological leadership or character traits but focus on how Greta became a social object with a vast social network following her, including more than 5.5 million X/Twitter followers, a new documentary film about her, and mainstream media coverage across the globe.

Greta has become a social phenomenon, a 'global sensation' according to *Time* magazine, which made her Time Person of the Year 2019. Sixteen months after commencing her lone 'School Strike for Climate' she 'addressed heads of state at the UN, met with the Pope, sparred with the President of the United States and inspired 4 million people to join the global climate strike on September 20, 2019, in what was the largest climate demonstration in human history'.[35]

Greta inspires, angers, attracts, and fascinates many, but what social meanings do these identifications and emotions reveal about wider society and our collective thinking? I am not making a case for or against 'Greta' and the environmental cause she champions. Millions of people coalesce around and identify with Greta, both positively and negatively. What is it that Greta represents and plays back to us?

There is not a singular explanation of the meaning of Greta, only a plurality of meanings that emerge from the diverse identifications we project onto her and introject (take in) from her. Personal identifications merge to form the collective narratives that bind a movement together. It is these unconscious identifications that produce meanings and attachments, creating a strong emotional bond (a libidinal economy) that has propelled Greta to fame and mobilised many more to become activists in the environmental movement.

Messages and meanings

'The medium is the message'[36]

Greta draws from, inspires, and mobilises the environmentalist movement. In 1967, McLuhan and Fiore famously stated the 'medium is the message', claiming that meaning was no longer communicated only through the content of what is said. They held that a deeper and more powerful meaning comes from the medium through which it is communicated. Looking at Greta through this lens, we see she gains maximum attention not via the words and the content of her talks but by how she, as 'the messenger', presents, delivers, and embodies the message.

Greta acts as an embodied *sign or message* to wider society. The globally transmitted images of Greta, the 'child-leader' admonishing the world's most powerful leaders, are hugely important when trying to understand the meaning and impact of Greta. The environmental message is so much more powerful when delivered via Greta than when delivered by yet another scientist, green politician, media celebrity, or environmental activist.

Greta the messenger

I have identified five core messages delivered by Greta, acknowledging that these are partial and not a full account. Beneath each message, I share a hypothesis of the meanings she mobilises for others.

Message 1: Vulnerability

Greta presents as vulnerable. 'Thunberg is 16 but looks 12. She usually wears her light brown hair pulled into two braids, parted in the middle.'[37] This small schoolgirl, whose growth was stunted by a previous eating disorder, openly acknowledges her Asperger's diagnosis, past depression, and OCD; she presents as vulnerable and fragile. She often looks a little bewildered in the public sphere. When I first saw Greta on TV, I immediately felt this sense of vulnerability, becoming worried about her safety. How would she (and her family) cope with her media exposure, the pressures of fame, the mass love and hate projections that she was receiving? This worry hasn't left me. Yet from this place of vulnerability, she speaks with a fearless voice and often, when speaking publicly, with an aggressive and angry tone.

The meaning

Greta's self-presentation embodies a vulnerability that others identify with and is a powerful signifier to wider society. Greta's vulnerability signifies three more systemic meanings:

1. The vulnerability of planet Earth.
2. The vulnerability of millions at risk and all those who feel anxious about the impact of climate change.
3. How vulnerability and strength can be combined. Vulnerability does not mean we have to be paralysed by it.

Vulnerability is the very essence of what many feel when facing the escalating environmental crisis. The disruptive turbulence of the digital age also creates more social vulnerability, which has been amplified by the Covid-19 pandemic. Greta embodies this vulnerability and plays it back to us loud and clear. Millions personally and collectively identify with Greta's vulnerability. Her presence aligns with how they personally feel vulnerable and worried for their children and grandchildren and for those who live in the most precarious places. Her fragility and vulnerability mirror the precarity of the planet we live on, and Greta's presence embodies this.

There are two parts to this. First, Greta embodies the vulnerability we feel, and second, her strength, anger, and presence reassure and awaken us. Greta conveys that being vulnerable does not mean being passive. It is possible to be both vulnerable and strong, to live precariously and to be active and courageous.

Greta's message resonates strongly with those who feel both vulnerable and impotent; it gives new meaning and vitality to their experience.

It is particularly powerful to those in the environmentalist movement who have a heightened awareness of the vulnerability of the planet and all its human and non-human inhabitants.

Message 2: Not-patriarchy

Greta presents as the polar opposite of patriarchy, and in particular to the macho, toxic patriarchy presented by populist male leaders who champion climate change denial.

Greta really gets under the skin of these patriarchs. Brazil's President Bolsonaro said of Greta, 'It's amazing how much space the press gives this kind of *pirralha*,' using a Portuguese word that loosely translates as 'little brat' or 'pest'. President Trump posted a derogatory tweet about her needing to chill out. Greta, to the delight of her supporters, puts their tweets on her Twitter feed as an ironic badge of honour. In 2020, after Trump's election defeat, Greta recycled Trump's tweet telling him to chill out when he was having a post-election rant.

Feminism and environmentalism have a long-coupled history. Gaia theory, the Pagan Goddess, and Mother Earth offer alternative accounts of human engagement with the natural world and counter patriarchal structures that have dominated in religious, philosophical, and scientific circles. Yet Greta doesn't fit into a normative feminist narrative, perhaps because of her young age, perhaps because her focus is solely on the environment. Suzanne Moore, the *Guardian* columnist, writes: 'The extraordinary reactions of certain men to Greta Thunberg, which have nothing to do with her urgent and necessary message on the climate emergency, tells you exactly what happens when a young woman simply refuses to be sexualised. It makes them deeply uncomfortable .... She is a 16-year-old, and these are grown men. And they are terrified. Wonderful. Who knew you could shake the patriarchy simply by refusing to smile for it, dress for it or demur to it? A refusal to acquiesce to the male gaze has these dinosaurs squirming.'[38]

Moore projects her feminist desire onto Greta, delighting in imagining that Greta wilfully refuses 'to acquiesce to the male gaze'. Yet is this a feminist refusal or simply that Greta hasn't developed into, or was not yet interested in becoming, a teenager who felt the pressure to socially conform to gendered and sexuality norms? Greta is Greta, a schoolgirl who writes on her Twitter handle, 'Climate and environmental activist with Asperger's. Born at 375ppm' (accounting for the CO_2 level at her birth).

Greta's socialisation has been problematic, her salvation from deep unhappiness, social isolation, and withdrawal, according to her and her parents, has been to fight the environmental cause. This situates her outside the social norms that Moore implicates. What is correct is that Greta definitely impacts particular men, as Robert Shrimsley reports in his *Financial Times* article titled, 'Why middle-aged men hate Greta'. He writes, 'Of course, the main reason why some right-wingers are so agitated about her is that they do not like her message, but the messenger herself obviously riles them too.'[39] He argues that her presence as a role model to others, in other words a 'stroppy teenager' who berates adults and forces her parents to become vegan strikes fear into these angry men.

Greta clearly mobilises strong identifications that are particularly disturbing and unsettling to patriarchal men. Their egos and their internalised idea of how power operates are directly confronted and undone by Greta. Her nonconformist presence, her openness about her Asperger's, and her appearance as a young schoolgirl have been the ultimate antithesis to the power games and status accumulation, which is their currency. To be precise, she epitomises 'not-patriarchy'.

The meaning

Greta plays back to wider society a vision that a mainly white, male-dominated world is not the only possible world: another world is possible. The negative identifications from male patriarchs are countered by powerfully positive identifications from many women, men, and thousands of schoolchildren who identify with Greta and who don't identify with patriarchy. This is not a clarion call for feminism; it goes beyond feminism vs patriarchy, male vs female. Greta's persona and physical presence transcend this binary. Schoolboys and schoolgirls, young people, men and women who desire a different future all identify with Greta.

The radical change Greta speaks for demands 'not-patriarchy'. Patriarchy got us into this mess. While her school strike protesters chant 'system change not climate change', there is a realisation that system change is not only an environmental, economic, or political demand, it also demands personal, cultural, and social change. Not-patriarchy demands new power structures and different relationships between human and non-human actors. Complex societies demand less binary and more fluid identifications. New social movements are at the forefront of these changes. Greta's presence reveals to us how nonconformist, non-binary and not-patriarchal 'ways of being in the world' can open a new space for the transformation of society.

Message 3: Giving voice to the voiceless

History can become punctuated by a single voice, one that articulates the voice of a generation. A voice that speaks for the marginalised and voiceless. Bob Dylan became the voice of his generation in the 1960s. Greta has become this generational voice for our times, mobilising 4 million to go on school climate strikes. Varshini Prakash, twenty-six, writes of Greta: 'She symbolizes the agony, the frustration, the desperation, the anger—at some level, the hope—of many young people who won't even be of age to vote by the time their futures are doomed.'[40] Many environmentalists' messages are similar to Greta's; her message is not original or unique, but her presence is. Greta's physical presence embodies the innocence of a voiceless schoolchild, becoming a spokesperson and articulating the concerns of millions. She talks on behalf of young people with confidence.

'The problems we care about the most are usually not the ones that are being prioritized the highest. Young people are very concerned about the climate crisis and ecological crisis, and that is very under-represented' (Thunberg cited in Meyer, 2019).[41]

Neither Dylan nor Greta operate in a vacuum; they are part of a much wider ecology of social struggle. However, they both, in their own ways, managed to capture a generational mood. Dylan in his poetic, rebellious way; Greta in her persistent, stark, and rational way. Dylan presented himself as a 'rebel youth', while Greta presents herself as a vulnerable schoolchild determined to stand up for her truth and her generation's future. Both transmit the anger of their generation and awaken the world to the reality that 'the times, they are a changing'.

The meaning

To be voiceless is to be powerless, and the disempowered seek a vessel to carry their projections and feelings. They identify with someone who shares their language and desires, who speaks for them and with them so their voices can be heard. Young people on school strike, through the medium of Greta, have discovered a power and a voice they didn't have before. Greta speaks on behalf of many voiceless constituents, amplifying and making legitimate activists' voices across the world. Some of the voiceless she speaks for are:

- School-age children who will inherit climate and bio-diversity devastation.
- Marginalised environmental activists.
- The 'voiceless' environment: the fauna and flora that are being decimated by biodiversity damage, the Amazon rain forest, the polar regions.
- Indigenous people, sub-Saharan Africans, and impoverished people who are most at risk of the impacts of climate crisis.[42]

Greta's voice has captured a zeitgeist, her school strike movement has gone global, and she has become a voice for the voiceless while, more importantly, mobilising many to find their own voices.

Message 4: Prophetic messenger

'Greta Thunberg is a prophet, preacher, rulebreaker, avenging angel,' wrote Fintan O'Toole following her UN address in 2019.[43] From this small girl on stage comes the quavering voice of Greta Thunberg, like the cry of an Old Testament prophet, she transmits the anger of others that speak through her. At Davos in 2019, Greta spoke to world leaders, 'Oceans will rise. Cities will flood. Millions of people will suffer ... I want you to panic ... I want you to feel the fear I feel every day. And then I want you to act.'[44]

The environmental movement claims not to like charismatic leaders (or leaders at all), and yet Greta has become a beloved 'messiah leader'. Margaret Atwood said of Greta: 'She's wonderful ... She's sort of the Joan of Arc of the environment. I think she needs a big white horse.'[45] Joan of Arc was perceived to be the holy virgin fulfilling prophesies to work miracles and restore France. I imagine Atwood connects Greta and Joan of Arc due to their gender, young age, the purity projected onto both and due to Atwood's own desire for a saviour. Greta presents as a young school-age child, untainted by worldly things, speaking with absolute conviction as if inspired by a greater power.

While O'Toole's and Atwood's comments are written in good faith, it is worth remembering the fate of Joan of Arc, who was martyred. This again raises the vulnerability of Greta, who holds so much worldly attention. A colleague of mine recently attended a business and sustainability course at Schumacher College. She reported how Greta inspired awe and wonder among the climate activists she met and was surprised that there was no space for dissent in this groupthink. This echoes my experience when observing Extinction Rebellion events in London, where Greta is sanctified by the activists I mixed with. Paradoxically, environmental activists abhor power elites, aiming for egalitarian, leaderless, self-managing movements, yet a huge blind spot exists towards the messianic worship of their new idol.

Prophetic voices are necessary for new social movements that lead change, and yet these voices can quickly gain cult followings. Greta adds to her prophetic identity by referring to Asperger's as her superpower, using the hashtag #aspiepower.[46] Environmental activists use drum circles to call on the spirits, drawing on indigenous traditions of shamanism, and Greta perhaps enters their social imaginary as a Nordic folklore heroine. Ireland's powerful folklore tradition perhaps speaks through Fintan O'Toole's 2019 article, where he describes her as 'a ghost of the future, who presents herself as an avenging angel'.[47] I experience the rising of an unconscious desire for our disenchanted modern world to be re-enchanted once again with pagan spirits,[48] particularly in environmentalist and alternative communities. Melucci proposes that new social movements challenge society in three symbolic ways, the first being prophecy. He writes: 'Prophecy is the act of announcing, based on personal experiences, that alternative frameworks of meaning are possible.'[49] Greta's personal experience of undertaking a lone school strike at the age of fifteen, which became a global movement, offers such an alternative meaning to society. Her lived experience demonstrates that a child's voice can be heard at the highest tables, that the seemingly impossible is possible, and that with the will to speak truth to power, things can change.

The meaning

Three meanings are revealed from Greta's prophetic voice.

1. A prophetic voice breaks through normative consensus, shattering complacency and denial.
2. Greta's lived personal experience is prophetic. If Greta can rise to lead a global movement, then people can rise to demand system change, and politicians can rise to deliver. Prophecy announces a new future.
3. A collective desire for salvation. Her adoring followers unconsciously desire salvation. A desire for a transcendent force, a charismatic superhero, a new prophet to lead them to the promised land. Greta reverses the common idealised notion of a messiah leader, yet in achieving 'prophetic status', she propels herself even higher into the salvation stratosphere. This desire for salvation is a desire to overcome anxiety and impotence, to create an emotional landscape where we feel bound together in solidarity.

Caution is required for those who hold Greta up as a prophet with superhuman powers. The desire for salvation quickly becomes a dysfunctional fantasy if the prophetic saviour riding in on a white horse, leading us to a utopian, egalitarian future is not challenged. Prophetic voices only work when they mobilise activists and movements rather than become spectacles of hope.

Prophets have a tendency to be martyred and painfully taken down from their pedestal. Those who treat Greta like a prophet need to reclaim their projections and unconscious desires for a saviour, not only to take care of Greta but also to keep the environmental movement focused on its mission. Greta is not a prophet, but she is a prophetic messenger. She doesn't have magical qualities or even a radical new message. What Greta has is her personal experience and presence that communicates a message of radical transformation, which I address next.

Message 5: Turning the world upside down

Greta's presence signifies a world turned upside down. Global leadership figures that hold the world's attention are not sixteen-year-old shy children with a neuro-developmental disorder and a recent past of eating disorders and depression. Schoolchildren rarely confront world leaders on an international stage, admonishing their immature behaviour, asking 'Where are the adults in the room?' Greta is a wounded healer who millions identify with, turning her Asperger's diagnosis into a super-power. She says she is rarely angry, but in front of an audience, she is like an avatar channelling her supporters' rage.

'How dare you? You have stolen my dreams and my childhood'; 'People are underestimating the force of angry kids'; 'We are angry and frustrated, and that is because of good reason. If they want us to stop being angry then maybe they should stop making us angry'[50]—Greta speaking at a rally in Bristol in 2020.

Returning to Melucci's three forms of symbolic challenge:

1. Prophecy: the act of announcing, based on personal experiences, that alternative frameworks of meaning are possible.
2. Paradox: the reversal of dominant codes by their exaggeration.
3. Representation: the movement plays back to society itself, revealing contradictions and irrationality.

We addressed Prophecy in the last section. The other two, Paradox and Representation, are addressed here.

Paradox: The reversal of dominant codes by exaggeration is precisely what Greta does. When she says, 'World leaders are behaving like children, so it falls on us to be the adults in the room,' this is the perfect example of Melucci's symbolic challenge. A 'powerless' unelected school child telling the world's most powerful politicians to stop behaving like children reverses the dominant codes and, in doing so, reveals the mess we are in. A school child taking a leadership role, berating world leaders, plays back to society the irrationality of what is going on.

Melucci's third form of symbolic challenge, Representation: 'The movement plays back to society itself, revealing contradictions and irrationality,' is also what Greta does. With an army of schoolchildren on strike, shouting 'System change, not climate change', this movement plays back to society the irrationality of the inaction of politicians in the face of a human-made catastrophe. It reveals the absurd situation whereby children are taking responsibility for the future of the planet, telling adults what is important, ethical, and right.

The meaning

Greta's presence reveals the irrationality and contradictions that exist as the world struggles to address the environmental emergency. When a schoolchild is talking more sense than powerful adult leaders, the meaning is clear. The world is turned upside down. It is an irrational world where thousands of schoolchildren have to strike to activate adults and world leaders to address the environmental emergency. Greta is a messenger revealing how the world is turned upside-down, with powerful political leaders hiding in the face of disaster. She also evokes an uncomfortable truth that to take a corrective path, the world needs to be 'turned upside down'. That the current ways of doing things cannot continue. A radical reimagining of economics and social organising is required to deliver the system change needed.

Conclusion

Exploring the meaning of Greta is a way of returning meaning to ourselves. Environmentalists, alongside other social movement activists, can easily become distracted and indulge themselves by gaining excess pleasure through enjoying berating the bad-other capitalists and taking refuge in their moral righteousness.[51] When this happens, it undermines their primary task of working to deliver system change to alleviate environmental destruction.

Greta can fall into this trap when speaking. Like populist politicians, Greta calls on 'the people' to stand up against the powerful elites, identifying herself and her followers as the good tribe vs the bad other. She finds herself as a leadership actor in a passionate movement, and it is fraught with the same dangers we see in populist movements. Thus far, Greta steers on the energising side of this fragile balancing act and keeps her focus clearly on the environment. As she claims herself, Asperger's syndrome gives her a super power because it keeps her completely focused on the task, and my guess is she also has good advisors supporting her.

The meaning of Greta

Greta's five messages come together to form a collective meaning she brings to the world. Greta, as a messenger, acts as a sign that heightens society's awareness of what we repress and deny. She operates in a similar way to a pre-modern shaman/oracle, or a psychoanalyst with a patient, or how new social movements act in relation to society. All three aim to reveal that which is concealed and to make visible what is repressed and hidden. This process of unveiling brings the repressed knowledge into conscious awareness, and then it can be worked with. The meaning we can extrapolate from how Greta presents as a messenger is as follows:

We are all vulnerable, and the planet is vulnerable; patriarchy has failed; the voiceless need to be heard, and we need prophetic voices to cut through the current coalition of power and repression. The human species is acting irrationally and turning a blind eye in the face of the greatest existential threat we have ever faced. The meaning of Greta is that the world is turned upside down, we claim to be rational beings yet are acting in a self-destructive and irrational way. A schoolchild berating world leaders reflects this logic of our times. The meaning of Greta is that the world needs a new 'turning-upside-down' to deliver system change.

Greta does not provide answers, but her messages provide us with meanings. We should pay attention.

CHAPTER 10

The rise of woke

The 'rise of woke' is a commentary on how identity politics have been weaponised to undermine the causes of social justice that 'woke' originally aspired to change. The essay was written at the end of 2022 after Robert DeSantis was re-elected as the Republican governor of Florida, where he made the term 'woke ideology' a central feature of his campaign. The essay explores the origins of 'woke' and how it is used by both the right and the left and finishes by making a distinction between fake-woke and awake-woke, that is, between virtue signalling and acting for social justice.

Introduction

Woke is a hot topic these days. In the USA, Europe, and beyond, right-wing politicians use the term 'woke' as a derogatory shorthand for the liberal views of progressives. As the culture wars spread fast, woke is utilised to raise fear and divide further. Woke, once an object of desire for leftists, has been transformed into a term of derision by the populist right.

Robert DeSantis, re-elected with an increased majority as Republican Florida governor and hot-tipped to run for president, utilises 'woke ideology' as a centrepiece for his campaigning. He positions woke as the evil enemy to fight against. Recently, he attacked Democratic governors and leaders as being infected with a 'woke mind virus'. As with all populist political attacks, they begin with a grain of truth that enables them to gain credibility within their partisan groups, and then they explode it. Political correctness, cancel culture, identity, gender, and sexual politics have indeed gone viral, particularly on university campuses and within certain demographic groups. This movement from class politics to identity politics has been liberating for some and oppressive for others. Identity politics have made some more visible and given them a greater voice, for example, the LGBTQI+ community, and for others, it has made them feel even more disempowered, for example, the economically impoverished, white, working class, and rustbelt communities. DeSantis and others play the woke card to polarise society and to gain political leverage.

In his governor's victory speech, DeSantis said: 'We have embraced freedom .... We have maintained law and order. We have protected the rights of parents. We have respected our taxpayers and we reject "woke" ideology.'

He continued to a cheering crowd, mirroring the famous Winston Churchill 'we will fight them on the beaches' speech: 'We fight the woke in the legislature, we fight the woke in the schools, we fight the woke in the corporations. We will never ever surrender to the woke mob. Florida is where woke goes to die.'[52]

DeSantis and Trump are the best-known advocates of using woke to attack opponents, and this 'successful strategy' has led to woke becoming the essence of the culture wars across many parts of the world. UK conservatives and other Europeans use anti-woke sentiments to win right-wing votes. Rishi Sunak vowed to stop 'woke nonsense and left-wing agitators' when campaigning to be prime minister.[53] On university campuses and in many political fights, woke has become a battleground. Russian and other authoritarian-patriarchal states utilise the politics of woke to dismiss their liberal-Westernised opponents. This has huge implications for social justice issues; if you are gay and live in Russia you live in a dangerous world.

Until recently, woke was a term to be proud of, as Simon Hatterstone of *The Guardian* proudly claimed, 'I am woke' when critiquing antisemitism.[54]

Woke: Its original meaning

Woke first came from the black community in the USA; its meaning here was to be awake to issues of social injustice and particularly to racism. Barbara Lee sums it up neatly:

> But we will only succeed if we reject the growing pressure to retreat into cynicism and hopelessness ... We have a moral obligation to 'stay woke', take a stand and be active; challenging injustices and racism in our communities and fighting hatred and discrimination wherever it rises.[55]

In 1962, *The New York Times* published an article on 'phrases and words you might hear today in Harlem', a neighbourhood in New York City where many African Americans live. The African American novelist William Melvin Kelley wrote the earliest known use of the word under its new definition in an article titled, 'If you're woke, you dig it'.

Ten years later, in 1972, a character in Barry Beckham's play about pan-Africanist Marcus Garvey says: 'I been sleeping all my life. And now that Mr Garvey done woke me up, I'm gon' stay woke. And I'm gon' help him wake up other black folk.'[56]

Woke entered mainstream language during the Black Lives Matter movement, which used the hashtag #staywoke in the wake of racial injustices spreading across the US.

Woke ideology literally means an ideology that demands we wake up to injustice. When DeSantis says he will fight woke ideology, what he is really saying is this: 'We fight woke in the legislature, in the schools, in the corporations,' in other words, we fight people waking up to injustice in the legislature, schools, and corporations.

'We will never ever surrender to the woke mob,' or, we will never surrender to people who are awake to social injustice and racism.

'Florida is where woke goes to die,' meaning Florida is where we will crush those who are awake to social injustice and racism.

When you look at it this way, to be against woke is a damning project which will inevitably fail because social justice issues do not disappear.

What DeSantis and other right-wing politicians are actually doing is appealing to those voters who feel left behind, who believe that cancel culture and identity politics are being used to impose others' way of living on the majority. However, using woke in this way can have terrible consequences.

When a large proportion of a population supports 'not being awake' to social injustice and openly discriminates against marginalised groups, blaming them for their economic and social problems, history reveals that dreadful things happen. Reactionary politics are simply that, a fearful reaction, an unconscious displacement of anxiety and fear projected onto a convenient 'bad other'. Reactionary, nationalist, and populist politics rely on people turning a blind eye to what they know, choosing to be asleep rather than take a more thoughtful, but perhaps difficult position, of being 'awake' and facing the deeper underlying issues that require addressing.

To be awake-woke means to acknowledge our own biases and prejudices and not project our fears onto the easily identifiable targets chosen by 'anti-woke' political forces, namely immigrants, Jews, Muslims, people of colour, or ethnically diverse communities, including travellers, Roma, and LGBTQI+ communities, among others.

What politicians and media on the populist right have understood very well is that bipartisan culture wars pay off; stirring a passionate hatred of the other offers a release of anger and fear and creates a tribal response of 'we the people' against a common enemy. Yet, this only works in the short term. The underlying causes of anxiety, fear, and resentment do not go away when we repress them. Being anti-woke provides a short-term sugar rush solution but leaves the deeper causes of the problems unresolved, and fear, anxiety, and resentment soon return.

Awake-woke

This short-term pleasure hit gained from fighting culture wars has become a left-progressive problem, too. There are some 'woke progressives' who gain (unconscious) pleasure from being self-righteous and demonising the bad 'populist other'. They began a journey in good faith to join the fight for social justice but got lost in identity politics along the way. Today, many woke warriors gain their pleasure not from fighting for social justice but from partaking in the 'culture wars'. Their libido energy and unconscious pleasure come from creating a good tribe vs an evil tribe, mirroring the reactionary splitting, which is not at all awake-woke.

When activists/progressives enjoy their activism identities too much,[57] it is a sign that a true awake position and the fight for social justice has been lost. Enjoying the culture war too much, rather than trying to understand the anxieties and social issues that underpin the fears that cause it, is not being woke. I use the term awake-woke to differentiate those who strive for social justice from culture war liberals who get caught up in unconscious dynamics, which lead to taking a fake-woke position.

Fake-woke

We are not awake-woke if we attach ourselves to tribal politics of the cultural war. The line between awake-woke and fake-woke can be blurred. Consciously, woke warriors really believe in social justice, but unconsciously, they are 'getting off' on alienating and attacking their 'bad other' enemies. In Lacanian psychoanalysis, this unconscious enjoyment, this 'getting off', relates to how we attain our unconscious pleasure or 'jouissance'.

Woke late-night-comedy liberal-progressive TV hosts in the US thrive on being fake-woke. They show how clever they are, and their audiences feel clever too, laughing at how stupid the 'bad other' is. The elite, self-gratifying audience delight in demonstrating their educated insider awareness, their woke credentials, and making fun of the lower caste 'deplorable' other (to coin Hillary Clinton's fateful language).

Fake-woke is also a common practice by corporates and public organisations who see woke as a positive branding exercise. They spend large sums on rainbow-washing to create PC language cultures to promote themselves as cool companies while doing little about the systemic and structural changes needed to address social justice issues. Many in the LGBTQI+ community are disgusted by how annual pride marches have lost their radical activist edge and become brand opportunities for rainbow-washing global corporations.

Fake-woke and cancel culture

Silencing free speech, de-platforming, and closing down the other also feeds the narrative spread by DeSantis and others that woke means 'woke police' who shut down freedoms and will take over public spaces.

Excess enjoyment reveals fake-woke

A good way to spot fake-woke is to notice when excess enjoyment takes place. Sharing jokes and feeling warmth and solidarity with others is important, but when 'surplus enjoyment' is present, take this as a warning. Excess pleasure reveals a manic reaction that signals anxiety and displacement of energy. When we are awake-woke, we are thoughtful and reflective, when we are fake-woke, we are manic, and anxiety speaks through us. When this occurs, we have drifted into enjoying tribal politics too much, and this just feeds the beast. The populist right then has some justification in claiming 'virtue signalling' (albeit loaded to undermine), that is, woke is being used as an identity indicator and has nothing to do with real change. The hunger for and pleasure taken in the culture wars on both sides undoes the real battle for social justice.

Fake-woke emerges when liberal progressives become puritans, when their good identity becomes more important than driving change. Sometimes, being with a cultural warrior from the progressive left is similar to being with a fundamentalist Christian, as they believe that they are the chosen ones and theirs is the only interpretation of the truth. The paradox is that when Evangelical Christians, religious fundamentalists, market fundamentalists, and populist nationalists preach their puritan truths, the fake-woke liberal tribe are incensed, unable to see the plank in their own eye.

Using language as power

We are not awake-woke if we claim to be social justice warriors and, at the same time, use the power of language, knowledge, and educational elitism to undermine and silence others with less power or language skills. I once heard a psychoanalyst say we have become a nation of stutterers, referring to how many people hesitate and stutter due to the anxiety caused by misspeaking about politically correct identity issues.

We are not awake-woke if we shout for social justice while posturing and virtue signalling to feed our egos, to get attention and 'likes', instead of acting to progress social justice.

What is to be done?

First, to strive towards being an awake-woke activist, let go of the culture war adrenaline buzz, and realise that enjoying bipartisan politics too much just feeds the culture war, which isn't helping social change take place.

Second, be alert to 'surplus-enjoyment politics' on both sides. The excess enjoyment at Trump rallies offers a clear signal of the danger. Not only have right-populists enjoyed Trump too much, but so did the liberal press, such as *The New York Times* and *The Guardian*, who feasted on Trump's transgressions. 'Enjoying too much' the dystopian spectacle he creates boosted their sales and also boosted the Trump libido and its followers, feeding into the culture war on which they thrive.

The truly radical position is to engage with the other, calling out injustice and speaking truth to power, but also being awake to our own biases and tribal behaviours that create pleasurable bonds between us. Enjoy the bonds of solidarity, for they provide the strength and courage to make change, but don't enjoy so much as to forget the struggle.

Holding open a space for people to enter into dialogue, challenge each other, and wake each other up is the real work to be done. Let's fight for social justice and strive to reach out to the marginalised who need our solidarity. Let's also reach out to the discontented others who are being seduced by anti-woke rhetoric.

It is telling that a social justice movement focused on awakening black people to the issues of structural racism that began in the black community and was re-energised by the Black Lives Matter movement has found itself attacked by white politicians. It is also telling that educated university students and others have become much more consumed by identity politics and culture wars, leaving others to strive for the most pressing social justice issues, dominated by economic poverty, immigration, class barriers, ethnicity, and the urgent need to make a socially just environmental transition to a green economy.

Today, to be woke is needed more than ever; that is awake-woke, not fake-woke.

CHAPTER 11

The politics of dissonance

This essay responds to a recognition that dissonance has undergone a silent but powerful change. Until recently, experiencing dissonance was an uncomfortable experience, but that has changed. Political movements are at the heart of this change, which opens up a new political front.

Introduction

> ***Dissonance: a definition***
> A tension or clash resulting from the combination of two disharmonious or unsuitable elements
>
> *Cognitive dissonance:*
> The state of having inconsistent thoughts, beliefs, or attitudes

This chapter discusses how dissonance has become a central artefact in political discourse and explores how it has been embraced in both populist and progressive politics. Dissonance was always considered a problem, something to overcome, yet recently, it has been celebrated by right-wing populists and accommodated by left progressives. The chapter explores how the politics of dissonance plays out and concludes by reflecting on the eco-systemic forces working in society at large.

Dissonance as tension

Dissonance, and in particular cognitive dissonance, has long been considered a problematic state of affairs. Dissonance led to disharmony and tensions that would lead to inner conflict and/or external conflict. Psychoanalysts, psychologists, and sociologists from Freud onwards put forward theories of how internal or social tensions brought about by living with dissonance, individually and collectively, would create anxieties, stress, depression, somatised illnesses, and even civil conflict and war. Leon Festinger proposed that human beings strive for internal psychological consistency to function mentally in the real world.[58] This idea of humans trying to find unity and harmony in their life-worlds has been around for a long time, showing up in diverse philosophies and religions. In China, for example, a long history of seeking social harmony exists, such as the balancing of Yin and Yang.

> Traditionally, the Chinese have 'the ability … to hold different propositions simultaneously without distress' (Cotterell, 2002, p. 30). The mindset derived from the Yin of Confucian paternalism and the Yang of Taoist holistic thinking does not see opposites but rather different aspects of the same system … (Li, 2012).[59]

The capacity to hold difference and paradox together in the East comes in sharp contrast to the West, which favours clarity and is troubled by paradox and conflicting ideas and behaviours. The above authors reveal that dissonance and distress are less present in Chinese culture when difference arises because difference is held within a holistic and systemic space, with the greater shared purpose of maintaining social harmony.

The current situation of living in a communist state with capitalist economics is a living example. There are many tensions, but so far, they are holding together and achieving outstanding economic results. Dissonance seems to bring about tensions and problems when the difference pulls against individual and social harmony. In the West, this tension is exacerbated by a rigidity of linear thinking that lacks a systemic perspective. This emanates from the belief in science, rationality, order, and hierarchy, which draws on reductionist thinking rather than holistic thinking. The environmental crisis is a result of this lack of holistic thinking.

As modernity took hold in the West, a new faith in science and reason dominated the culture. It was considered rational if behaviours aligned with beliefs and irrational if they did not. Cognitive dissonance occurred when behaviours and beliefs diverged. Festinger explains how people rationalised their thinking to avoid suffering the tensions and anxieties any dissonance caused, 'Tell him you disagree and he turns away. Show him facts or figures and he questions your sources. Appeal to logic and he fails to see your point.'[60]

The idea that dissonance creates discomfort, anxiety, embarrassment, regret, shame, and stress has long been held by psychologists and also by mainstream society. Media commentators would quickly pick up the dissonance in a politician's speech or actions, challenging them to explain discrepancies, and their failure to do so would undermine their legitimacy.

At the heart of modernity lies the promise of an ordered world where things become categorised and boundaries are clear. An ordered society demanded an ordered mind, one where reason ruled. When dissonance occurred individually or socially, it had to be addressed and either repaired or rationalised. Dissonance emerging from disordered minds could lead to a disordered society. Disordered minds were disciplined by society and sent to asylums, prisons, and clinics.[61] Dissonance occurred when the Big Other of society demanded certain behaviours and the individual/group believed or experienced something different. Before legalisation, homosexuality was disciplined by law and by moral codes (social disapproval), meaning that most gay men and women lived in a state of dissonance, often struggling to live with their own deviance from what was established as a social norm.

Dissonance as desirable

Yet something has changed in our engagement with dissonance. Modernity has become troubled and is fragmenting as we enter a new age; some call it postmodernity, late-modernity, liquid modernity,[62] or the Anthropocene.

Modernity's grand narrative that the world relies on order and reason, which served us for more than three centuries, has become precarious and, in many places, lost. Fake news, conspiracy theories, and distrust of science and experts (bad elites) are symptoms of wider changes. Culture wars are taking place in the USA, across Europe and in other regions, challenging the social norms from both directions. As the old order fragments, one of the changes we can observe is that dissonance, once something to be wary of, has become a desirable part of the political norm.

In progressive politics, dissonance remains problematic but has become normalised and accommodated, largely unconsciously. In right-wing populism, dissonance has been transformed from a state where it previously created anxiety and conflict to a state where tensions have become erased, and dissonance is happily played with in a bricolage of enjoyment.

Populist pleasure of dissonance

Right-wing populists have managed to bypass the tensions that arise from individual and collective dissonance; they don't appear to experience the shame or anxiety it previously created. Donald Trump role models this lack of dissonance for the wider masses. This goes beyond the usual attributions of narcissistic behaviour or defence mechanisms and grandiosity. His contradictory and often absurd statements are no longer problematic to his supporters. Millions of populists follow authoritarian leaders with the nostalgic dream of recreating an ordered (white-patriarchal) society. Yet paradoxically, they follow bizarre, disordered thinking from conspiracy theorists such as QAnon.

Trump, in a recent interview heading into the 2024 election, said that the Democrats support not only abortion but also killing babies after they are born.[63] This is clearly untrue and a little bizarre; it should create dissonance between facts and fiction. Previously, it would make the speaker of such an untruth unelectable, and they would be judged to be acting bizarrely. Yet cheering crowds and populist followers embrace and enjoy this without suffering any dissonance, and the tired mainstream media mention it in passing as an untruth.

Viktor Orbán, the rightist premier of Hungary and Putin supporter, openly calls for illiberal democracy, a phrase that embraces dissonance.

Democracy and liberalism go hand in hand. A democracy cannot survive without a liberal free press, and it dies when the rule of law loses its independence; both these things are openly undermined by Orbán.

Yet they don't care, nor do they feel the need to answer this paradox or work through the tensions. The signifiers 'democracy and freedom' sound good, so those on the right remain attached to those ideas, and alongside them, the idea of a nationalist, authoritarian strong man protecting them sounds good too; so just put democracy alongside illiberal authoritarianism … the dissonance is your problem, not ours!

The populists live in a dissonant space, engaging in disordered thinking while paradoxically demanding a return to an idealised, ordered world. Yet, they do so without experiencing the tensions that this dissonance usually brings. They embrace dissonance unapologetically and thrive in it.

More than this, they gain great pleasure from the dismay their lack of dissonance creates in progressive circles. The populist right has rewritten the sociopolitical rules, and for them, creating political dissonance (without tension) is now a desirable political strategy.

Progressive accommodation of dissonance

On the progressive left, too, inconsistencies and dissonance have become part of their discourse and lived experience. Dissonance has not been welcomed as blatantly as on the populist right, but it has arrived subliminally into the mainstream, and it thrives. While the liberal-progressive left argues for the politics of emancipation, they have discarded the struggles for free speech and substituted this with new covert authoritarian politics, opting for cancel cultures. Their identity politics have become the politics of individual emancipation for some and the politics of oppression for others: it is also the politics of dissonance.

These liberals are labelled as woke police by opponents when using de-platforming and cancel-culture tactics. However, the most worrying aspect is how self and peer surveillance create an inner-world police state. So-called progressives passionately police themselves and each other, attacking liberal university professors for misspeaking, accusing each other of microaggressions, and imposing thought and speech control on those who cannot keep up with the increasing complexities of gender, race, and identity politics. Trans women and 'TERF'[64] feminists battle each other in vicious online attacks with both claiming to support solidarity and emancipatory politics.

Progressive dissonance is observable but unacknowledged. Emancipatory politics are delivered by authoritarian means.

Dissonance 1. Illiberal liberalism: Fighting for social and personal emancipation while imprisoning the self/group in authoritarian illiberal thinking and behaviours.

Dissonance 2. Harmony vs conflict: Calling for social unity, harmony, solidarity, and peace while amplifying/enjoying the culture wars and attacking those outside their identity tribe (and often those within it).

On the one hand, progressive identitarians have delivered new freedoms. Queer culture has brought gay pride and trans rights to the mainstream, with gay marriages accepted in many countries now. On the other hand, they bring about a new authoritarian culture that is oppressive both to themselves and to others. This 'illiberal liberalism' makes dissonance a lived experience in progressive circles.

Progressives repress and rationalise their dissonance. Unlike the populists, they don't enjoy it but try to retain a rationalist stance that demands reason and an ordered mind. However, they have become adept at accommodating dissonance and are less active in working through the tensions and conflicts it causes. One of the ways they bypass their own dissonance is to unconsciously project their unwanted feelings and inner conflicts onto an external 'bad other'. 'See how crazy Trump is! How authoritarian!!' 'We are the good people. We are the rational ones!'

An ecosystemic perspective

Perhaps it's not surprising that dissonance has been embraced across the political spectrum when we look at social changes that have taken place over the past thirty years. Contemporary tensions and social pressures have given rise to an amplification of the dissonance we experience, which is echoed in the politics of dissonance we now see.

To live today means compartmentalising and repressing the daily dissonance we experience, as it is impossible to work through the volume of dissonance we face each day.

The environmental emergency, biodiversity loss, and levels of pollution we experience are examples of having to live alongside the knowledge that the way we live our daily lives is damaging the planet, and unless we change, we are heading towards catastrophe. To address this dissonance, some turn to climate denial, others to taking limited action and rationalising their life choices, others to activism, and others get environmental-infused depression and internalise a sense of hopelessness.

There are many factors as to why our ecosystems of life have produced a social state whereby dissonance can no longer be tolerated. I highlight three examples below:

Factor 1. The impossibility of living ethically and well

Each time we fly, each time we eat, each time we drive, each time we consume, each time we … Each time we do anything, we have to face the knowledge that we are damaging the planet and/or ourselves and each other.

There is no escape from the superego injunction of society's Big Other, insistently reminding us we are co-producers of an environmental catastrophe and that whatever we eat or consume comes with a health risk and/or a production process that damages both the environment and has social justice consequences as it exploits downstream labour.

Factor 2. The overwhelm of bad news

We live in a time of mass communication as never before. This globalisation of awareness, alongside our mobile devices delivering 24/7 updates on news, means we receive a proliferation of images of war and suffering from 'natural' disasters that are overwhelming.

Factor 3. The constant production of the idealised self

Our social media platforms, such as Facebook, Instagram, TikTok, and LinkedIn, enable us to present our best selves to the world, and we co-produce the happiness imperative. We can be having a dreadful day, but the one shot we show the world is the smiley shot … This positivism and idealisation of our lives by image add to the existing celebrity culture media frenzy. Together, these forces create an aspirational lifestyle, a simulacrum of life which constantly makes us feel inadequate. The social imperative is fulfilling the happiness imperative, while our personal experience is very different, often one of alienation and disenchantment.

Dissonance: Accept it and just do it!

There has been a collective disavowal of dissonance. We have become desensitised to our individual and collective dissonance because it is overwhelming to engage with.

Populist politicians promote freedom from feeling bad, creating fantasy worldviews that embrace dissonance; they play with it and use it as a political strategy: just enjoy it, and as Nike pronounced in 1988 when the rise in dissonance started … Just do it!

What is to be done?

The task at hand is to rediscover how to live with dissonance but in a different way.

The populists' resolution is to overcome dissonance, to use it as a strategy, to weaponise it, and to celebrate and enjoy the absurdity of their positions. This is what Lacan names as surplus enjoyment (*plus-de-jouir*). There is a surplus, an excess of manic enjoyment in the way populists take pleasure from destruction. Whether it is hateful attacks on immigrants or politicians, whether it's the pleasure of chanting 'drill drill drill' when the planet is burning, with the full knowledge that this will cause more environmental damage and lead to more migration. The inconsistencies, the lies, and the pleasure taken from the pain of others are all a form of retreat from reality, an escapist fantasy that leads to annihilation and self-destruction.

The progressives' accommodation of dissonance is also a subtle retreat from reality. It shows a lack of courage in the face of real danger.

There are models to address the inescapable dissonance we face differently. I pointed to the Chinese way previously, with their long history of managing paradox within an ecosystem framework. Dissonance is reduced when social harmony and living in balance with nature are systemic and shared aims. Indigenous peoples have many examples of living more in harmony with the cosmos, which removes the sharp linear edges of right and wrong that modernity inflicts on us.

Richard Rohr writes from a Christian perspective focusing on the word 'shalom':

> *Shalom* embodies wholeness, completeness, and love. It is strikingly similar to many Indigenous constructs of 'harmony,' which emphasize the interconnectedness and interdependency of all things, the need for balance, and the primacy of community. And if that is what Jesus' kingdom was about—radical *shalom* and harmony—it is helpful to translate this metaphor into something like *community of creation*, a phrase infused with Indigenous meaning, which more readily emphasizes that all living things are participating in this new peace that the Creator is bringing about through Christ …
>
> The metaphor of an ecosystem could work in a similar way: we are currently living in an imbalanced, self-destructive ecosystem, but God is inviting us to live in a new network of relationships that will produce balance, harmony, and health.[65]

If we take these holistic ecosystem approaches, the dissonance we feel from modernity is changed. No longer do we split ourselves and strive for an idealised need for order, domination, and control that produces a hard dissonance. We are freed from the great tension to find ways to resolve the binary paradox or dilemma. The ecosystemic and interdependent approaches allow us to engage in a more accepting, thoughtful way with the dilemmas and inconsistencies we face. This ecosystem approach reduces anxiety, which is the first stage in enabling us to really think deeply about the challenges rather than react to them or repress them. An ecosystem approach enables us to see ourselves as a small part of a greater whole, to see others' differences as part of that whole, and to work together towards a common good and a healthy cosmos. Dissonance then becomes a part of the whole, not something to be weaponised or repressed.

CHAPTER 12

The wounded-self and celebrated-self

This essay emerged from a long-standing interest in my observations of how people often find themselves unconsciously entrapped in experiencing the world from a wounded-self or celebrated-self perspective. I first wrote about this when researching for my book, *Coaching and Mentoring: A Critical Text.*[66] Since then, I have incorporated the wounded- and celebrated-self concepts into my coach training work. I think it's very important and something that gets missed. I have colleagues who are experts in the group relations and psychoanalytic traditions, but are completely entrapped in the wounded-self discourse. If it is challenged then a highly defensive response results due to the unconscious attachment to the wounded-self as an identity. Individuals and groups find themselves repeating damaging relationships or living in ways that limit them, because they are trapped in one of these polarised ways of being in the world.

Introduction

Two distinct and powerful emotional identities have emerged in society over the past sixty years. Both individuals and groups have internalised them, becoming unconsciously attached to either the wounded-self (WS) or the celebrated-self (CS). These two 'selves' are not fixed positions, and clearly, there is a spectrum. Some people and groups cross the boundaries between them with ease, depending on the context and situation they are in, yet many get stuck in one place or the other. In my experience as an executive coach, therapist, and organisational consultant, I have observed how individuals and groups become polarised and follow groups, narratives, people, and the media that align with their 'chosen' position.

Below, I summarise the wounded-self and celebrated-self identities before describing how therapy culture emerged. I then briefly reflect on how these identities impact society before concluding.

The wounded-self (WS)

Those who identify with the WS frame the external world as a persecutory or dangerous place. Individuals and groups tend to look for problems and unconsciously see the shadow side of human relations and veer towards pessimism. They often take up a victim identity, which can be mild or extreme, framing their past and present as a series of wounds they are working to heal or simply to find acceptance and integrate into their lives. When excessive, the WS position is debilitating and entraps individuals and groups in a mindset that limits their capacity to enjoy life or engage in a process that leads to change.

However, being able to access the WS position is vitally important as it enables us to tap into our pain and sadness and to empathise with others. A good therapist or coach will be able to contain the sadness, grief, hurt, or trauma a client brings, and this is only possible if the coach/therapist has been able to face and experience their own pain. The therapist or coach's skill is to be able to visit the WS without entrapping the client in a victim life script. Having access to our own WS can enable us to identify with others and put our empathy to work to drive positive change; for example, to set up charities for suffering others, campaign for refugees, or face up to the reality of the climate crisis and engage to mitigate it. The illustration below sets out the core aspects of the wounded-self.

The celebrated-self (CS)

The CS identifies with personal empowerment and frames the external world as filled with opportunity and abundance. The CS individual is sovereign, believing we make our own happiness and can fulfil any dream if we are passionate enough.

The CS individual believes we each have a pure inner state, that if recovered from society's negative impacts, we can unleash our unlimited potential. Those identifying with the CS veer towards optimism, on the surface at least. The importance of seeing opportunities and focusing on strengths is abundantly clear. However, when the CS gets excessive, it produces toxic positivity that damages individuals and groups. Aggression, anxiety, and sadness are denied and repressed as they are 'negative emotions'. This leads to unconscious acting out, such as passive aggression or displacement into manic activity. Depression, somatised problems, and ill health can result from not facing the more difficult emotions that all humans experience. Turning a blind eye to real-world challenges in personal, relational, and global political issues becomes a problem for CS individuals and those around them.

Leave the past behind

The CS pushes us to leave the past behind, focusing on what we can become rather than what we were. Cobb sums up the CS mindset:

> Trust your feelings, have faith in yourself, follow your bliss, do your own thing, listen to your inner child, do what feels right, and be true to yourself. These messages are offered as formulas for salvation ... Therapeutic values that are worthy of organizing one's life around, such as self-esteem, self-fulfilment, self-realisation and self-expression have come to be accepted as axiomatic, occupying the normative heights once controlled by such counter values as self-discipline, self-control and self-denial.[67]

The CS demands an optimisation of the self. The aim is self-actualisation, that is, to realise one's potential through personal growth in order to improve happiness and well-being. To be happy, in recent years, became a social imperative, it became a social demand rather than a personal desire. Society moved from a repressive and hierarchical 'society of prohibition' in the 1950s to the 'society of commanded enjoyment'[68] in the 1970s. Happiness was no longer an option but a need. If you weren't happy, you were failing both yourself and others. To celebrate the self also meant identifying with celebrity culture: each of us could now aspire to become a celebrity, which begins by sharing celebrity moments on social media.

New Age spirituality

CS identities merged with the growing individualistic spirituality that filled the void left as institutional religion rapidly declined in Europe and more slowly in the USA. Eva Moskowitz claimed that therapy became a new religion, noting that in the 1990s, Americans spent $69 billion a year attending to their emotional health.[69] New Age spirituality emerged alongside and fed into the celebrated-self, taking inspiration from the transcendentalists, the beat generation, and Eastern philosophies. Eckhart Tolle, author of *The Power of Now* (1999), became a leading figure in the New Age scene:

> Tolle talks like a contemporary Buddhist but without the religious baggage—the personal narrative that sells his story claims he became enlightened like the Buddha, but whereas Buddha sat under the Bhodi Tree to become 'the awakened one', Tolle found a contemporary place to become awakened; he sat on a park bench for two years in a London park. Tolle is a New Age phenomenon; the message is about how to live in the present and how to live calmly in the face of modernity's distress—Tolle simply says, 'Let go.'[70]

New Age spirituality takes individual empowerment beyond improving our personal lives, reaching into a narcissistic grandiosity that suggests each of us can change the world. Ken Wilber, a leading guru, concludes his book *Religion of Tomorrow*, saying, 'It is possible to remake the world because you—the very deepest you—are its one and only author .... Grab yourself, grab the world, re-awaken and remake both.'[71]

CS culture and new spirituality entered the workplace via leadership development and coaching programmes. It can be found in abundance in management texts and magazines on airport bookshelves. To become a successful transformational and visionary leader, one must align oneself with the dogma of the CS.

Celebrated-self goes mainstream

A myriad of techniques and interventions exist to help individuals discover and celebrate their true inner selves: meditation, yoga, chanting, Eastern philosophy, Buddhist teachings, crystals, tarot cards, NLP, Reiki ... the list is endless. Life coaching, in particular, has encompassed the CS and New Age philosophy. The New Age movement and CS are big business in financial terms and also in social terms, moving from the edges to the centre of social thinking. Oprah Winfrey became a leading figure in promoting therapy culture, mostly the celebrated-self movement, and her phenomenal success reached millions. In 2008, Oprah Winfrey invited Eckhart Tolle to co-host a series of ten 'webinars' which were downloaded by 38 million people. Paul Heelas describes the CS community as 'expressivists':

> Expressivists live their lives in terms of what they take to be a much richer and authenticated account of what it is to be human. They are intent on discovering and cultivating their 'true' nature, delving in to experience the wealth of life itself.[72]

Are we not all expressivists now?

The illustration below sets out the core elements of the celebrated-self.

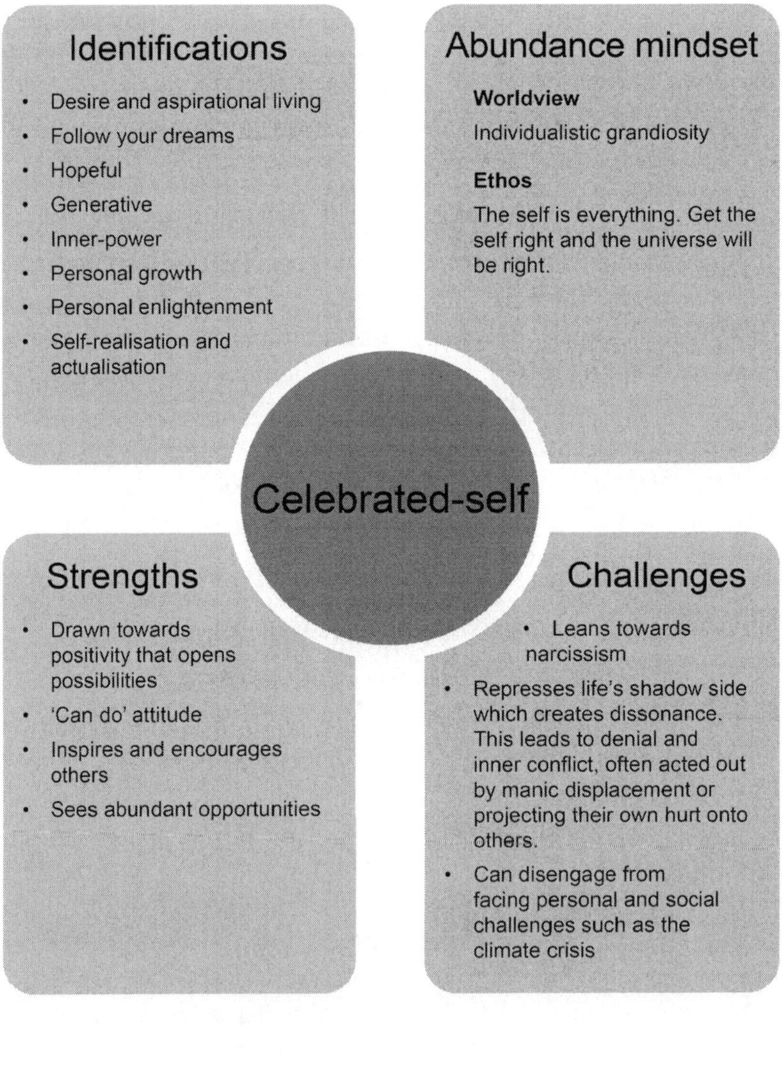

Overview: Wounded- and celebrated-selves

In the world of therapy and coaching it's rare to engage in critical theory and examine the structural power dynamics that underpin therapeutic work. This lack led me to write *Coaching and Mentoring: A Critical Text*, where I first identified these two polemic selves to show how they inform and unconsciously frame the work of coaches.[73] Coaches are often split between these two camps, entrapped in one of these positions, but without recognising it. WS inspired coaches look for wounds and seek problems to cure, and (unconsciously) identify with their role as a 'healer'. CS influenced coaches ban 'problem talk' as it leads to negativity. They are solution-focused, seeing themselves as modern-day shamans, enlivening the spirits of their clients. Clients often find therapists/coaches that match their identification with either WS or CS, seeking solace in sharing and reaffirming their perceptions and beliefs.

When the coach or therapist is very attached (unconsciously) to one of these positions, they create dependency cultures in their clients. The WS therapist needs a WS client to maintain their identity of healer, so (unconsciously) keeps their client in the victim position. The CS coach needs to constantly receive positive feedback to fuel their own CS ego. They create dependency relationships in which the client relies on their wonderful 'shaman' to assure their well-being. To self-actualise is a lifetime journey of personal development, so the need for life coaching/therapy has no end (which happens to be a good business model).

Blind spots

Therapeutic clinicians claim a false neutrality; therapists, counsellors, and coaches identify as being non-judgemental, and yet they come filled with the baggage of unconscious assumptions and informed by social-cultural influences. This also applies to the WS and CS folk who are not therapists or coaches. Unless we undertake a critical perspective, our assumptions about the world go unquestioned.

When supervising Chinese MBA students, I quickly realised that the individualistic/therapeutic assumptions I had grown up with were a foreign emotional landscape to these students, coming from collectivist cultures where taking group time to share personal feelings was frowned upon. Having supervised therapists and coaches, I observed how their unconscious attachments and investments in their own WS or CS determined how they interpreted a client's experience.

Ideally, a skilled coach or therapist (or any of us) will have an awareness of our biases towards the WS or CS. However, the ideal is often lacking. When the unconscious bias is identified, many go into denial. The reason for the denial is that challenging these positions goes beyond challenging an idea; it is to challenge the person's very identity and their whole way of being in the world.

I will next explore how WS and CS emerged.

The rise of therapy culture: How WS and CS emerged

Psychoanalysis and psychotherapy, known as 'the talking cure', were founded as a new treatment for the wounded-self at the beginning of the twentieth century. Freud and others recognised a need to address our emotional and psychological wounded-selves, and they developed a framework of psychological understanding. Many variations of psychotherapy emerged, and in recent decades, there has been a huge proliferation, such as cognitive behavioural therapy, solutions focused therapy, and neurolinguistic programming. What all therapies initially had in common was the treatment of 'suffering' patients in a clinical setting.

> 'If you have problems, it's good to talk; if you don't talk, you have problems.'

The 1960s counter-culture heralded rapid social change, which enabled therapy to transcend the clinic and enter into popular culture. At the centre of this social transformation was the rise of individualism, free choice, a challenge to authority, and a 'turn to subjectivity'.[74] Expressing our feelings and emotions flourished, and soon, the focus on our identities followed. The complexities of modern life also increased, alongside the demise of traditional sites where solace was found, such as the extended family and the church. This opened a space for therapeutic culture to expand into.

> 'Therapy is too good to be limited to the sick.'[75]

Therapy culture transcended the limits of treatment in a clinical setting and became pervasive across the whole of society. Therapy culture was a response to these social changes, providing ways to cope, create meaning, and manage feelings and relationships. It also became an important driver of these social changes. 'Therapy speak' appeared everywhere, in popular talk shows, self-help books, support groups, and family conversations. Our feelings, relationships, and psychic injuries, once hidden, now became part of everyday life. As it expanded into everyday life, it followed two paths: the WS and the CS.

The diagram below traces how therapy culture was influenced by two sources, 1) psychotherapy and 2) wider culture, and then how therapy culture manifests in two directions.

The emergence of the wounded-self and celebrated-self

Under the psychotherapy column, psychoanalysis launched a psychological movement that became dominant and diverse. It went beyond treating our problems to also informing how we think about ourselves. Carl Rogers, the 1950s American psychologist, was instrumental in democratising what he saw as elitist psychotherapy. He de-medicalised psychotherapy training and invented person-centred counselling.[76] This enabled counselling/therapy to escape the limits of the clinic and make 'therapy' more publicly available, such as in schools.

Rogers' therapeutic work, alongside many others, was also focused on self-realisation. They believed in utilising therapy techniques beyond alleviating suffering to emancipate an individual's full potential. This shift towards the CS was part of a post-Second World War movement towards optimistic self-actualisation[77] driven by the human potential movement.

The 'macho' workplace was one of the last sites to accept therapeutic culture into its domain. Successful corporate leaders (mostly male) could not show weakness, therapy was considered to be for wounded people, not successful executives. Coaching brought therapy culture into the domain of work by drawing on CS approaches. Executive coaching began as a remedial treatment for failing leaders with little success, but when it was re-branded as a CS intervention for successful leaders, it became a badge of honour to have a coach. New Age therapies proliferated alongside more traditional therapy approaches from the 1970s onwards, with the Esalen Institute in the USA leading the way. Therapy culture had transitioned successfully from the clinic to become a major economic and ideological bedrock of westernised society.

The wider cultural influences that produced therapy culture and WS and CS can be traced via the post-war years, leading to economic growth and mass production, which then led to mass consumption. For the first time, a rising middle class had spending power and could choose how to express their identities through consumption choices, such as their houses, cars, and fashion. The 1968 counter-culture took individualism to new levels, throwing off the yoke of authoritarianism and demanding choice and free expression.

Individualism and identity moved to the fore in westernised society. Expressivism became the norm, and emotions no longer were to be bravely concealed but openly expressed. The rise of feminism and the deconstruction of patriarchy also had a big impact on wider society, encouraging all to be more emotionally aware. The human relations movement utilised psychology, sociology, and anthropology in the workplace to bring therapeutic and psychological understandings to motivate workers to raise performance. These changes gave rise to a new era where people gained societal permission and a new emotional-therapeutic language to explore and express themselves.

Globalisation increased both economic growth and cultural exchanges, bringing Eastern philosophy and practices such as meditation, mindfulness, and yoga to mainstream culture and opening the door for even more therapeutic intervention. Finally, neoliberalism and free-market economics amplified the ideology of individualism. The counter-cultural ideas of the 1960s were successfully appropriated by corporations for the service of profit. Hyper-consumerism emerged, binding personal growth to economic growth. The happiness imperative[78] became tied to marketing and consumerism: 'Buy this and it will make you happy'.

These two overlapping forces, coming from psychotherapy and wider cultural changes, brought therapy culture into popular culture. Therapy culture is then separated into two distinct directions: either as a means of healing wounds or for self-actualising.

Case example

A client, 'Sally' comes to therapy/coaching having had a difficult childhood. Her father was a product of his age, where men and fathers were socially expected to be more emotionally distanced. He had a short temper and was unable to bond closely with his daughter or his wife, who divorced him.

Sally first visited a wounded-self psychodynamic therapist, to reflect on how this impacted on her adult life. The therapist focused on the hurt and asked about trauma and its impacts, hoping Sally would gain deeper insights into how this early traumatic experience impacts her current relationships. They worked on reparation and integration of this hurt into her current day situation. This was partially successful and enabled Sally to revisit her pain, but she felt the therapist trapped her in the victim role, and didn't appreciate her strengths or achievements.

She also felt the father became an object of blame in the sessions, that didn't feel right to her.

Sally later worked with a celebrated-self life coach, who spent no time on these 'negative emotions' and focused on helping Sally to think more positively. Her focus was to get Sally to self-improve and fulfil her dreams to find happiness. The life coach worked with Sally by setting out clear goals and they worked together to try to attain these.

These therapeutic stances are mirrored in wider social settings, with individuals, friends, and families siding with these positions. Sally's sister takes a CS stance: 'It wasn't so bad with Dad, he just got angry at times, you know he loved you. Don't dwell on the past, you have a great job and a new boyfriend and you're doing great!' Her WS best friend asks, 'What did your Dad do? Was it emotional abuse? You must find it so hard to trust men these days. You keep changing relationships and are never stable. I am sure it's due to your relationship with your Dad ... I really feel your pain. Read this self-help book on abusive parents, it will really help.'

When the pathway is polemic, problems always arise. Sally got stuck with the WS therapist feeling she was going in circles, and she didn't enjoy being trapped in the victim position. The CS life coach kept pushing her to achieve personal goals, and she felt infantalised. The coach was like an over-anxious parent trying to get their infant to walk, exuding positive feedback when small gains were made.

Sally finally found a therapist who could bridge the WS and CS. This therapist only worked for a short period with her, as they both agreed she was doing well now that she had acknowledged her suffering and troubles with her father and also realised how he was trapped in his own social code of behaviour, unable to express himself and how he struggled with his own inability to form close relationships. This awareness allowed movement in their relationship, and Sally began to see her father in a different light, and herself as well. Her relationship with her Dad improved over time and when he died she felt she had resolved much of the childhood angst she carried. She felt more whole and more energised and worked on her relationships with men in general, and found a long-term partner in the process.

Nancy Pelosi 'You gotta be proud of your wounds'[79]

Nancy Pelosi, the eighty-four-year-old veteran politician known for her ability to fight for what she believes in, rose to become the most powerful woman in US politics. Referring to a prayer that a Sierra Leone preacher shared with her, Nancy restated the need to be proud of your wounds … 'When meeting their maker and their creator they will say … show me your wounds. And if I have no wounds he will say: was nothing worth fighting for?'

Nancy is acknowledging the need to look at the wounds and to be proud of the wounds that come from fighting for social justice. This ability to put a WS energy to work for change is very different from identifying as a victim, which leads to introspection and paralysis.

Critical reflections

There are many critiques of therapy culture and of the wounded- and celebrated-self. Most critiques are concerned with how therapeutic culture has co-opted the WS and CS, creating a narcissistic culture at the expense of collective solidarity.

The happiness imperative feeds unhappiness

The CS is underpinned by what Berardi calls the 'happiness imperative',[80] that is, a social injunction that tells us it is our duty to be happy, and if we are not happy, we are failing.

Self-optimisation

We are constantly being posed the questions: 'Am I happy?', 'Am I depressed?', 'Am I stressed?', 'Is my body perfect?', 'Is my sex life adequate?', all with the following question: how can I optimise myself … to be a better person, to improve my work performance and my performance as a parent, a partner, in the gym … The pressure to continually undergo personal growth is relentless.

Commercial interests play a big part in products and services, promising everything from beautifying you to optimising you as a person. The pharmaceutical and therapy industries commercially profit from the increase in self-focus, with massive sales of antidepressants and other drugs to treat the huge increase in the diagnostic criteria of psychological-physical ills such as ADHD, stress, post-traumatic stress disorder, autistic syndromes, depression, and anxiety.

Narcissistic culture and victimhood

Many claim that therapy culture creates a narcissistic, selfish, and introspective society, focusing on 'I' instead of 'we'. Rather than liberating individuals from their concerns, it entraps them in an increasingly widening array of 'ills'.[81] Fitzpatrick writes that social approval demands a victim identity these days: 'A therapeutic culture has become pervasive. It is apparent in the emotional "esteem" and "support"; displays of emotional incontinence and claims of victimhood are guaranteed social approval.'[82]

Cultural influences

The two selves are shaped by society around us. The greater our engagement with therapy culture, the more we see WS and CS identifications. The USA is the centre of therapy culture; it has a strong WS but is dominated by a CS culture which emerged from consumerism, individualism, and American Dream ideology. The United States Declaration of Independence famously pronounced 'life, liberty, and the pursuit of happiness' as being the inalienable right of all men.

Our unique life stories draw us unconsciously towards these different emotional states. Individuals invested in the WS find themselves comfortable in groups that affirm their position. These groups utilise peer pressure to maintain group norms, creating circular causality. If you're drawn to a WS group, you will be peer-policed to express your victim status. If you are drawn to the CS group, you will post images celebrating your life on Instagram/TikTok and engage with like-minded souls, listening to self-optimising podcasts and reading spiritual well-being magazines.

Each position becomes reinforced by peer pressure, social media, and the algorithms that push individuals towards their interests. Younger people who have grown up with identity politics and social media all around them are more likely to take stronger WS and CS positions.

Return of the repressed

Both sides have a shadow. Psychoanalysis teaches us that when something is repressed and hidden from our conscious awareness, it returns to haunt us in different ways. CS identities maintain positivity by repressing sadness and by disavowing challenges in oneself and the world. WS identities often miss opportunities, repressing the possibilities of hope because they are trapped by gaining unconscious 'pleasure from their displeasure'.[83] WS people consciously complain about their situation yet gain satisfaction from their dissatisfaction, unconsciously enjoying their suffering.

As a family therapist, I also witnessed on many occasions how parents, deeply worried about a child, would keep the child/family trapped in the problem. If the 'problem' family member got well, another member took up the ill/victim role in the family. The dynamics in each family were different, but a common situation was when a parent needed a 'problem' child to keep their parental role as family carer. Similarly, CS families would be in denial, not acknowledging an underlying family issue until the problem had become so severe they had to seek help. Both CS and WS identities become polarised when a big part of themselves is repressed.

Polemic combinations

When the WS and CS are both present in an individual or group but not in an integrated way, they create split dynamics. Everything is black and white, good or bad. Individuals flip from victim mindsets to positivity speak, unable to integrate the positions.

I noticed how talk shows and self-help literature move through the WS-CS positions without integration as if they are steps on a path to salvation. This replicates the salvation narratives from a Christian cultural tradition. Talk show hosts created the 'new confessional' where a celebrity would be invited to confess publicly their misdemeanours in order to be forgiven and start afresh, usually following these four steps (the Christianised narrative in italics):

Confession: The wounded-self is exposed in confessional culture. I was an alcoholic and abused my partner. *I fell from grace, and I was a sinner*!

The lost sheep: I struggled and lost my way ... I turned to drink ... *the devil took control.*

Lost sheep found: I went to rehabilitation. My therapist led me to recovery, and I realised my mistakes. *I was lost, but now I'm found. The light of Christ showed me the way.*

Salvation: Since my confession and my personal growth work, I have found redemption, self-actualised, and rediscovered my pure and true self. *I have been saved. Halleluiah!*

This secular adaptation of the Christian path shows how our cultural underpinnings speak through us.

We see the WS and CS also play out in polemic politics. Populist-nationalist politicians initially preached WS politics, as in 'The world is doomed, we are all victims of the elite, and of immigrants, the country is broken.' They then jump to the politics of the CS: 'I am great, follow me! We, the people, are great! Let's make America great again!' A left-wing polemic narrative does similar work, initially taking a WS stance: 'The capitalists have stolen our world, it's a disaster, and we are all suffering', before pointing to the CS stance of the promised socialist future when they gain power. However, more recently, the left has had a problem identifying an emancipatory world and has lost faith in a CS future, which is why maybe they are suffering and losing power to right-wing populism. For even when hope is a fantasy, it is better than no hope at all.

Last thoughts

Therapeutic culture is now integral to our lives, and the WS and CS identities have become central to how we make sense of the world and live our lives. As we recall, some believe the WS and CS lead to hyper-individualist and even narcissistic norms that undermine social solidarity and create greater unhappiness. Others argue that therapeutic cultures are essential to help us navigate our fast-changing age. Having emotional and reflective capacity empowers us and helps us to make meaning, to find autonomy, and to realise our potential in this complex age.[84] The four steps below set out possibilities that enable a more integrated way of being in the world.

1. **Stop binary splitting:** When we split ourselves into binary positions of WS or CS, we lose a part of ourselves and shut out a full

engagement with the world. A part of us and a part of others become repressed, and a return of the repressed will always take place to the detriment of all.

2. **Building bridges:** By acknowledging both the WS and the CS in ourselves, we create a bridge that begins to enable integration and synthesis and is helpful for a more balanced future. Helping each other achieve this is the work of a good coach, therapist, family, or friend.
3. **Decentring ourselves:** The constant focus on the self, whether WS or CS, isn't healthy! If we decentre ourselves, we can discover new pleasures in collaboration, relationships with others, and mutuality. This can lead to supporting the suffering other, engaging with the creative other, and facing micro and macro problems with others in common purpose.
4. **The holistic self:** Introducing a third position. The WS and CS are always leaning towards polarity. The holistic self works towards connectivity and interdependence rather than autonomy and independence. Our connectivity and engagement with the wider environment create a missing element in the WS and CS identities. Reclaiming our place in the universe, to live alongside the multi-species companions we share our planet with, is vital both for our survival and also to regain our sense of wholeness.

Depending on our personal and cultural influences, we gravitate unconsciously towards either the WS or CS. Individuals, groups, and even nations can become entrapped in excess positivity or victimhood, with each having a detrimental impact, while also providing some unconscious pleasure (jouissance). Becoming aware of these unconscious pulls can be a liberating experience, freeing ourselves from patterns that inhibit who we really are, and who we want to become.

CHAPTER 13

What is your true desire?

This question of following our true desire is one that has been a companion of mine for my whole adult life. As a young rebel anarchist, I was confronted by challenging questions such as 'What are you doing and why are you doing it?' and by slogans such as 'Never work!' from Guy Debord and the Situationists,[85] who I admired because they asked about the very meaning of work and our identities, not just what career do you want. I pushed myself to answer these questions in the way I lived my life. Since then, my psychoanalytic journey has taken me further to understand and question human desire. This essay emerged from recent work on the journey of helping others to discover their true desire.

Introduction

This essay explores how we navigate our desires in the current social landscape. The stimulation for this piece comes from my coaching experience. In the 'coaching confessional', individuals share their intimate personal feelings and thoughts in confidential safety. They often speak about desires, surprising themselves with their own thoughts and reflections. In recent years, I have trained coaches to ask,

'What is your desire?' because it lands so powerfully with people. It resonates because our desires, what we want for ourselves, and what we think will make us happy have become increasingly important to our current social imaginary. Collectively, our idea that we can find happiness through free choice and by working hard to optimise ourselves has become ever more powerful. To find this elusive happiness means to follow our true desires. What is striking is that although this fundamental question resonates very strongly, it seems we have done little work on thinking about what shapes our desires, where they come from, and how others influence our desires. This essay explores these questions.

Why desire has become central?

Desire has moved from being one of many influences on us to becoming a very central influence. This follows a larger drift towards individualism, consumerism, and a growing focus on personal identity. Who we desire to be, what we desire to become, and how we desire that others see us have become central to our very personhood, to the question of 'Who are you?'.

People strive to find the elusive state of happiness that society constantly encourages us to seek. To be our best selves, to follow our passion, to choose the right job or career or the perfect partner who will make us happy, we first have to understand what we really desire for ourselves. Unless we identify our true desires, we may spend a lifetime chasing false hopes and dreams.

This question of desire has become amplified and distorted by rampant individualism and the happiness fetish that has been rocket-boosted by relentless marketing. Our desires are the target and the essential element of consumer capitalism.

The previous chapter explains the rise of therapy culture and how the WS and CS emerged as dominant social identities. To identify with the WS is to realise that our desires are unfulfilled. To follow the logic of the CS, we are constantly trying to decipher and fulfil our desires.

Surface levels of understanding our desires lead us into an abyss. We have to deepen our exploration of the question, 'What is our true desire?'. Different ways of looking at the question take it beyond an individual quest. Desire is relational. Psychoanalysis teaches us that our desire is vital to what it means to be human in our modern times and that it is influenced by conscious, unconscious, and societal forces.

Exploring desire is vital, not only to help individuals transcend consumerist and narcissistic cultures but also to discover less destructive and more positive ways to live well with each other and with the environment.

Exploring desire

To understand desire, I turn to psychoanalysis and, in particular, to Jacques Lacan. Engaging with the unconscious seems vital to get beyond the superficial ideas propagated by our consumer society that desires can be fulfilled by short-term pleasure hits. I take from psychoanalysis selectively and make my own sense of it, as Lacan and other psychoanalytical approaches can be overly complicated to the point of distraction, and yet within them, nuggets of wisdom help us understand the human condition.

Desire is a conscious and unconscious process

One of Freud's great insights was that we are doubly subjected to a) the conscious thoughts we are aware of, and b) the unconscious attachments, investments, and drives that shape our thinking and behaviours but that we are not fully aware of. Our desires are often caught between these two. Consciously, we know what we want, while our unconscious desires demand some other form of gratification and often sabotage the fulfilment of our conscious desires.

'Desire is always the desire of the other'

> Desire full stop is always the desire of the Other. Which basically means that we are always asking the Other what he/she desires.[86]
> —Lacan

This has two main parts. First, our desires are not simply what we want, they are relational and entangled with other people. Second, our desires are closely linked with a need to be recognised by important

Others. Lacan identifies how desire is not something that comes from deep within us but is thrust upon us from early encounters with the Other. From infancy, our desire is to fulfil the desire of the other, such as to please and gain recognition from a parent figure, who signals to the infant what is pleasing and what is not. This means that to fulfil our desires is a constant process of wondering what the Other desires. Lacan's insight is hugely valuable; we are social and relational beings, and our desires and thoughts are never taken in isolation; 'No man (or woman) is an island.'[87]

The desire of the big Other

The Other from whom we desire recognition comes from two sources. First, our main carers through our infancy and childhood: parents, grandparents, nannies, friends, and as we grow up, other influential or inspirational individuals such as an important teacher. The second force that shapes our desires is known as the 'big Other'. The big Other is the social voice we internalise, which comes from society at large and from the groups we belong to, such as a church or a sports club. These influence and often impose the values, morals, and social expectations we are expected to follow. Our desires are shaped by these forces, and how our personal desires are shaped in the 2020s will be different to how they were shaped in the 1950s. We carry the voice of the big Other within us, and our desires are influenced consciously by clear expectations set out in rules and laws and also unconsciously through taken-for-granted norms and cultural perceptions of what is right or good and what success and happiness mean. To get to university, have a successful career, be a good husband, wife, or parent, become wealthy, own a nice house, or become a celebrity, our desires cannot escape what society inscribes upon us. Expectations relating to our age, gender, sexuality, career expectations, and social entitlements are all shaped by the big Other.

We desire recognition and to gain this, we interpret what the other/big Other wants in order to feel fulfilled. Even when we rebel against the other or big Other, we cannot escape their influence. The desire of the other is not a negative per se, it may be an important guide or it may limit us. What is important is our relationship to this desire, and the underlying cause of the desire, that is, how we discover our enjoyment.

Lack and prohibition create desire

Two things often create desire: 1) 'You can't have it' … 'I want it!' The thing we are prohibited becomes desirable; parents know this well! 2) Lack is a cause of desire. If we lack something, we experience an emptiness, something is missing, and we then desire what we lack. The challenge here is that we can feel emptiness without knowing exactly what we are lacking.

Lacan said that we seek an *objet à*, this is an object that becomes a cover for our lack, something that stands in the place of what is lacking. We seek to fill our feeling of emptiness with some object or activity that takes away the empty feeling, for example, shopping or marathon running. When this happens, we fail to work on discovering our true desire, we just keep buying or being active to avoid feeling empty, which can lead to dysfunctional behaviours which undermine us. We buy a new car or dress or get plastic surgery, and we feel good for a fleeting moment, then that empty feeling returns, which haunts so many. That's how consumer capitalism works, in a ferocious cycle: lack creates desire, buy to fill the gap, lack returns after fleeting pleasure, which then creates new desire which activates us to buy the next product or service … repeat.

Satisfaction kills desire

As soon as our desires are satisfied, we no longer feel desire. If we managed to fulfil our desires through consumption, the car, or the job we wanted, we would no longer buy stuff or work hard to chase more imaginary dreams. Lacan refers to the object cause of desire, saying that desire is not what we need to satisfy, it is the object cause of our desire we need to understand, the hidden part of ourselves that is lacking. This cannot be discovered through rational thought; we can only find traces of our lack when we observe our unconscious, such as how we seek pleasure or comfort through patterns of behaviour, for example.

Case example: Discovering one's desire

A young man from a high-income family spent years rebelling against his parents' desire for him to become a lawyer and his private school's desire that he should go to a top university. He became a punk, dropped out of school, got into trouble, and became lost and unhappy. He self-referred for counselling and he spoke proudly that he was rebelling against his father and society. Yet in counselling, he came to realise that his rebellion was still an entrapment. He was not following his own desire, he was tied into rebelling with anger against his parents' desire, rather than discovering what he really desired for himself. His acting out was seeking recognition that he was his own person, but paradoxically, he was entrapping himself in the role of an angry child, unable to free himself. This insight freed him from his 'acting out' behaviour and he began to search for his own path, which led him over a two year period to take up horticultural studies and work in landscaping. While he was always in relation to his parents and society's big Other's desire to be successful, he was no longer determined by it. His parents reconciled with him after realising their son had found his own path. Both were freed from their enmeshed relationship and discovered a new enjoyment together.

The personal is political

Exploring our true desires and seeking to understand the desire of the other/big Other gives us not only increased personal agency and an opportunity to radically reshape our lives, it also has a sociopolitical perspective. Working to understand our true desires and how they relate to others is a consciousness-raising exercise that can undermine consumer capitalism's desire to turn us into 'buying machines'. It is not until we step out of our societal norms that the shock of the mass branding and marketing ideology imposed on us becomes real.

Back in the 1990s, I travelled to communist East Germany and Poland. I recall the shock of returning to West Germany/Berlin at night. From zero advertising in the East to being bombarded with flashing advertising lights and billboards screaming at us to desire and buy! Since Naomi Klein wrote *No Logo* in 1999, the infiltration of branded marketing has become endemic. Also, exposing big Other desires, such as patriarchy that were once taken-for-granted norms, can liberate men, women, and non-binary folk alike from gender-essentialised behaviours and prohibitions.

In my work as a family therapist, I explored relationships within families and how wider social codes shaped individuals' and families' understanding of what their desires were for themselves, the family, and different family members. It is revelatory for them to gain insights and to realise how they desire to gain recognition from parents and parents from children.

We are not trapped in fixed relationships with the other, nor are we determined by the big Other's desire. However, we are shaped by the other's desires and how we respond to these desires. Exploring how we want to please mothers/fathers or to be like them (or not) can help reveal how our desires are shaped in the real world. We unconsciously transfer infant desires onto present-day relationships.

Case example

Daria, who was always trying to gain positive recognition from her parents through performing being 'nice', became the employee who always tried to please her boss. When she received constructive 'negative' feedback from the boss, she was devastated. For Daria, it wasn't feedback, it felt like an attack on her whole identity, which had been constructed by her, of being 'good Daria'. Her need to please was evident during her one-to-one coaching sessions, as she spent the first few sessions trying to please me the coach rather than do the 'real work'. We were able to work on her 'not-pleasing the coach' to help her free herself from this entrapment and become aware of her own desires and separate these from striving for recognition from authority figures in her life.

Buddhist desire

There are many variations of Buddhist teaching in the West, telling us that desire is the root of our unhappiness, the cause of suffering and evil. Buddhists teach that to end our suffering is to lose our desire and our ego. This may be one solution to solving the human condition, but let's be honest, how many of us get anywhere close to this? And is it really possible or desirable to lose desire and ego? While excess of both leads to problems and requires rebalancing, having desire is an important driver of creativity and progressive social (and personal) change. When we put our desires and egos to positive work for ourselves and for society, then the array of negative effects is reduced, and good things can be achieved.

There is a strong critique of how Buddhism has been appropriated by the West, which claims that it has become distorted and is used instrumentally. Mindfulness, for example, has become a desired corporate training method, as it helps employees with their stress levels. Critical theorists claim that it also aims to create a compliant, uncritical, and hardworking workforce. This is not the intention of mindfulness but how it has been selectively used. This approach undermines the desire for structural, political, and systemic changes. Perhaps the stress workers feel is because the company has them working unrelenting hours, and the stress should not be personalised but read as a sign that organisational change is needed.

From a psychoanalytic perspective, desire and ego are part of human subjectivity. Perhaps an occasional Bodhisattva is found wandering the earth, living a saintly life, but for the rest of us, the question of how to live well with our desires is an important quest. I am very aware that Buddhism comes in many forms and that what I am discussing is the appropriation of Buddhism and how it is misunderstood and misused in society.

Conclusion

The question 'What is our true desire?' is of paramount importance today. Our distorted desires have led to rising mental health issues, feelings of disenchantment and depression, and contribute to social justice issues and the environmental crisis through our consumerism.

Now is the time to question our relationship to our desires. The answers lie in recognising the underlying drivers of our desires and discovering our true desires, which will include how we gain recognition from others.

Tips for the journey ahead

Staying with the trouble: Liberating ourselves from the immediate desire to get rid of the emptiness caused by lack. Taking time to explore what the lack really means for us.

Gaining recognition from the other/big Other in a conscious way that is chosen rather than an unconscious, reactive response.

Emancipating ourselves from the desire of the capitalist big Other to free ourselves from being compliant consumer subjects.

Co-creating a collective desire to live well on our planet alongside our multi-species companions. This entails developing a decentring of the self, which frees us from so many social pressures.

CHAPTER 14

'Helpless helping'

'I swear I am helping'. Artwork by Niamh Swanton

The title of this art photo is 'I swear I am helping', and it inspired me to write this short essay. The photo is created by the talented Irish artist Niamh Swanton,[88] and when I wrote this essay it was on display in one of my favourite Galway cafés. When ordering my morning flat white, I take time to look at the picture. My first reaction was that it made me smile, I enjoyed the humorous image. Later, I found it thought-provoking: perhaps it wasn't so amusing, but this reaction to crisis is actually quite commonplace. My third response after seeing it a few times was that the picture made me feel emotionally moved.

Introduction

The photo imagery speaks to my experience of our times and also reminds me of the many instances when I have witnessed what I will call 'helpless helping', when individuals, groups, or businesses may seem to be helping, but in reality, they are not acting in 'good faith'. Their actions can be driven by conscious or unconscious desires and sometimes cause more harm than good. Below, I explore the underlying causes of this 'helpless helping'.

Three underlying causes

I will share examples of each cause in the following paragraphs.

1. **Self-interest:** Helpless helping, in this case, is a calculated conscious act driven by selfish desires, in that we pretend to help, but we are serving our own purposes while fully aware that our actions are not really helping at all.
2. **Unconscious repression:** We have a conscious desire to help, but unconsciously, we undermine, limit, or distort the help we want to give in order to satisfy our own needs and desires. In this case, we repress our lack of commitment to helping the other fully, to protect our idealised self. Our ego-identity of being a 'good person' won't allow us to see our true selves, and the shame of our selfishness is buried and rationalised away while we convince ourselves 'I swear I am helping'.
3. **Performative helping:** This stance is often blurred between the conscious act in point 1 and the unconscious act in point 2. We see

the need of the suffering other and want to help, yet we also see benefits to ourselves. For example, to get attention and make others think about how generous we are. In this case, our helping becomes performative and often overshadows the actual need of the suffering other we are helping. This creates a conflict within ourselves and/or within the group we are acting with. We have to wrestle with our conscience, but too often, the help we give is distorted towards 'helpless helping' as our priority becomes the performance of helping to make us look good.

Often, our helpless helping goes beyond a lack of help; it can also cause more harm.

Examples of the three causes are below:

Pharmaceutical companies pushing dangerous drugs: 'I swear I am helping'

Pharmaceutical companies sell opioid drugs to 'help patients' control pain. Yet these companies have acknowledged that they were putting profit before patient welfare. Pharmaceutical companies have made incredible profits from pushing these dangerously addictive medications, which has led to terrible consequences. Many Americans with opioid use disorder have shifted from taking prescription pain pills to street fentanyl, a synthetic opioid that is far more powerful and lethal. Drug overdoses now kill more than 100,000 people in the USA each year.[89]

'As today's plea to felony charges shows, pharmaceutical company Purdue put opioid profits ahead of people and corrupted the sacred doctor–patient relationship,' said Christina Nolan, US attorney for the State of Vermont.[90]

These pharmaceutical companies cynically put self-interest and profits first.

Corporate greenwashing: 'I swear I am helping'

In the picture, the planet/chair burns and many corporations and political actors perform acts of 'helpless helping' that are more about promoting an ethical brand than really making a difference. Sometimes, this comes from position 1, where self-interest rules and profits are put before ethics, and sometimes from positions 2 and 3, where there is a desire to be greener, but self-interest trumps the desire to actually help the planet. This is then either rationalised through unconscious repression or, more often, the performative greenwashing takes precedence over actual change.

These two examples of greenwashing are shared by Ibrahim Okunade:[91]

1. *Innocent Drinks:* Innocent Drinks was accused of greenwashing for pushing adverts that claim that buying their smoothies can help save the environment. Innocent Drinks is a subsidiary of Coca-Cola, and the beverage company is widely regarded as one of the worst plastic polluters globally.
2. *Volkswagen:* Another famous example of greenwashing is the case of Volkswagen's 'Clean Diesel' campaign. In the mid-2000s, Volkswagen marketed its diesel vehicles as environmentally friendly, claiming they had lower carbon dioxide emissions and better fuel efficiency. However, in 2015, it was revealed that Volkswagen had installed software in their vehicles that manipulated emissions tests, allowing the cars to pass regulatory standards while emitting much higher levels of pollutants in real-world driving conditions.

The invasion of Iraq: 'I swear I am helping'

In my humble opinion, Tony Blair and George Bush, when they pushed for the Iraq invasion, were acting from position 3. They did want to get rid of a dictator and 'help', and they also wanted to serve their own political agendas at home. The performative act of 'helping Iraq' by killing the dictator Saddam Hussein turned into a humanitarian disaster. To really help, a very different path would need to have been followed.

Helpless helping closer to home

Bringing it closer to home, I interpreted the picture as a reflection of our narcissistic cultural response to the many challenges we face. I have witnessed so many situations where individuals focus on themselves, incapable of making the connection to the needs of the other ... even when the suffering is great.

In workplaces, many people suffer mental health challenges due to toxic cultures or work demands, and yet the organisation's rhetoric will claim to be one of well-being and employee engagement. The HR departments and senior leadership teams metaphorically pour water over their own heads in a performative act, such as offering mindfulness classes to show they are helping, while the structural and systemic causes, such as a bullying culture or hyper-workloads, go unchallenged. Many in the organisation suffer while they are told by their leaders, 'We swear we are helping.'

As a family therapist, I would so often see caring parents undermine their children through unconscious acts of 'helpless helping'. For example, parents who do everything for a child to 'help them' without seeing how their help was undermining the child's development to become more independent. The parents would rationalise their behaviour as 'We are only trying to help' while their behaviour served an unconscious purpose to keep the parents in 'control' and therefore alleviate the parental anxiety about their child going into the dangerous external world. Even when a child would rebel in a dangerous way, such as self-harming, the parents would often struggle to change their dominating and controlling behaviour, saying, 'But we are only trying to help.'

Conclusion

Some people make a conscious choice when they are in a dilemma between self-interest and helping others, and they put aside their own needs to offer help. Others turn to rationalising their approach, defending their ideal good selves with everything they can, and often blame others when their help is identified as, at best, performative.

The Eco-Leadership Institute, which I founded, has the stated purpose of supporting leaders to act in 'good faith' to create the 'good society'.

To act in 'good faith' means not only to perform good deeds, it means to take on Jean-Paul Sartre's challenge to really look deeply at ourselves and to question ourselves with an honesty and transparency that can be painfully revealing. Our idealised good selves are not always as ideal as we would like them to be. Only when we undertake this deep soul searching, with ourselves and with others, can we avoid acting in bad faith and challenge the 'helpless helping' that we observe, enact, and collude with.

Facing ourselves in this way has two upsides. First, after an initial painful reality check that reveals to ourselves who we really are, it's quite liberating to see ourselves more clearly and to see how our unconscious works to repress things we don't like about ourselves. We then regain some power to make real choices that can be life-affirming. Second, when we shift from helpless helping to really helping, the rewards are immense.

Real helping means

1. **Acting in good faith:** This is achieved by challenging and critiquing ourselves, our teams, and our organisations to rise to the challenge of doing our very best in any given context and not performing or deviating from undertaking the help that is needed.
2. **Putting our egos to work:** Some people advocate getting rid of ego. Perhaps this works for a Buddhist monk who spends his life working towards this aim. However, for those who engage in psychoanalysis like myself, getting rid of your ego is like saying get rid of your left arm ... it's not going to happen! We all have egos, and those with strong ego drives can become narcissistic and self-orientated, or they can put their egos to work for the good of society. Recognising our ego drives, our needs, and our talents helps us to direct our energies towards the help that is needed.
3. **Mutualism, not saviourism:**[92] Saviourism affirms a good and powerful me and keeps the suffering other in a position of dependency and weakness. The humanitarian sector is struggling with this challenge of saviourism, and they are criticised for maintaining the white-saviour complex, such as using poverty porn to raise funds in the short-term, while in the long-term reproducing the perception that Africa is underdeveloped and full of poor helpless people who need the 'we know best' help from the global North. To really help is to engage with mutuality; this is not to ignore real differentials in terms of power and resource control but to acknowledge that those in need of help also have agency and power. The task

is not to empower them, as that just means giving a bit of our power to the less powerful. The task is to think, act, and be mutualistic in our engagement with others.

What mutuality means

- Helping becomes a co-produced act.
- It enables the recipient of help to have the strongest voice possible in what kind of help they need.
- It makes helping become more sustainable, as those being helped are engaged in the process, working with others collaboratively for longer-term solutions.

None of us is perfect, we all act in self-interest at times, we unconsciously repress parts of ourselves we don't want to face, and our egos like to be stroked, so we perform our best selves in order to feel good. Yet we are also able to be courageous, to think critically, to question ourselves and others. Stopping to ask ourselves, 'Is this helpless helping or is it real helping?' is one important question we should ask regularly.

CHAPTER 15

Free yourself from the happiness imperative

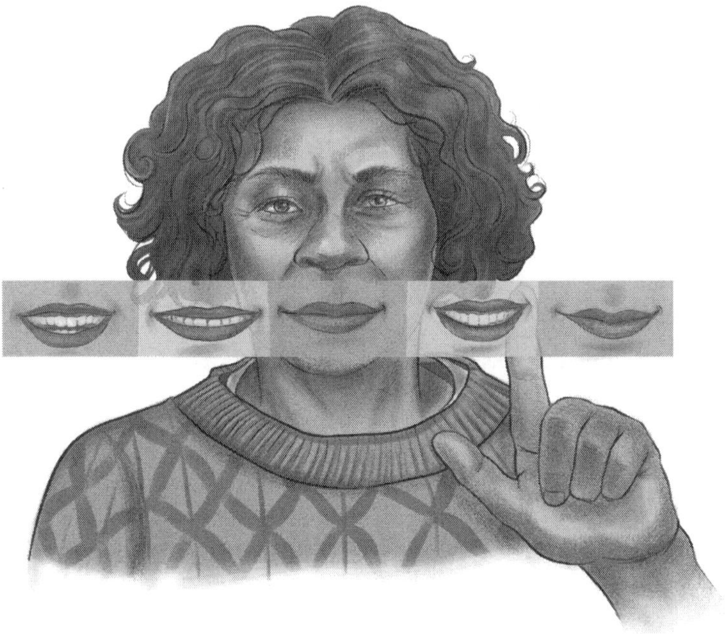

Original artwork, hand-drawn by Martyna Adamska

I wrote this essay after discovering that the UN had introduced an International Happiness Day. It sparked these reflections.

Introduction

This chapter explores a new social demand that has slowly crept up on us. Its message is simple, 'It is your duty to be happy', but this message has a profound impact. In the recent past, fleeting happy moments were to be enjoyed, remembered, and cherished. Happiness was accepted as being one part of a diverse fabric of life that included other emotions such as suffering, boredom, joy, love, sadness, and melancholy. Yet today, happiness has become something we should feel entitled to, elevated to become a human right. Social expectations are that each of us deserves to be happy. More than this, happiness is not only a desire or expectation, it has become a duty. If we are not happy, we are failing ourselves, our families and friends, and society. This chapter explores how this 'happiness imperative'[93] crept up on us and the paradox that this demand to be happy leads to less happy societies and individuals, not happier ones.

The big Other

The big Other is a psychoanalytic term to describe the voice of society that speaks directly to our unconscious. The big Other acts upon us like a parental or godlike voice that we internalise, and it impacts our values, conscience, and perceptions of what is good and bad. The big Other lets us know when we transgress social rules, when we are enjoying a forbidden pleasure, and when we are being good citizens. The big Other conforms and socialises us to the norms of society. Each of us experiences the voice of the big Other differently and uniquely, yet there is commonality to the messages depending on which social groups we are a part of. If you belong to a mosque, church, or temple, the big Other will have a particular flavour, very different from a feminist activist social group, for example.

In today's society, the big Other speaks across these diverse groups with a clear message that rarely changes; it instructs us to be happy. This external voice screams at us to be happy from multiple platforms and places. From social media, Instagram, TikTok, Facebook, on marketing billboards, in shops, magazines, and branded objects, and from our TVs and radios. This voice has become so expansive, pervasive, unrelenting, and repetitive that 'being happy' has become an internalised norm. It is now taken for granted that it is our duty to be happy.

The 'Society of Prohibition'[94] existed pre-1960s, where the social injunction was 'thou shalt not!'. Institutions such as the Church, schools, monarchy, government, and major media outlets like the BBC spoke as the big Other with a voice of authority, which was widely respected and accepted, even as it was resisted and resented by a minority. The voice of this big Other said, 'No! Your role in life is not to seek personal enjoyment but to serve society and know your position in the social hierarchy.' In the UK, this meant with the monarch, God, politicians, and the Church at the top of the pyramid.[95]

In the Society of Prohibition, happiness and satisfaction took two forms. First, finding your place in society, being part of a community, and enjoying the small personal pleasures that existed, perhaps being with family, with friends in the pub, watching sport, or working on your allotment. The other way of gaining pleasure was to transgress the prohibitive rules, as in the excitement/danger of having transgressive sex before marriage. Todd McGowan writes:

> A society of prohibition requires all its members to sacrifice their individual, private ways of obtaining enjoyment for the sake of the social order as a whole. That is to say, one receives an identity from society in exchange for one's immediate access to enjoyment, which one must give up.[96]

A society of commanded enjoyment[97]

The 'society of commanded enjoyment' emerged in the 1960s counter-culture. Institutional authority was challenged, privileging individualism and the freedom to choose how we live, which emerged into today's identity politics. A new space was opened for what Berardi calls 'the happiness imperative' to emerge.[98] The counter-cultural social movements that led to riots in Paris in 1968 and demonstrations across the USA initially threatened the status quo. However, political and commercial interests quickly realised that this new desire for individual choice could become the perfect business model and, at the same time, undermine social solidarity and political activism. Consumer capitalism co-opted the ideas and the energy of the individualistic movement. The society of commanded enjoyment developed because it was a perfect neoliberal political solution. Hyper-individualism and mass consumption in search of the perfect happy life went hand in hand with the demise of social solidarity. This meant that resistance to social injustice and inequity brought about by capitalism was undermined.

> Rather than demanding that its members give up their individual enjoyment for the sake of the whole, the society of enjoyment commands their enjoyment—private enjoyment becomes of paramount importance—and the importance of the social order as a whole seems to recede.[99]

Yannis Stavrakakis writes that 'commanded enjoyment' refers to the way modern society pressures individuals to pursue pleasure and fulfilment, often through consumerism and the media.[100] However, individuals often feel a deep sense of dissatisfaction or alienation. Paradoxically, the abundant options for enjoyment constantly make us feel lacking as if we always need something else to make us happy. When we buy the next service or product to fulfil our lack, the fleeting moment of happiness passes, and we are back where we started, an individual desperately trying to fulfil the command to be happy. Communal well-being and social solidarity, which create feelings of connectedness and deep satisfaction, became marginalised in the society of commanded enjoyment. Also, the pleasures gained from transgressing prohibitive rules were lost. The only prohibition to your happiness was your own inability to be happy.

Reflections

Both of these social injunctions, 'prohibition and enjoyment', are problematic in different ways. I am not advocating a return to the society of prohibition, which was overtly stratified by class, paternalism, and authoritarianism. Striving to fulfil our potential and to seek our happiness can liberate us from the former constraining forces that told us 'to know our place, and accept authority'. Yet constantly having to strive for happiness and to perform being happy, even to ourselves, is an impossible burden to carry. The emotional labour involved in this happiness culture takes its toll on our mental and emotional health.

The pressure to fulfil our duty and entitlement to be happy actually makes us discontented, as it is impossible to fully satisfy our desires that always seem out of reach. Following the happiness imperative means judging ourselves against the imaginary 'happy others' we see on mainstream and social media. We strive to match their upbeat presentations and their manufactured beauty. The rise of beauty treatments and cosmetic surgery has expanded exponentially as individuals try to fulfil the social pressures that demand you to look a certain way to be happy. Individualisation and identity politics have exploded, and social media platforms propagate the 'happiness imperative' with new vigour. We perform being happy on Instagram, Facebook, and TikTok as we want to share our best selves.

In 2012, the UN introduced International Happiness Day, stating 'happiness as a fundamental human right and goal for all'. Positive psychologists, life coaches, self-help books, and now politicians and the UN are all demanding that we strive for happiness. The 'happiness imperative' has become institutionalised and normalised to such an extent that it is no longer questioned.

On the surface, it is hard to argue against the wish that we all want to be happy, and don't we all deserve to be happy? And yet … something is unsettling about happiness being a fundamental human right.

Maybe being happy isn't all it's cracked up to be!

Mental health crisis, depression and anxiety, loneliness

Frank Furedi and Franco Berardi[101] claim that the happiness imperative creates the opposite effect of what is intended, citing the devastating amounts of depression, anxiety, and unhappiness since society adopted this stance. Barbara Ehrenreich, focusing on the happiness imperative in the USA, claims 'that on a personal level, it leads to self-blame and a morbid preoccupation with stamping out "negative thoughts" … On a national level, it has brought us an era of irrational optimism resulting in disaster.'[102]

It is worth noting that in the USA, where positive psychology thrives, and the happiness imperative is most prevalent, Americans account for two-thirds of the global market for antidepressants, which are the most commonly prescribed drugs in the USA. Mental health concerns for young people, who are particularly vulnerable to the happiness imperative, are soaring. The happiness imperative has gone viral. Even those who believe they are living alternative lifestyles use the same mantras as in consumer capitalism. Take up yoga and be happy; mindfulness will bring you inner happiness. The well-being and new-age spirituality movements have now become big business. Gwyneth Paltrow's company, Goop, was valued at approximately $1 billion in 2021. Happiness has been instrumentalised and co-opted by the market.

The connections are clear. The unrelenting pressures to meet the impossible demands to be happy, alongside the demise of social solidarity and community, have a great cost. Dissatisfaction now appears as something that one need not experience.

Free yourself from the happiness imperative!

To be human is to experience a whole range of emotional states, happiness being just one of many that are vital for us to live engaged and fulfilling lives. To be reflective, sad, contented, loved, unloved, melancholic, angry, excited, bored, frustrated, delighted, and many more feelings and experiences are what it means to live a full life.

To be happy comes in fleeting moments, it arrives surreptitiously as a by-product of living a full life. As soon as we strive for happiness itself as a life goal, we instrumentalise happiness, and we lose it.

Realising the double bind this puts us in, let us rid ourselves of this perverse demand that encourages us to chase an illusory fantasy of always being happy and positive.

Below are some thoughts to help free us from the happiness imperative:

- Give yourself permission to not always feel positive/happy.
- Don't accept the big Other's voice in your head … refuse it! Notice the demands to be happy all around you, and let them pass you by.
- Allow yourself to feel human with all that entails, accepting limitations with humility, welcoming into your life the full range of feelings: sadness, grieving, loss, pain, love, hope, joy, contentment,

melancholy, and the ambivalence of many confusing feelings. It is the combination and richness of these feelings, thoughts, and emotions that makes our lives so liveable.
- Social bonds—find your way back into relationships with others, and remember 'that to give is a greater thing than to receive'.
- Become part of the whole, remember the cosmos. Find your way to get in touch with nature and engage with the transcendent. To find solace in being a tiny molecule in a spectacular whole.

Contentment and moments of happiness come to us as a by-product of living a good life. When we set happiness as a goal, we discover we are on the wrong journey.

CHAPTER 16

Enjoy your limitations!

Original artwork, hand-drawn by Martyna Adamska

This essay was written in response to a commercial advert stating 'No human is limited' which jarred with me immediately!

Introduction

In 2019, Kenyan distance runner Eliud Kipchoge became the first person in history to run a marathon in under two hours. News of the incredible feat sparked excitement around the world, and the runner's personal mantra of 'No human is limited' became corporatised by Ineos, a global chemical company and sponsor of Eliud Kipchoge.

From the Ineos website:

> His legacy may be one for the history books, but this is his chance to inspire people to do great things, even beyond sport, to challenge themselves in a way they may never have dared ... .
>
> 'Any human being can go beyond their limits' he said.
>
> It is this philosophy that is shared by INEOS and an exceptional group of men and women involved in sport, which has inspired the launch of No Human is Limited.[103]

While hugely admiring Kipchoge and others who achieve remarkable feats, the #nohumanislimited memes following his marathon troubled me. After a period of reflection, I was moved to write this chapter, critiquing not Kipchoge or his aspirational-inspired meme but a wider issue that is endemic in our society and pushed by corporate power.

The idea of having no limitations promotes a wider culture of narcissistic grandiosity. This fantasy whereby humans can totally master themselves is not unrelated to the idea that humans can also master each other and that we can also master nature. While Kipchoge is clearly aiming to inspire people, I am not convinced his commercial sponsors have the same altruistic agenda.

The capacity for individuals and teams to do remarkable things beyond what is considered 'normal limits' is admirable and uplifting. Yet ideas like 'No humans are limited' go beyond a single athlete trying to be aspirational. This idea has been commandeered, manipulated, and reproduced to become part of a dominant ideology that speaks directly to our unconscious. We internalise the idea of having unlimited aspirations, following a social injunction, 'You can become whatever you desire', which aligns with the social injunction, 'It is your duty to be happy'.

This chapter draws on psychoanalysis to show how these positivistic mantras undermine us rather than empower us.

You are not master in your own house

When Freud said 'we are not masters in our own house'[104] he referred to how the unconscious influences so much of what we think and do, without our conscious awareness. We are 'doubly subjected'; first, we are subjects responding to our conscious thoughts, desires, and fears, and second, we are subjects responding to our unconscious dynamics, which often are in tension with and undermine our conscious desires and rational reasoning. The idea of humans having no limits has long been promoted by capitalist forces and their marketing teams who direct their message at our unconscious drive, one that desires unlimited pleasure, which Lacan calls jouissance.

Pleasure principle and reality principle

Having no limitations relates to the pleasure principle, which demands immediate gratification and unlimited pleasure. Freud offered two conflicting principles that we all struggle with:[105]

1. The pleasure principle—emanating from our deep unconscious is the voice of 'no limitations', an inner voice that tells us we deserve pleasure and we should fulfil our desires and gain immediate gratification without accounting for others or for limitations.
2. The reality principle—is in opposition to the pleasure principle and is the voice of reason based on an assessment of real-world contexts. It takes account of our limits, including our mortality and the ageing process.

The pleasure principle inspires mantras that are commonly found in the marketing of corporate brands, such as #nohumanislimited and Nike's 'Just do it'. Great sporting achievements are also great commercial opportunities when the memes align. 'Buy our brand and identify with being super-human without limits!' Politicians learnt from this, and Obama's successful 'Yes We Can' political campaign was both inspiring and also worried me at the time for overpromising, leading to later widespread disappointment with the limitations of his achievements in power.

To discover and accept limitations, such as the way our bodies are and the ageing process, can be truly transformational. The beauty industry exploits the 'there is no limitation' idea to vulnerable men and women who are buying cosmetic surgery and drugs at unprecedented rates, trying to reverse the ageing process. To accept limitations means we can accept that our body changes, enabling us to grow old with grace, enjoying a good life rather than living a life of disappointment at our limited and failing body.

The idea that no human has limitations also erases social justice issues. Those in poverty have many more limitations than the wealthy. To not have enough food, to live in a war zone, to have ill health without medical attention, and to have no education is to have limitations imposed on whole communities. We are not all equal, nor do we have equality of opportunity. Human limitations are often structural and political, and to have corporations pushing the message that we are all free individuals without limitations is an act of political manipulation that we shouldn't accept.

Enjoy your limitations

To find unique ways to live a good life, individually and collectively, we must traverse the fantasy that no human is limited. Paradoxically, acknowledging our limits is not a self-limiting exercise. It is a liberating process that opens up new possibilities for how we choose to live well, both for ourselves and for society. Below, I offer two main thoughts on why we should enjoy our limitations.

Knowing our limitations is liberating

Individually and collectively, recognising our limits is liberating for the reasons set out below.

Focusing on success

Recognising our limits as an individual, team, or organisation does not diminish our aspirations but actually helps us towards success. When we realise our limitations, we make better choices as to where we put our energy and time. We don't waste energy chasing unrealistic dreams, which takes an emotional toll. This doesn't mean not having high aspirations or challenging ourselves to go further, but it does mean not entering a fantasy world where we believe we are omnipotent and can achieve anything ... we can't, and that's OK!

Emancipated from relentless 'better' and 'more'

Recognising limits emancipates us from the never-ending cycle of feeling we are never good enough. Constantly striving for unlimited success at work and for the perfect relationships is exhausting. Today's paralysing social injunctions condemn us to the relentless internalised pressure that produces a general feeling of dissatisfaction.

Improved relationships through accepting others

Acknowledging our own limits can help us to acknowledge the limitations of others. We can make space and recognise both the strengths and the limitations of others. We can then empathise with their struggle and admire their resilience in the face of limitations. When I was a hospital nurse, what most inspired me was to see people discover new ways of living well when new limitations beset them. I recall stroke patients, unable to return to their lives as before, who strived to find new ways to live fully and well. Those who accepted their physical limitations would put all their energy into discovering how to live to their full potential. Those unable to accept the changes struggled and were often living with anger and resentment, unable to direct their energies into living their best lives. Accepting our own limitations and others' limitations puts us more at ease with others and makes us less judgemental, better partners, family members, and team players.

Recognising limitations is vital if we are to live well on planet Earth

Global corporations are crucial to addressing the urgent social inequalities and environmental issues we face. They must urgently address the madness of a no-limitations approach to commercial growth that continues to burn fossil fuels and create the climate crisis. We live on a planet with finite resources, a planet that has reached its limit in terms of biodiversity destruction and climate warming. There is a limit to how humans exploit the environment and a limit to the social inequalities that are acceptable. To prevent social unrest and climate catastrophe, ditching the ideology of no-limitations is vital.

Reflections

Kipchoge is a brilliant athlete who works tirelessly to break records. His genuine desire to inspire others is welcomed. Yet we must retain our critical faculties when corporate sponsors use the meme of #nohumanislimited to sell their brands. These supposedly innocuous inspirational slogans carry an ideological message of individualism, of free choice, and that there are no limits.

These slogans and memes are not isolated incidents, they are endemic. The rhetoric of politicians, leaders, and marketeers who seduce us by telling us we live in individual bubbles separate from societal realities and can be anything we want is pervasive and damaging.

'No human is limited' speaks to our irrational selves and puts the pleasure principle before the reality principle. It creates an unsustainable world for ourselves, our organisations, and our planet.

Imperfections and limitations are little discussed in today's 'just do it' (just buy it) world. Yet, at the same time, we face deep discontentment in society with rising levels of stress, depression, and mental health issues.

Jean-Paul Sartre famously said, 'We are condemned to be free.'[106] Surely, our freedom requires us to take responsibility and to acknowledge limitations in order to live well and in solidarity with our human and non-human companions on this fragile planet.

Balancing our aspirations and desires with the reality principle sets us free to be who we really are, to spend time on what is attainable, and enables us to become who we can truly become rather than chasing utopian fantasies.

To liberate ourselves from constantly striving for the impossible and to reverse the excesses that have created social inequality and environmental crisis, let us enjoy our limitations!

CHAPTER 17

Staying with the trouble: Psychosocial insights into working with diversity issues

Diversity is in the news a lot these days and is a hot topic in workplaces, politics, and across all media. This short essay explores why diversity is troublesome and that to work with diversity means we have to 'stay with the trouble'.[107] I invite you to read this chapter, noting what troubles you. Observe your reactions and your attachments to what you strongly agree or disagree with. As you read, try to avoid being judgemental or reactive, just 'stay with the trouble' and make sense of your reactions.

Diversity is troublesome

Diversity is troublesome, and it troubles me. Diversity is troubling because it is not easy to speak of, and when we do speak of diversity, it impacts the essence of who we are as individuals and collective groups. What is at stake here is not something abstract but our personal and group identities. Diversity troubles me because so much commentary and dialogue in the diversity space is polarised, with a good side and a bad side, or the trouble is swept under the carpet as rhetoric replaces real dialogue and engagement.

Speaking about diversity puts our identities on the line, and therefore, it evokes strong feelings, sometimes conscious and often unconscious. Whether we identify ourselves with a minority group that desires recognition, inclusion, and equity or whether we are part of a majority group whose identity feels threatened by minority groups, the reaction on either side is to defend our identities.

Populist politicians amplify fears that 'traditional' group identities are being diluted and overwhelmed by a 'foreign body'. These politicians amplify insecurity and create a 'bad other' who they claim will undermine 'the people' they represent. They treat this 'bad other', for example, immigrants, Muslims, Jews, gays, Roma, or other minority groups, as if they were a deadly virus.

In the field of diversity, the idea of purity looms largely. The pure race and the impure other are ideas that have underpinned racist and misogynist thinking for more than a century. The science of eugenics was fairly mainstream in westernised thought in the 1930s, taken to extremes by the Nazi regime, and the idea of cleansing the nation of impurity is rising again. White supremacists circulate ideas such as the 'great replacement theory', which maintains that there is a grand plan to replace white populations with immigrant non-whites/Muslims. Less extreme views are held by other groups; some feminists are worried that trans women are diluting the purity of biological women, and 'TERFs' and trans groups fight with vitriol over their identity rights.

A paradox exists at the heart of the diversity issue. Those who support diversity and inclusion believe in promoting unity and solidarity to create a more equitable world. Yet, in promoting diversity, more differences are encouraged, and we see ever more categories and identities being passionately claimed. Creating more divisions to create more unity is paradoxical and plays into the hands of those who thrive on division.

The recent turn to right-wing populism reveals how identity politics, charged with emotions, have become more important to many voters than economic politics. The rise of nationalist populism in the USA, Hungary, Poland, India, Brazil, Germany, the UK, France, and more, has had devastating impacts on wider issues such as human rights and distracts from deeper issues such as addressing climate change. Culture wars are fought over identity issues, and both sides relish the fight.

The prevalence of diversity forces us to look at ourselves and at others and to make identity choices. We cannot engage with diversity issues without reflecting on and defining who we are and how we relate to others and they to us. This is a deeply personal issue, and it is also a sociopolitical one.

Organisational diversity

In organisations, diversity is big business. Diversity and inclusion are put high on the agenda as a badge of honour in companies because having a positive brand identity is vitally important to organisations. Companies want to be identified as progressive to attract and retain staff. To be a cool brand is especially important, and the brand can be even more important than their products. Coke was a famously early adopter of diversity issues. In 1971, their famous 'I'd like to teach the world to sing' advert showed diverse young people singing in unity and drinking Coke—the message being that to drink Coke is to be cool and progressive. Bad news diversity stories, such as the mistreatment of minority groups, can be devastating to a business, as customers, suppliers, and even governments can quickly turn away from them.

Having worked in many public, non-profit, and private 'progressive' organisations, I know the gap between diversity rhetoric and reality can be wide. Woke capitalism or rainbow washing are the new terms being used to describe corporations that co-opt progressive agendas, such as diversity, and use them to increase profit without delivering real change.

Diversity is not straightforward, and emotions run high. When discussing diversity issues, there quickly appear oppressors and the oppressed, the good 'us' and the bad 'other', the victims and the perpetrators. You can be named a perpetrator without even being aware of your 'unconscious biases', or you may be collectively named as a perpetrator of racism by being associated with an 'institutionally racist' organisation, such as the London Metropolitan Police in 1999. Also, as a minority person, you can find yourself being neatly placed and labelled such as BME (Black Minority Ethnic), and/or treated as a victim by individuals or institutions who claim to wish to defend you (white saviourism). Yet the person/group may not identify at all with the acronym label given to them and not as a victim at all.

Names and acronyms

Diversity is troubling. Names and acronyms are part of the trouble; DEI stands for diversity, equity, and inclusion, and LGBTQI+ is the latest inclusive acronym I am aware of, but usually I am a couple of years behind. Language and acronyms can amplify existing identities, and they create in-groups and out-groups, those who know and use the politically correct language, and those who are excluded because they don't know the latest terms, or what they mean. In the culture wars, between the progressive-liberal tribe and the populist-conservative tribe, both enjoy creating a 'bad other', and both utilise aggression and control to deepen their own 'good self' identities.

Using pronouns is another example of how language is used in the diversity stakes. Using pronouns is liberating for some people who have felt boxed in by normative assumptions, when finally they can express their non-binary or gender preference. Yet using pronouns is not only a personal statement about how you identify yourself, it also says, 'I am part of the liberal-progressive tribe,' which excludes many because of cultural, class, regional, or political differences. I recently worked on an online international experiential learning event where a Chinese member expressed total confusion by the use of pronouns that showed up on the screens of mainly American members, and their explanations did not clarify the situation for her.

The use of pronouns also highlights another diversity issue which is the hierarchy of diversity issues. Pronouns say what gender preference you have but not your age, ethnicity, sexual preference, economic class, or religion. They privilege gender diversity over other forms of our diverse identities.

Kimberlé Crenshaw coined the term intersectionality in 1989 to describe how people from diverse backgrounds encounter the world differently.[108] Diverse women's experiences cannot be reduced to a single experience. The experiences of discrimination faced by a black woman will be different from the experiences of a white woman; the lived experiences of a white woman living in poverty will be different from those of a wealthy black or brown woman.

Intersectionality is very helpful, and yet it has been weaponised by both conservative and progressive activists. Intersectionality recognises the differences within diversity. It was originally used to support more equity in the legal field so that a black woman's experience could be accounted for, not only as a woman or only as a black person but by acknowledging both when differing identities intersect. Today, there emerges a hierarchy of victimhood and privilege, some say a new caste system that overturns the old order. Conservative pundit Ben Shapiro described intersectionality as 'a form of identity politics in which the value of your opinion depends on how many victim groups you belong to. At the bottom of the totem pole is the person everybody loves to hate: the straight white male.'[109]

I find intersectionality very useful, especially as it enables economic class to be accounted for, which is so often omitted from diversity discussions and education. However, the danger is that it becomes weaponised or used prescriptively. Structural and systemic issues can be overlooked as internal battles within liberal diversity groups take place.

When I initially typed DEI in this chapter, I mistakenly put the I before the E, writing DIE. It didn't look right, so I checked and corrected it. I then realised that maybe I had made a Freudian slip, and my unconscious was alerting me to the mortal danger that is very real in this space. People do DIE due to the negative impact experienced because of their identities, and often, their trauma is supported by a state apparatus as well. People are oppressed, imprisoned, and murdered for being gay, black, trans, Muslim, Jewish, Roma, and marginalised groups suffer mental health issues and suicide rates at much higher levels than the majority population. The white working class are dying, too, from suicide, drugs, and violence. Black Lives Matter is a very necessary movement, and perhaps DIE is the appropriate way around to signify the real dangers that diversity issues raise.

Language matters and it is troubling

When talking of ethnicity, some talk of black people, which can annoy those who identify as brown or in other ways. In some parts of the world, 'people of colour' is acceptable, whereas in other places and spaces, this language is regarded as old-fashioned and derogatory: 'I am not a person of colour, I am black and proud!' Black and white are used as if these binary groups are homogenous, as if all white people or black people are the same. There is a partial truth to this. For example, in apartheid in

South Africa or in the USA in the 1950s, having black/brown skin put you in a different legal category and limited your human, educational, and civil rights.

Today in the USA, you may be a privileged and wealthy black man, but if you drive an expensive car, you (like all black men) remain fearful of getting pulled over and mistreated, even shot by the police, simply because your skin colour will draw police associations with crime, drugs, and theft. A successful black colleague of mine was very keen to move his teenage boys back to the UK from the USA precisely because of the dangers young black men face in the USA. Living in a comfortable neighbourhood meant that if his black teenagers were seen driving a nice car they were in real danger, mainly from the police.

The diversity that exists within the terms black or white is vast. There are huge cultural and economic class divides within these groups and diverse categorisations such as sex, age, and ability differences. The post-industrial world has undermined proud working-class communities. In his book *Chavs*, Owen Jones explores how the 'working class has gone from salt of the earth to scum of the earth'.[110] Irish travellers face terrible discrimination in Ireland and the UK, and in the USA the term 'white trash' is used to describe the underclass. Not all whites are privileged! The economically poor remain the most deprived of all groups, across all measures: mental health, life expectancy, physical health, suicide, education, and in this late-modern era the lives of poor people, from whatever background, become more and more precarious. In the USA, violence between African American males has been rampant for years with the highest death/murder rates recorded in these groups, and other tensions exist between diverse ethnic groups as well as between white and black ethnicities.

When we talk about diversity, it is not a simple binary of black and white, and language is both important and troubling. Language is a signifier, and it can close down a conversation as well as open it up.

Gender and sexuality

Gender and sexuality are emerging as core diversity issues, with new language and identities emerging each year. There have been many gains: non-binary, queer identities, and trans people are gaining more recognition and visibility. However, this visibility also brings aggression, fear, and anxiety. The tensions between feminists and the trans community (if the term community makes any sense) are making the news. Some are shocked at the vitriolic hatred and trolling that is taking place as feminists have often essentialised such aggression as a male characteristic. The essentialism of gender and other differences produces dangerous tropes that undermine the realities of difference and box people into categories. 'Women are more …', 'Men are more …', 'Black men are …', 'Jewish people are good at …'. These tropes remain common in the public space and are apparently thriving in non-public social media spaces.

A colleague once remarked that we have become a 'nation of stutterers', referring to the hesitation and anxiety of speaking wrongly about diversity issues. As I write this, I feel the stuttering sensation on the keyboard. Will I make a mistake? Will I be trolled? Another trouble comes with the word 'woke', which I address in Chapter 10. This word emerged from black culture to mean being awake to issues of social injustice, particularly racism. It has now been appropriated by political conservatives and used as a derogatory term for someone who is politically correct or ultra-liberal. I had a right-wing friend who called me out for being woke whenever we touched on political issues. It's a cheap and lazy shot and avoids the work and engagement it takes to 'stay with the trouble'.

Staying with the trouble

Donna Haraway, in her excellent book, invites us to 'stay with the trouble'.[111]

When we feel we are getting into trouble, our instincts tell us to problem-solve, and to seek solutions that remove the trouble or take flight to escape the trouble and the discomfort it brings. To stay with the trouble is to work with the issues and challenges we meet without expecting quick solutions or fixes. To stay with the trouble means shifting our thinking from 'We must get rid of this bad trouble' to 'What does the trouble mean?'

Can we think about the context? Is there a structural or systemic challenge that this challenge is a symptom of? Can we engage with the discomfort, not seeking immediate answers but exploring the issue to gain a deeper understanding?

Staying with the trouble is to recognise the complexities of the challenges we face, and diversity is one of these complex, knotty challenges. Staying with the trouble is very counter-cultural in a world that demands quick fixes, and it takes practice, resilience, awareness, and courage to face ourselves, our biases, and our fears.

To work with diversity in any meaningful way can only be achieved if we learn how to stay with the trouble. This means holding onto our curiosity in the face of the discomfort and anxiety caused by whatever is troubling us. It draws on the psychoanalysts' position of working with 'negative capability',[112] whereby the psychoanalyst suspends their judgement and lets go of their 'memory and desire' to pay full attention to their client in the moment. Yet Haraway's position goes beyond vacating our minds to learn something new from the here and now. It asks us to pay attention to the actual trouble we face, while not grasping at solutions or going into flight mode.

When engaging in the field of diversity and equity, we have to face three challenges to enable us to 'stay with the trouble'. Ask yourself and the group you are working with these three questions before and during working on diversity issues:

- **The trouble in ourselves:** What troublesome issues arise in me, in us? What defences, desires, attachments, and investments do I/we hold which are evoked by this conversation?
- **Lack and gaps—avoiding the trouble:** What particular and/or general troublesome issues are not being addressed in this diversity conversation? What greater implications do the challenges we face have beyond the immediate issues being discussed? What is not being spoken of, what is lurking beneath the surface?
- **Troublesome relationships:** What troublesome relationships and group identities are evoked here? Where is power? Who is dominant, vulnerable, upset, or angry in this space? Who is included and who is excluded in this discussion/process? What am I/we projecting onto others, and what are they projecting onto me/us?

The first challenge is the biggest. Only if we do the work on ourselves do we have a chance of doing the work in areas two and three. To work on ourselves means locating ourselves in our own histories and experiences and in relation to others. For example, as a white male, I will often carry the 'bad object' identity in diversity conversations; this may be named explicitly, with white supremacist, white privilege, and 'male and stale' language used, or it might be expressed more passive-aggressively. In this scenario, my identity of having a 'good self' (mostly) is threatened. This is the time I have to stay with the trouble and not become reactive and defensive. Yet I also have to hold onto my voice and not be silenced or resentful. To be silenced perpetuates the trouble for all.

To stay with the trouble is to ask the meaning of being identified as a 'problem' systemically. Perhaps it reveals that these diversity conversations are a rare space where others who have been silenced and oppressed elsewhere have permission to feel equity or privilege in a conversation, and are able to share pent-up frustrations and anger. As a white, heterosexual, cisgender male, I am likely to be the object of these angry feelings. Making sense of these relational dynamics is not easy. It means managing my feelings of being objectified, I lose 'the Simon' and become an object representing all 'privileged' white males. When we communicate, two things are always present: the conscious content of the speech and the unconscious communication. In this case, the objectification of me is an unconscious way of showing me how minority groups are treated and objectified all the time .... Unconsciously, the communication is, 'Now see how it feels, Simon!' My task is to hold onto being Simon and not react with some angry or defensive stereotypical response. Staying with the trouble means holding onto thinking, that is, to be able to think in the face of anxiety.

We can learn from the wider experiences of the unconscious projections we receive. The projections (positive and negative) I receive as a white male academic, author, and consultant in diversity settings vary between being the expert, 'the one who is supposed to know' (Lacan), and being the privileged one who doesn't understand oppression. This is very different from the internalised feelings that stay with me from childhood. From being the boy thrown out of school at sixteen years old, working in a factory, and having never attended full-time university. The experience of getting past both the lack of education and the childhood narrative that I was 'stupid' is ongoing (I have to stay with my own trouble).

We need to draw on our own experience. My experience of being 'othered' stays with me: first, as a male nurse in a female dominated profession, and later being othered as a young male single parent in an all-woman mother and toddler group. These experiences were very challenging but also very rewarding. I can draw on them to help make some sense of the experiences of others who are marginalised, while also acknowledging my experiences are not the equivalent or the same. Remembering to not make stereotypical assumptions about individuals and how the hidden injuries of class and 'personal history' are not visible when the physical body turns up is vital in this work.

The work of diversity is complex and challenging. It is deeply personal, yet at the same time, it is about collective identities, power structures, and systemic oppression. To stay with the trouble takes practice, but more than this, it takes the commitment and the courage to begin by staying with the trouble in ourselves.

CHAPTER 18

Space invaders

Photograph taken by author in Rotterdam's Markthal food market, 2023

This essay followed a brief visit to Rotterdam, where I had a powerful experience finding some spaces to be inclusive and welcoming to all, while others were starkly the opposite, exclusive and unwelcoming to some.

Introduction

In and around the wonderful modern architecture of the Markthal food market in Rotterdam, I enjoyed a multicultural and diverse experience. Wandering and enjoying the wonderful food stalls were people from diverse ethnicities, cultures, nationalities, and ages. A group of teenage 'goths' mixed happily alongside Muslim men and women. Families with children ate next to groups of young women of Asian descent, hanging out together, while elderly women passed by shopping at the fruit stalls. I encountered food from the Netherlands, Turkey, Spain, Italy, the Middle East, China, Japan, Korea, India, and France, which reflected the human diversity in the market. The market itself was designed to be filled with light and to have mixed use, with more than 200 apartments that arch around the market space below, which then opens onto a public market square. The market is a modern and striking building, an architectural space designed to welcome all. This was an inclusive space.

Exclusive spaces

I ate my Korean Bibimbap inside the market and then cycled across town to the Rotterdam Philharmonic to listen to a delightful classical concert. What caught me unexpectedly was the dramatic difference in terms of diversity. The beautiful concert hall was a 'white space'. From what I could see, all of the audience and the musicians were white; the only exception was two female violinists of Asian ethnicity. At the interval, I looked out of the window to see a very different, diverse space in the streets below. I recalled Nirmal Puwar's book *Space Invaders: Race, Gender and Bodies Out of Place*,[113] which describes how the spaces we live and work in are not neutral but filled with history and meaning. Puwar explores how certain bodies are 'naturally entitled' to certain spaces while others are not. She cites Winston Churchill's reaction to Nancy Astor, the first woman MP to enter the House of Parliament, Churchill said: 'I find a woman's intrusion into the House of Commons as embarrassing as if she burst into my bathroom when I had nothing with which to defend myself, not even a sponge.'[114]

Those who feel entitled to be in a space generally will not recognise the absence of a different 'other' until, like Winston Churchill, they are awakened by difference being thrust upon them when a diverse other 'invades their space'.

Space policing

Some spaces explicitly exclude others, utilising state laws, as in racial segregation in South Africa, pre-civil rights in the USA, and women in today's Afghanistan. Other spaces are policed by local rules, such as all male or female clubs or groups. Male clubs are often regarded as 'bad' in the sense that they reproduce patriarchy. Marylebone Cricket Club at Lord's Cricket Ground would only allow male members for its first 211 years, and yet when this was challenged in the 1990s, the club was surprised to discover that there was nothing in its rules to prevent a woman from becoming a member, any person could apply. This is a classic case whereby 'a person' was assumed to mean 'a male person', and it reflects many other cases whereby unconscious bias determines who is in and who is out. Feminists often advocate for women-only spaces, and this creates an interesting question about when is a space that excludes others an ethically good space. What determines these ethics, and who decides?

Most spaces become exclusive because of 'soft space policing', in other words cultural norms and unspoken social rules make the spaces welcoming or not. A few years ago, I wrote about my personal experience.

> We particularly notice 'otherness' when our difference transgresses normal spaces. My own experience alerts me to this as I have transgressed normative gender boundaries at different times in my life. As a young man, I worked as a general nurse when it was a 95% female profession, and later as a single parent walking into mother and toddler groups in the early 1980s as the sole male figure. My experience was that I was not treated as 'me' but as an 'object' either to be exoticised or feared. To some, I was a threat that might

> contaminate the homogeneous group. As a nurse, I was asked to leave lectures on women's anatomy and was not allowed to work on female wards. In the mother and toddler group, I was either to be flirted with or treated as an object of pity to be 'mothered'. Women experience this objectification and are made to feel like space invaders in many work situations, such as all-male boardrooms.

For the person entering an exclusive space, there is discomfort, anxiety, and sometimes a physical fear. The minority person/s entering an exclusive space will often feel objectified and 'fixed', as Frantz Fanon so brilliantly describes in his book *Black Skin, White Masks.*[115] Fanon writes about arriving in France in 1950, as a black man from the French colony of Martinique. He describes his experience of transgressing boundaries and the effect of the 'gaze' of the other: 'The movements, the attitudes, the glances of the other fixed me there, in the sense that a chemical solution is fixed by a dye ... sealed into that crushing objecthood the look imprisoned me.'

A space invader often has a visibly recognisable difference: skin colour, ethnicity, age, gender, disability, or religious affiliation marked by a dress code. Carrying a visible minority difference, such as a body inscribed by age, ethnicity, gender, or physical disability, can mean the person is repeatedly exposed to being objectified. Frantz Fanon captures how he discovered his blackness and how the white gaze fixed him as an object: 'I discovered my blackness, my ethnic characteristics; and I was battered down by tom-toms, cannibalism, intellectual deficiency, fetishism, racial defects, slave-ships.'

While things have moved on since the 1950s, the experience of being fixed by the gaze of the other when you are a minority entering a majority space will be familiar to many.

Those with a non-visible minority difference, such as class or sexuality, may not be immediately 'outed' and objectified, yet they still feel uncomfortable and out of place and fear exposure at any time.

When I entered university for the first time in my mid-thirties, I was too overwhelmed to enter the library for the first six months of my master's degree. I was the working class boy who failed school, and this huge library was an intimidating space: it signified elite knowledge that was not my space. The university space screamed at me, 'What are you doing here? ... get out!' Later, when I attended my first academic conference to present my PhD research, I was mistaken for a waiter by another academic who asked me to bring him a drink. Wearing my black tee shirt and hovering around the back of the conference room was my unconscious acting out of feeling like a space invader.

Spaces are sometimes policed by hard boundaries via laws and rules but more often by soft boundaries via unspoken social codes. There are different levels of acceptance and rejection, depending on what difference the person or group brings into a space and how threatening this might be.

Space invaders in organisations

Our organisations replicate wider society, and many spaces are less than welcoming. It's interesting to observe one's reactions when gender and racial stereotypes are challenged, such as male nurses, female builders, or the reactions to a black president in the US. Elijah Anderson, professor of sociology, African American studies, writes:

> Black people now inhabit all levels of the class and occupational structure. They attend the best schools, pursue the professions of their choosing, and occupy various positions of power, privilege, and prestige. But for these people, in the shadows lurks the spectre of the iconic ghetto—it is always in the background, shaping the dominant white society's conception of the anonymous Black person as well as the circumstances of Black people in all walks of life.[116]

The questions below can be helpful in thinking about diversity in the workplace.

Spaces at work

- Who inhabits which spaces?
- Who is excluded and why?
- What happens if the space is transgressed by 'the other'?
- What happens when a woman walks into a boardroom full of men?
- What happens when a black person enters an all-white establishment or a disabled person enters an able-person-dominated space?

- Does the new 'other' have to be assimilated?
- Do they have to learn to be like the majority group, like women executives proving their maleness, or black executives their whiteness?
- Is there a negotiation and co-existence tacitly agreed whereby the 'other' conforms to the existing norm?
- Does an outsider become an 'exotic other' performing 'otherness' for the majority as their only way to find acceptance in an excluding space?
- Does the rhetoric 'we are inclusive' match the reality?
- What spaces have you experienced that are open and welcoming to diversity?
- How do you react to a person of difference entering an existing space?
- Does your organisation have spaces that exclude?
- What can you do to create welcoming spaces for all?

Diversity and inclusion are often discussed in terms of language and identity. Physical spaces are rarely included in our thinking, but perhaps we should think more about the spaces we inhabit and who is welcomed and who is not.

CHAPTER 19

The network society is a disruptive society

Photograph taken by author

Today's 'network society' is a society infused with and shaped by digital technologies.[117] New mobile technologies and the rise of social media alongside AI and quantum computing are creating a hyper-connected network society (NS). The NS creates new opportunities and challenges, with one of its main impacts being constant disruption. This essay was written in response to the changes I was personally experiencing in my life and work because of technological influences.

Introduction

The NS is renowned for disrupting business with new technological innovations, yet what is often missed is just how much it disrupts almost every aspect of our lives. Disruption can be experienced as a positive or a negative and is often both, depending on the context and perspective. Disruptions create precarity, and hyper-connectivity creates interdependencies. Together, these have contributed to the creation of the PI-Age in which we now live (Precarious-Interdependent Age—see Chapter 26).

Business-workplace disruptions

Technology companies and start-ups love to be disruptors, aiming to knock traditional businesses off their parapets by offering new business models rather than just developing new products. To be a disruptor is cool in the tech world. Amazon and Apple were famous disruptors. Amazon changed the way we buy and sell products and became the dominant retailer, and Apple changed the way we listen to and buy music and how we communicate via smartphone technologies. The NS is hyper-connected, and the success of Apple and Amazon are entangled. The iPhone app platform generates huge income for both Amazon and Apple, making purchasing super easy. It adds value to consumers, producers, and platforms. Yet disruption can also be traumatic and damaging, with many existing/traditional businesses being forced out.

The constant and relentless speed of change in the NS is disruptive in itself. No sooner have we mastered one new technology than the next is upon us. Tesla headlined the electric vehicle (EV) car revolution, and all other manufacturers jumped to transition, investing billions, believing their future was bleak or non-existent if they didn't switch to EVs. Yet EVs are now being questioned, and plug-in hybrids are now the latest car currently dominating the market. Workplace changes have always followed technology innovation, and some call this the fourth industrial revolution. Nearly all work is mediated via computer technology, and many of us spend our lives facing a keyboard and screen. Algorithmic management replaces people managers; we are constantly surveyed by machines measuring our performance and productivity. Those working in the gig economy know this well, but it is also true of professionals in many fields.

Sociopolitical disruptions

It is unlikely that Trump would have become president of the USA without social media and the NS. Algorithms organise and direct our attention towards our 'interests', which become increasingly polarised and radicalised, as the more feisty the content, the more attention it gets. People are funnelled towards punchy and catchy headlines on social media, which get noticed in our 'attention economy'. Trump and other populists used Twitter and other outlets to gain huge traction, offering constant memes of their attention-grabbing content. Mainstream media, TV, and news outlets were disrupted by social media. Many people simply bypass traditional news these days.

Paradoxically, while the NS produces mass communication as never before and new opportunities to connect across the globe, we have become ever more parochial, detached from a cosmopolitan worldview, and have retracted ourselves into our comfortable ponds of likeness. Techno-utopians, who dreamt of the NS democratising and opening up society, have been replaced by a techno-dystopian view of humans who have sleepwalked into being addictively attached to their phones/machines, compromised by algorithms that have turned them into 'quantified selves'. We are measured at work and are encouraged to measure our performance in all aspects of our lives. Our phones measure our fitness, our sleep, our movement, our steps, and our purchases. We give and get stars for our purchasing ability and find ourselves under constant surveillance by ourselves and our peers, mediated through the

NS machinery. There are positive sides to NS disruptions; we can talk to our family when apart through video conferencing, and grandparents can stay connected to distant grandchildren, watching them grow. We can find ourselves in a new city, jump on an electric scooter, follow an online map, and explore with joy.

The environmental crisis is impacted by new technologies. The rapid rise in renewable energy has been a huge success and will be an important factor in addressing the climate emergency. Networks of renewable power, charging our vehicles and heating our homes are exciting developments. On the other hand, networks of mass tourism work in the opposite direction, and the rise of AI and the demands data centres place on the grid are a massive challenge. The way wars are fought changes radically with new technology. NS produces soft warfare, with bots impacting national politics, while drone warfare is being conducted from mobile phones on the front lines of Ukraine.

The printing press was not only a new technology for our convenience; it led to the radicalisation of society by enabling the democratisation of information. Reading became widespread and Bibles available, which meant it was read without elite priests and churches interpreting what the lay people should hear. The poor shall inherit the earth! Across Europe, the printing press lit a fire of rebellion, and common people distributed radical pamphlets that challenged mainstream elite power. Much like the internet revolution does today, conspiracies and wild stories spread alongside important messages from the margins. The printing press played a huge part in triggering the democratisation of Europe, and the new digital revolution has already played its part in the Arab Spring uprising and other social movements, such as Occupy, that have challenged the existing order. This, in turn, has led to repercussive retributions. In authoritarian states, at the first sign of trouble, the first reaction is to switch off the internet.

Personal–relational disruptions

'It is not what computers can do for us, it is what computers do to us'—Sherry Turkle.[118]

What remains under the radar is how the NS impacts our subjectivity, how we feel, how we communicate, and how we form our identities.

The NS disrupts how we parent and creates social divides as well as connections: divides between rich and poor, young and old, and those with and those without access to technology.

I wonder what the long-term impact of constant connectedness to the internet will be on us. Children are tethered to their parents with their mobile technologies, never free to roam without their parents only a click away. Interestingly, quantum computing is about getting beyond the binary limitations of existing computing technologies, while in parallel, gender identities are on a similar disruptive path, with trans and non-binary gender identities coming more into our awareness. These things are entangled.

'The baker makes the bread, and the bread makes the baker'; this saying reflects the reality that technology does not just provide new tools for our use, it also shapes us individually, our bodies as well as our relationships, and it always has. The traditional French baker had a right-sided body much stronger than the left due to the kneading of the dough; their body shape, sleep patterns, and relations with families and the community were shaped by the rhythms and cycles of breadmaking. The bread made the baker. Does the mobile phone make the adolescent?

Today's advances are exceptional because of the speed of change that is occurring and because of the interconnectedness which produces unknown and unpredictable consequences.

Conclusion

The NS is a disruptive society; it disrupts our normative 'ways of being' in the world. Learning to balance ourselves in the midst of being thrown off balance in these turbulent times is becoming a vital life skill. We are being forced to learn and adapt quickly, to navigate through our hyper-change and hyper-choice society, and to resist and manage the seductions and coercive pulls in different directions. We have to walk the high wire each day, sustaining a sense of balance in order to live well.

CHAPTER 20

The making and unmaking of borders

I wrote this in response to two things: first, a disturbing memory that stayed with me of walking through a wealthy area in Johannesburg where every house had huge security gates, a guard, and barbed wire everywhere. These gated communities offered a dystopian vision of the future that haunted me. The second was my daily frustration with passwords, trying to cross the internet borders, and blocking my access to information I needed.

Introduction

'We live in a world of borders. Territorial, political, juridical and economic borders of all kinds quite literally define every aspect of life in the 21st century.'[119]

This short essay explores how borders are increasingly important in today's world. Individual and social anxieties are rising in response to borders being 'made and unmade' at a phenomenal pace in the past few years. The phrase 'crossing borders' unleashes a chain of associations and meanings in society today. When we think of crossing borders, national boundaries, immigrants, and passport controls may immediately come to mind. Walls, fences, security barriers, and checkpoints are all associated with borders, yet many other borders exist that we have to negotiate crossing multiple times each day.

As borders become unstable and fluid, individuals and collective groups can become anxious and threatened. The unmaking of borders and the dismantling and loosening of border regimes remove obstacles and create radical new opportunities for some while creating anxiety and threatening others. The making of new borders and the tightening of border regimes create hardship and marginalisation for some and a feeling of greater security for others.

Borders and movement

A border controls flows of movement.[120] A border can act as a barrier, returning a flow of movement back on itself, or as a filter that allows some things to pass and others not. A border may also be a boundary or an edge. It can be man-made, such as the Berlin Wall, or naturally occur in the environment, like the Himalayan mountains bordering India, Nepal, and China.

Borders are not only material manifestations, they are also found in the virtual world. Some open-source spaces minimise borders and other virtual spaces maximise borders. Borders monitor the movement between physical and virtual spaces, controlling the flow of accessibility to the virtual world via passwords, for example.

Borders also occur within us and between us. Emotions, affects, and thoughts flow and are inhibited by internal borders within us and across our communications and relationships. Borders are an intrapsychic phenomenon; our psychic landscapes consist of conscious and unconscious borderlands. For example, in Freudian structural psychoanalytic terms, our superego negotiates the borderland between the ego seeking the reality principle, and the id seeking instant and instinctual gratification. These borders within us, in reality, are less transactional and often ambiguous and blurred; they are also entangled with our relations to others, never only internal. We are all aware of how cognitive dissonance creates tensions within us and between us when a border divides and splits us, denying an integrated or holistic understanding of a context. Borders operate in interpersonal, relational, and social ways. Individuals and groups open or close access to others, both emotionally and physically, in a variety of ways.

> Borders … determine the extent to which we are included, or excluded, from membership in groups […] the 'us' and the 'here' being located inside the border while the 'other' and the 'there' is everything beyond the border.[121]

Border regimes within us

In my work as a therapist, coach, and organisational consultant, I am constantly crossing the borderlands between the conscious and unconscious worlds. Psychoanalysis teaches us that something important is at stake when the client shows resistance to an interpretation, that is, their defence mechanisms act as a border and try to block access to something within them which makes them uncomfortable. We have intrapsychic borders that keep material repressed and hidden from our conscious minds, yet our bodies experience what our minds cannot think. These psychoanalytic concepts, 'defences and resistance', echo military language; when a force encounters an enemy's border, it too meets defences and resistance. This mirroring of language reveals how closely our internal borders relate to external borders. Our internal worlds impact and shape the external world and vice versa.

Weaponising border regimes

'I saw that beautiful barbed wire going up,' (President Trump, 3 November 2018).[122]

Populist politicians weaponise border talk to amplify existing fears and gain the support of anxious and disillusioned voters. Donald Trump's election rallies in 2016 elicited two main chants: first, 'build the wall', referencing the border wall to keep immigrants out, and second, 'lock her up', referencing putting Hillary Clinton behind the security walls of a prison.

The demand to build walls and lock people up signifies the internal desire for punitive security borders to be inflicted on the 'bad other'. The promise of new border regimes is a very evocative way to symbolise how to make people feel safe and secure, at both physical and at emotional-identity levels. Build a wall and we keep people behind it … problem solved! Yet, as we know, these symbolic solutions are far more problematic and complex in real life. Populist politicians are great advocates of building walls and borders because they create borders in the mind. They create a binary scenario; 'us', the people who belong this side of a border against 'them', the elites and the immigrants who belong the other side of the border.

The Brexit cry of 'take back control' is a classic example of politicians mobilising border talk. Taking back control signifies the remaking of a lost border (between Britain and Europe), claiming to prevent the free flow of people and act as a barrier to block European laws. Take back control also aims to create an emotional border, supporting a stronger identity of being British. Brexit supporters felt strongly that a new border regime would restore Britain, and its opponents felt very sad that this new border regime would be divisive, creating harmful barriers with our European allies and friends.

Emotional borders

We create internal 'security' borders, behind which our repressed anxieties and dormant fears lie. However, like most borders, they are never 100% secure; leaks occur, and our unconscious life seeps into our consciousness, often in displaced ways that causes dysfunction. The conscious and unconscious borders within us, and the relational borders between us, constantly regulate our emotional lives. Our emotions and affects, our drive and psychic energy are regulated by the border regimes within us and those between us.

Internal mindsets produce external realities. Internal anxieties and fears produce nationalist politicians, external walls, scapegoats, repressive laws, and even wars. This also happens in reverse. Our internal worlds are shaped by external realities. When physical borders impose themselves on us each day, for example, the Berlin Wall during communism.

We internalise these walls and border regimes, and they create normative mindsets that limit and shape how we live. We internalise restrictive border walls, creating defensive and fearful mindsets.

In the workplace today there is much talk about psychological safety, and one has to ask, why this and why now? We live in times where everything around us is deemed risky; there is no escape from the health scares; what we eat, and the air we breathe are all a risk. In a landscape of fear, defensive borders will be erected with the hope of creating safe psychological spaces.

Luxurious prisons

When the rich and powerful build border walls to defend themselves against undesirable others, the wall impacts both sides. A wealthy gated community in a city acts as a defence against the poor, but it also encloses the rich in a (luxurious) prison, and both sides internalise the impact of this. A border controls both the flow in and out. While walking in Johannesburg's wealthy districts, I experienced the dystopian future that is becoming increasingly common in other cities. High walls, razor wire, security gates, security guards, and nobody walking or cycling, just people locked in their houses and cars. What mindsets and cultures are internalised when we live with border regimes that are so pervasive, defensive, and aesthetically troubling?

Digital border regimes

The internalisation of border regimes also occurs in our encounters within the virtual and financial world. We find ourselves constantly crossing virtual borders, signing in and using security passwords. Each time we shop, buy something online, or visit a website, we cross a border, each with its own way to control and restrict the flow of movement. This is not like crossing a physical border, like passing through a security gate, because to get into the virtual site we give up our data to the 'machine'. We are then placed under constant surveillance, with algorithms identifying our desires and trying to sell us stuff. We internalise the experience of being constantly monitored by these digital border regimes, checking we are human and not robots, surveillance systems watching every move, algorithmic systems putting us in boxes and categorising us. Other border regimes deny access or expel us from places beyond our reach. These new online border regimes are a dominant feature of our daily existence, and we unconsciously internalise this world of surveillance and borders.

The constant boundary crossing, the warnings of dangerous viruses and cyber-attacks, fears of being shut out and discriminated against, and the frustration at being refused entry create new anxieties, frustrations, and even rage in the digital age.

Yet the paradox is that the internet promised a new egalitarianism that erased elite borders, opening up new possibilities and making connections that were once impossible. Knowledge and information are now freely accessible, which was once only available to elites and required difficult border crossings. Yet corporate giants now create new borders to control access, and worse still, those who cross the borders into their lands (Amazon and Facebook, for example) become surveillance fodder for the corporate machine.

Techno-utopians still dream of radical new democracies powered by open-source technology and new possibilities of the commons, but the dystopian view of a surveillance society with walls and borders everywhere is now dominating.

We live in times where huge new potential exists and vast open spaces appear as so many borders have been dismantled in this digital era, while at the same time more borders exist than we could have possibly imagined in the past.

Shifting borders

We live in an age when borders are being made at unprecedented rates.

Despite the celebration of globalisation and the increasing necessity of global mobility, there are more types of borders today than ever before in history. In the last twenty years, but particularly since 9/11, hundreds of new borders have emerged around the world: miles of new razor-wire fences, tons of new concrete security walls, numerous offshore detention centres, biometric passport databases, and security checkpoints of all kinds in schools, airports, and along various roadways across the world.[123]

Yet borders are also being unmade at an unprecedented rate. This relationship between the making and unmaking of borders is symbiotic, with each force impacting the other. As borders are unmade, new anxieties are unleashed that create a drive to make more borders. As borders are being made, activists strive to open up new spaces and loosen border regimes.

Three examples reveal how contemporary borders are being made and unmade

1. **Trade borders:** Globalisation, neoliberal free trade, mass air travel, and the EU's four freedoms of movement (finance, people, goods, and services) are examples of a radical unmaking of borders in recent times. Neoliberal capitalism offered a vision, at least on the surface, of open trade and free markets, although many claim that elites created hidden borders under this rhetoric of freedom, excluding many from accessing a share of the wealth that was created. There is currently a counter-revolution against these globalising forces to create new borders that protect national trade and the movement of labour, such as Brexit and the rise of populist nationalism elsewhere.
2. **The digital age:** The digital age unmakes borders in ways we couldn't imagine in the last decade, unleashing new possibilities, huge opportunities, and also unforeseen consequences. As discussed earlier, there is also a rapid proliferation of borders in the virtual world. Microsoft is a good example of a company that managed to exploit the virtual world of border making to create vast profits. Through the licensing of its software (Word, Excel, etc.) and creating restrictive borders that prevented open use, it created a vast business empire.
3. **Identity borders:** Another unmaking of borders comes about through a radical changing of identity and emotional borders. Same-sex marriage and transgender rights are examples of the unmaking of border regimes. Non-binary and queer identities gain both legal and cultural recognition, challenging strict binary borders that defined identity norms for decades. The unmaking of these borders is hugely liberating for many and threatens the identity of others. The speed of this change is phenomenal. For example, Ireland, a conservative Catholic country until recent years, recently voted in a gay taoiseach (prime minister) and held a referendum that allowed same-sex marriage. These changing border regimes are part of what some call 'culture wars' taking place in the USA and the West. Some are fighting for more borders, some for less. Those who fight for fewer borders for immigrants

and to open societies' borders for marginalised people to gain rights (such as transgender rights) are seen by others to be imposing new authoritarian border regimes that restrict free speech and thinking. Borders are not straightforward, they are complex and enmeshed in power relations.

Conclusion

Changing border regimes impact us emotionally, physically, legally, virtually, and psychologically. Crossing borders in the recent past was probably less confusing and demanding. Institutions, social norms, and rituals made borders more rigid, and prior to the digital revolution and hyper-globalisation, borders were more stable.

Perhaps there were fewer borders, the commons of the past, for example, before the enclosures created free spaces that are rare today.

Borders today are prolific, and at the same time, they are being questioned. In the past, they were never fixed but were often more stable and less fluid than in today's disruptive world. We live in confusing times where more borders are appearing all the time and where many borders are disappearing or becoming more porous.

In today's world, we have to negotiate and accommodate fast-changing border regimes, which requires us to reflect on how these border regimes impact our intimate lives, as well as our political and social lives.

CHAPTER 21

Presence and absence: Melancholia and confusion in the digital age

Introduction

Today's digital society transforms not only the material world, such as how wars are fought but also how it produces psychosocial changes. Moving quickly between the virtual and real world changes how we relate psychologically and emotionally to ourselves, to each other, and to the social contexts in which we live and work. I offer a psychoanalytic interpretation of how working across the virtual and physical realms creates dissonance, detachment, melancholy, and confusion in the digital age.

The chapter draws on two examples from digital war zones. The first is from US Air Force drone pilots operating in Iraq in 2015 from a home base in the USA, attacking and killing enemies 'virtually' before returning to their family lives after their day's 'killing work'. The other example comes from a Ukrainian drone operator fighting on the front line against the Russian invasion in 2023. I explore how emotions and effects are also a life and death matter. Working between the virtual and real world complicates our emotional and psychological experience of being present and absent. I will discuss the impacts reported by these drone operators and then make links to how moving between the virtual world and the real-time world impacts us all more generally.

Case study 1. The experience of US drone operators

I draw on a *New York Times* article that interviews US military drone operators living with their families in the US, whose work was to kill and maim by operating drones in Iraq.[124] This led to them suffering stress on such an epidemic scale that drone flights had to be cut back. Our psychological and emotional states are not simply a direct reaction to our experience of the material world; our emotional states, and the world we experience are entangled and symbiotic to each other. The material world shapes our affective state and vice versa. In this case example from the USA, drone pilots are heavily impacted by their work, which in turn impacts their families. Drone flights had to be severely reduced due to high stress levels. Perhaps the errors made by the pilots were also linked to their high stress levels, which was ignored in the *NYT* article.

> Drone pilots are worn down by the unique stresses of their work. 'We're at an inflection point right now,' said Col. James Cluff, the commander of the Air Force's 432nd Wing.

Putting aside the question of whether or not USA drone attacks are ethical, rational, or desirable, I want to explore the impact of using computer technologies and operating in the virtual domain and how easily we make wrong assumptions about the psychosocial dynamics that occur. Below, I discuss three assumptions raised by *The New York Times* article, as well as two additional points that were not mentioned but are relevant to the conversation.

Assumption 1: Physical distance from the warzone makes the killing less real and less emotionally stressful for the pilot/drone operator.

Correction: Physical distance doesn't make any significant difference; in fact, it may be worse. In some ways, the drone operator is closer to the killing and gore because, unlike an airborne pilot who sees the damage from a great height and speed while flying over the strike area, the drone operator revisits the site, and the video replays are studied in close up detail to assess the strike. Whereas the drone operator is thousands of miles away, emotionally, they may be a lot closer to the consequences and violence inflicted on others by their actions. This is particularly horrifying when innocent civilians and children or their own men get killed in error.

Assumption 2: 'Virtual' killing mediated through a computer screen is less 'real' and therefore less stressful than when in the war zone.

Correction: The killing appears to be no less real in its impact on the operators.

The article states,

> A Defense Department study in 2013, the first of its kind, found that drone pilots had experienced mental health problems like depression, anxiety and post-traumatic stress disorder at the same rate as pilots of manned aircraft who were deployed to Iraq or Afghanistan.

The assumption that drone operators can emotionally and psychologically distance themselves because it's like a fantasy war game underestimates our human capacity to differentiate between reality and fantasy. Mature drone operators seem as equally vulnerable to stress as 'real' pilots, suggesting that they can clearly differentiate between fantasy virtual games and actual drone strikes that kill people. The repetition of going over the drone strike in close-up, as mentioned before, perhaps amplifies the stress of killing via virtual means. Whether the blurring between virtual and real happens in reverse is yet to be determined, meaning that when a susceptible person plays fantasy war games, they may be more vulnerable to commit a terrorist act if their real and virtual worlds become blurred. However, more research is required, and the diverse contexts of each individual would need to be accounted for.

Assumption 3: Being close to family and community gives the drone operator more support.

Correction: The stress of transitioning on a daily basis between war and Walmart, killing at work, then dropping the kids off at school, seems far too difficult to manage psychologically.

The stress levels for drone pilots are probably increased due to two other factors. First, because while air pilots are deployed to a war zone for a limited time period, the drone operators are 'perpetually deployed', there is no looking forward to an end of deployment. Second, because being deployed with a band of brothers/sisters in a war zone provides certain rituals and camaraderie that help contain and process the stress. Drone operators don't have this 'team support' in the same way.

> Having our folks make that mental shift every day, driving into the gate and thinking, 'All right, I've got my war face on, and I'm going to the fight,' and then driving out of the gate and stopping at Walmart to pick up a carton of milk ... and the fact that you can't talk about most of what you do at home ...

Assumption 4: The impact of killing while being free from danger oneself creates cognitive dissonance.

This point isn't mentioned in this *NYT* article, but I hypothesise that it might also be a factor in the drone operator's stress. Pilots and soldiers in a war zone put their lives at risk and see colleagues at risk. Drone operators unleash violence upon others (and sometimes on innocent others) when their lives are free from danger. Does this make the killing more difficult to rationalise internally? Even if consciously they believe their killing is an act of a 'just war', perhaps unconsciously it is less easy to adjust to killing from afar. Does killing in rational, clinical circumstances, without the danger and risk, without the adrenaline of being in the war zone, without fear, make those doing the killing more psychologically vulnerable to unacknowledged guilt? Does a cognitive dissonance between how the pilots rationalise their work and what they feel lead to excess anxiety, stress, and depression?

Assumption 5: A techno-utopian war without casualties is possible.

The drone operators may also be experiencing the fallout from the techno-utopian idea that a clean, digital war can be fought without casualties (on our side). This represses and disavows the reality that war is always ugly and violent. When something is repressed it always returns, but not in obvious ways. The return of the repressed here may occur in three ways:

1. 'Friendly fire'. The killing of their own soldiers by error brings the reality of war back in haunting ways.
2. Unleashing arbitrary terrorist acts on civilians back home that are almost impossible to defend against means that distancing and sanitising the war ends abruptly.
3. The repression returns in the form of internalised 'violence' against the self. The stress, depression, anxiety, and other forms of mental illness seen in the drone operators show that there are always casualties.

Case study 2. Ukrainian drone operator

The second case study comes from a recent *Guardian* article that tells the story of a Ukrainian drone operator fighting against Russian troops.[125] While the article doesn't go into depth of the challenges, it does offer a different perspective on drone-operated digital warfare. Oleksandr is a drone operator working in danger with comrades on the frontline, and drone operators are particularly targeted by Russians. Oleksandr describes his way of working and 'prefers not to think of the lives that have been taken in the process …'

> 'It's like playing a computer game, you know?' Oleksandr says of his deadly and unenviable task, which, in the pervasive climate of war, has become almost shockingly routine for him. 'It's fun, you know? When it's fun, when you relax, it's easy. When you are tense, it is not possible to work correctly. Anyone can do it.'

What can we learn from this?

1. Oleksandr offers a classic dissociative defence, turning his deadly activity (he is one of the most successful drone operators) into a 'computer game' explicitly linking it to the virtual world that millions of young men and women play to relax.
2. Preferring not to think about the death his drones bring about might also be a useful defence against the fear of his own death. In war, this is perhaps a necessary defence, but maybe it only works when you are in danger yourself, which was in contrast to the US drone pilots.

3. Another difference between his activity and the US pilots is that there is less focus on returning to the pictures that show the death and mayhem caused, which helps the dissociation to take place.
4. The drone attacks are also different. The Ukrainian attacks use smaller hand-built drones and target military vehicles rather than whole houses and villages, as in Iraq/Afghanistan, which led to greater civilian and child loss in the US examples.
5. Can dissociation last? Oleksandr is already in touch with reality a little, perhaps a greater experience of reality comes later?

> 'Oleksandr has footage to prove his deadly work. A video from Friday morning shows Russian soldiers, unaware of the peril from above, firing over the trench at Ukrainian soldiers seeking to storm their position, only for one of Oleksandr's Mavic 3 drones to make its lethal swoop.
>
> 'It is not to brag, however, that he has agreed to meet by a sunflower field in Zaporizhzhia, near to where he was killing and maiming just a few hours earlier. "War is nothing to boast about ..."'

Discussion: Melancholia, presence, and absence

Those who planned the drone operations believed that operators are less psychologically present due to their physical absence, but it seems much more complex than this. In some cases dissociation from 'the real' seems possible at least in the short term, in others not. The real, however, is never repressed for long, and its return often creates pain and dysfunction. Freud observed that when mourning and grieving don't get fully processed this leaves the person in a debilitating state of melancholia. Melancholia might help us understand the psychosocial dynamics that occur when we are constantly working between the real and the virtual. When working in the virtual domain, a loss occurs due to physical separation and to more nuanced factors, such as the engagement being mediated by a small flat screen. While we feel the effect of the physical absences, the loss, we rarely recognise what is actually lost when working between the virtual and physical domains. As Freud says, 'We experience the feeling of a loss but are not sure what has actually been lost,' and therefore we cannot mourn it, leaving us with the experience of melancholia.

Loss can also be enhanced by presence. Because we are not physically present this doesn't make us absent. For example, teenagers in constant contact with parents or friends on mobile devices and social media are virtually more present than before, but they may experience the loss of autonomy, freedom, and the personal space to be themselves. They are forever digitally tethered and surveyed by their parents and friends. The constant presence, in this case, creates a real loss to the individual.

Another example is that when making video calls with my children while working abroad, our live presence on the screen is a joy, but at the same time, it enhances the absence. The loss we feel, because we are physically apart, is amplified because of the virtual screen presence. My children become more present emotionally to me which leads to experiencing a greater loss of not being able to hug them. My absence from the family and home becomes ever more present within me and them. This cyclical reinforcing of emotions that dance between presence and absence, virtual and real, is a condition of our digital times. Often we choose not to connect as it can be emotionally difficult. While digital natives perhaps find this normative, the question remains as to what it does emotionally and psychologically to us and to our relationships.

The US drone operators experience a loss and melancholia that becomes somatised to depression or other mental health conditions. Perhaps Ukrainian drone pilots operating in the war zone process their killing and their own personal losses more fully because they have a tangible context to process this. They share an experience of living in difficult and dangerous conditions, fighting and killing with their units, and collectively mourn the loss of fallen comrades.

The US drone pilots' loss is unrecognised and unnamed; they cannot talk about their work to neighbours or family. The absence of the family is tough when deployed, but perhaps the presence of the family is tougher as it raises such inner conflicts and tensions. Finally, the unconscious guilt or dissonance that occurs when killing the other, when not in danger oneself, perhaps inflicts another hidden loss—a loss of humanity and of self-esteem at an unconscious level that cannot be integrated or spoken of.

We have a lot of work to do to understand the dynamics of our unfolding digital world and the psychosocial meanings and implications it evokes.

The blurring between the real and the virtual worlds is creating new dynamics that are not easy to read. When working on Zoom, I can experience an 'emotional crashing' after delivering a coaching or leadership course. From intense and often emotional group work on the screen, I crash back into family or solitary time, with no transitional space to navigate this. The screen shuts down, and I am left alone in an office with all the feelings swirling around. No transitional post-workshop coffees, debriefs, laughter, and chats. No travel time back home while I consciously and unconsciously process my experience. Assumptions about our emotional and psychological experience of physical distance and virtual engagement need constant reworking in this digital age.

Exploring the meaning of presence and absence is key to our understanding of the fluid boundaries between virtual and real.

CHAPTER 22

Networks of desire and NIPI

Preview

NIPI = networks, identity, power, and influence
Networks of desire = a new framing of organisations

This essay was written after I designed and directed two online Group Relations Conferences (experiential group learning events) with the theme 'Networks of Desire'. Working with organisations reframed from being machines to being networks of desire radically changes our perceptions of how organisations function. I used NIPI as an acronym to help the participants of these events focus on these four core issues, which are central to how networked organisations operate.

Introduction

The way we think about organisations shapes the way we work in them, how we engage with them, and how they shape us. As a leadership scholar, executive coach, and organisational consultant, I work in diverse organisations across the globe. Organisations fascinate me; like trees in a forest, they are both singular and interconnected: they cannot survive unless they interact with each other and the wider ecology. We grow up in organisations, born in hospitals and raised in nurseries and schools, and become adults at universities and colleges. We work in organisations, factories, offices, tech companies, banks, farms, and shops, and we socialise in sports and social clubs and attend religious organisations. We rely on organisations for all of our needs. Organisations are the lifeblood of society.

Currently, there is a dominant shared narrative that aspires to make organisations more agile, horizontal, decentralised, and ethical. The reasons are clear: agile organisations are vital to address the constant disruptions coming from three domains: technology, the environment, and rapid social change. Decentralised organisations mean distributing leadership; this leads to more engaged employees who are more autonomous and feel able to fulfil their potential at work. While the calls for agile, decentralised, and adaptive organisations are strong, on the ground there is resistance to change, and the resilience of hierarchical organisations remains steadfast. The reasons for this stuckness include a fear of change and powerful actors who are happy to retain the status quo. The greatest blocker to change is a knowledge, skills and awareness gap, which limits our capacity to lead organisational ecosystems. Our conditioning, training, and ways of thinking have been shaped to centralise, not decentralise, to think hierarchically and vertically, not horizontally and systemically, to reduce challenges to parts and miss holistic approaches.

Organisations are an important part of all of our lives and our futures. Radical change within organisations is required if we are to make the deep changes required to address climate change and to progress towards more socially just politics and economics. Organisations, in relation to society, are the equivalent of organs in relation to the body. If organisations/organs are dysfunctional or damaged, they have an impact on the holistic system, and the whole body/society becomes troubled.

Organisations need to radically change in order to meet the existential and disruptive social and environmental challenges we face. They have to become more agile and decentred to be able to adapt to challenging disruptions and to grasp opportunities.

Our experience at the Eco-Leadership Institute is that to organise organisations differently, we have to recalibrate how we think about organisations. This chapter is organised around two short provocations which aim to explore different ways of thinking about organisations in order to change them.

Provocation 1. 'Organisations are ecosystems within ecosystems'[126]

The first challenge is reimagining organisations as 'ecosystems within ecosystems'. In our social imaginaries, organisations are seen with the industrial gaze we have inherited from the recent past. Organisations-in-our-minds[127] are like 'machine-architectures'. The built environment of an organisation resembles what an office or workplace 'should look like'. Perhaps rows of desks filled with computers, micro-machines, material objects, and a water cooler. These spaces are filled with people who are structured in our imagination in linear hierarchies, as shown in organisational charts shaped like pyramids.

These mental images become a simulacrum that obscures the reality behind it. Organisations are not like this. They are more like webs of life, networks of activity, and ecosystems of engagement that are fluid and changing. Organisations are hybrid ecosystems that consist of technology, people, and the environment. These ecosystems are interconnected and interdependent and are so entangled it is hard to separate the technology, people, and environment.

The organisational ecosystem is in constant relation to many other ecosystems. Financial ecosystems, stakeholder ecosystems, political-regulatory ecosystems, environmental ecosystems, customer and competitor ecosystems, and also emotional ecosystems. The emotional lives of organisations are best described as networks of desire. In organisational ecosystems and their networks of desire, many things go viral: technology bugs or glitches, rumours and stories, positive and negative energy, and an array of emotions, all go viral.

These ecosystems are vibrant, fluid, overlapping, and both energy-consuming and energy-producing. Organisations thrive when (a) the organisational ecosystems are healthy, dynamic, and nurtured, and (b) when the organisation's relations with the wider ecosystems are dynamic and adaptive.

One of the four core principles of the Eco-Leadership approach is 'organisational belonging'. Organisations belong to local communities and to the global world. They don't live independently; they live interdependently. When an organisation belongs, it experiences the joys and sorrows of being fully engaged, a connected part of the whole.

Provocation 2: Networks, identity, power, and influence (NIPI)

Taking the perspective that 'organisations are ecosystems' opens up a new space for leaders to rethink how to organise and lead change. One useful way to think about this change is to contrast BART and NIPI approaches.

1. Boundaries, authority, role, and task (BART)
2. Networks, identity, power, and influence (NIPI)

These approaches represent two very different ways to think about how organisations work.

Boundaries, authority, role, and task (BART)

The BART acronym is used by organisational consultants and leaders. It was founded at the Tavistock Group Relations Conferences. The BART approach aims to support good organisational functioning through reflecting on and clarifying four key components of organisational life: boundaries, authority, role, and task. Clarifying and respecting boundaries is the beginning, that is, to be clear where something starts and ends, what is inside and outside, and to think about work in relation to the boundaries of time, territory, and task are seen as essential for good functioning. Authority relations relate to roles, tasks, and boundaries; position power is delegated from hierarchies to roles, and expert authority comes in relation to task. How we take up our authority in roles and relate to authority in others is explored in this model. Clarifying our roles in the organisational system, and whether we are working on the primary task, or perhaps off-task, are the final pieces of this model.

BART advocates apply this model to more networked and adaptive ways of working, yet I experience BART as fundamentally holding things back. BART represents a 'machine' organisation-in-the-mind, it is a functional and structural view of organising. Success is based on knowing our place (clear roles), staying within boundaries, deferring to the authority of those in senior roles, and focusing on a primary task. This approach reflects 'modernity's' desire to categorise and control the environment. Yet, in reality, organisations have blurred boundaries, we hold plural roles and multiple tasks and work dynamically with shifting authority relations. In this model, there is little space for the emergence of adaptive and fluid movement. Transcending the fantasy that humans can control their environments and that separation and categorisation create clear boundaries and roles is the first step.

Networks, identity, power, and influence (NIPI)

The NIPI acronym aims to help us think about organisations differently. It emerged from my work of observing and consulting with organisations and recognising them as ecosystems.

Highlighting NIPI's four interrelated themes changes our way of thinking about organisational ecosystems. We learnt from using NIPI approaches when we applied the acronym to guide our work in three group relations conferences and in multiple organisational consulting projects. NIPI changes our gaze and opens new opportunities and understandings when working to deliver organisational change. We will briefly work through the model.

Networks

> If you do not care about networks, the networks will care about you, anyway. For as long as you want to live in society, at this time and in this place, you will have to deal with the network society.[128]

Focusing on networks helps us work in contemporary organisations where boundaries and roles are more fluid, porous, and plural (see Chapter 19). Placing our attention on networks, new dimensions and new possibilities emerge. Networks are the connective tissue in organisational ecosystems, and they come in different forms. Digital networks, power networks, emotional networks, communication networks, social networks, conscious and unconscious networks, and seen and unseen networks. Networks imply connectivity, and in networks, nodal points appear that connect different organisational parts. Identifying important nodes and clusters in a network brings new insights into where change may emerge or where resistance to change lies. Hidden nodes of informal power and clusters of innovation can be found and co-created so they can be amplified and connected to other nodes and clusters in the network. This is how change happens in social movements and is mirrored in networked organisations. In network theory, they speak of 'edges' that connect nodes, and 'leaders working at the edges' are important in this new model. Sustainable change is more likely when mobilised through network connectivity, as many more actors are involved than when change is driven via top-down control.

The internet is the best-known network that is used and misused in organisations.

> The internet is a communication medium that allows for the first time, the communication of many to many, in chosen time, on a global scale.[129]

The term 'networks' has many meanings; in this context, it should not be reduced to either digital communications or networking to mean people meeting together with a view to gain influence. Networks are more profound and more permeating in organisations. An analogy is the 'wood wide web', a term first used in 1997 by the editors of the journal *Nature* to describe Suzanne Simards research into the underground network of mycorrhizal, fungi–tree networks. This symbiotic relationship allows for nutrient exchange, communication, and even sharing of resources among different species. Through this network, trees can warn each other about pests, share water, and support weaker plants, essentially creating a communal support system in forests. Similarly, informal networks in organisations communicate beneath the surface, allowing exchanges of ideas, practices, and resources that support organisational functioning and lead or resist change. Networks keep organisations alive, and they also transcend them. Networks don't stop at an arbitrary organisational boundary. Networks imply connectivity and interdependency. Networks make connections between other organisations, stakeholders, customers/service users, wider society, and the natural environment and are a key part of understanding that organisations are ecosystems within ecosystems.

Unless our gaze turns towards networks, we will misunderstand how organisations organise.

Identity

Identity has become increasingly important in contemporary society. Identity shapes our perceptions, interactions, and choices. Individual identity encompasses culture, ethnicity, gender, work, body, beliefs, and personal experiences. Identity is harnessed in the culture wars that have become a key battleground for politicians and social movement activists. In contemporary society, our identities, individual and collective, have become more fluid and unstable. This creates opportunities so that non-binary and transgendered people can be more open and visible. It also creates anxieties that lead to defensive behaviours, hence the turn to nationalistic politics in many countries. Our identities are not left at the door when we enter workplaces and organisations.

Identity also transcends individuals. Groups and organisations form identities. Brand identities are becoming increasingly important to organisations, and employees often take pride in their work/professional identity. Identity has become a core part of our subjective, social, political, and economic experience.

A strongly shared organisational identity enables a narrative that can bind the organisation together. Within any organisation multiple identities are competing and collaborating. A strong organisational culture thrives when diverse identities are dynamic, and difference is valued. Individuals and teams partly form their own identities, which are always fluid and changing. Identities are also formed by the gaze of the other, in that we are shaped by how others see us. Teams and organisations need to pay attention to how they are seen by others. Leaders and change agents need to pay attention to identity in the workplace because identity is central to how organisations function and how individuals and teams within the ecosystems feel and function.

Power

NIPI moves away from the authority highlighted in BART and turns to power because in social ecosystems and organisations, power is everywhere, and power underpins organisational functioning. Position power held by CEOs and leadership teams is easily recognised, and often, their importance is overplayed. Less recognised are the soft and informal power networks that often get missed. How often in organisations does an agreed strategy or change get undermined or resisted despite those in positions of power demanding it? In the digital age, horizontal networks of power can undermine vertical authority with a speed that has never been seen before. This does not mean that power is equalised or shared, but that we have to understand how power and authority operate differently between the vertical and horizontal. Power is everywhere,[130] not just at the top or centre. Power is not bad or good, power is simply part of any relational dynamic, and the question is how it can best be harnessed for the common good.

Ricoeur identifies three forms of power:[131]

1. Power from above: a leader's position empowers them, in that they are sanctioned and given resources.
2. Power from within: a leader or team enacts their leadership by drawing on their identity and characteristics, their expertise, social background, personality, skills, and experience.
3. Power from below: the power of grass-roots employees is immense. Sometimes, this power is transferred to a leader because they are admired and trusted, or because followers think it is in their best interests, or sometimes because they fear leaders. This power is undermined when followers are socially conditioned to be compliant, believing they have a certain place in a hierarchy.

Reflections on power

- Power is not only negative; it doesn't just say no.
- Power doesn't always come from the top down.
- Power isn't always where you think it is.
- Power is productive; it creates knowledge.
- Wherever you find power, you find powerful resistance.
- Power is enacted in discourses, language, and knowledge.
- We influence and control others and are controlled through subtle power we hardly notice.
- Power works at conscious and unconscious levels.
- Within networks and ecosystems, nodal points of power exist.
- Harnessing this nodal power is liberating, as small changes lead to big changes.
- Vertical power is symbiotic with lateral power in organisational ecosystems.

Eco-leaders in organisational ecosystems take the view that the power of grass-roots employees and wider stakeholders should be nurtured, embraced, and encouraged. The aim is to influence the ecosystem so that the diverse power from above, within, and below can be utilised to maximise the benefits of the many and work towards creating the good organisation and the good society.

Influence

Using NIPI to frame organisational dynamics helps us to discover where and how to influence change in organisational ecosystems. This approach draws on Eco-Leadership, which turns charismatic, individualistic, and top-down leadership on its head. Ecosystems cannot be controlled, and yet the influence of messiah, therapist, and controller leadership approaches cannot be ignored. Some espouse an evolution of leadership and organisations, creating a hierarchy that ends with leaderless, self-organising, and horizontal organisations. In my research on social movements, I show how leaderless organisations are a fantasy and that leadership exists under cover or under different names.[132] Others say that nature is our teacher, writing as if nature sits outside us. We can learn from ecology and the environment, but human nature, social structures, and organisational ecosystems are clearly not the same as a rainforest. They include power dynamics and technologies that scaffold our worlds and require accounting for.

To influence organisational ecosystems is not to deny power structures, resource accumulation, and position power, but to see them in relation to the whole ecosystem. Top-down influence creates controller regimes and dependency cultures which limit the capacity for self-organising, and for realising the potential of the whole. Eco-Leadership aims to influence ecosystems through distributing and decentring leadership by finding nodes of power and connecting them with other nodes and clusters, which leads to interdependency collaborative cultures. Influencing ecosystems is as much about paying attention and noticing as it is about being active and doing. Noticing where nodal power exists, paying attention to connectivity, and observing how emotions go viral. It is these qualities that reveal what and where action needs to be taken in order to influence an organisational ecosystem. Influencing isn't reduced to an individual leader acting; the idea is that influencing is a collective process that requires attention and nurturing.

Conclusion

The title I gave to the experiential group relations conferences I directed using NIPI was Networks of Desire. I used this title as a prompt to invite participants to connect the idea of networks and desire together. We face huge disruptions from technology and potentially devastating environmental and social catastrophes due to climate change and biodiversity loss. Organisations are society's change-makers, they are the lifeblood that can deliver healthy societies and reparations to the environment. Yet, to mobilise organisations, we need to think about them differently. 'Organisations are ecosystems within ecosystems', and they have to become 'networks of desire' in our minds if we are to transcend our current stuckness and disenchantment.

Organisations can only thrive if they are filled with human desire and if we recognise their connectivity through networks that make them interdependent with society and nature. Using NIPI as a lens in these experiential conferences, we explored how power circulated and how networks, nodes, and clusters formed. We reflected in small and large groups on questions of identity, how different individuals and groups identified themselves, and how they identified with others. We explored how, what, and who influenced the learning organisation ecosystem we had co-created.

Desire is a peculiarly human thing. It drives our behaviours and is charged with libido and emotions, and desire relies on relational connectedness. We never desire in isolation. The purpose of this essay is to reveal the potential of co-creating networks of desire so that our organisations and our wider ecosystems can thrive.

Postscript: Since writing this two 'Networks of Desire' Group Relations Conferences utilising the NIPI framework have taken place in person in Beijing, China, with fascinating results and very positive feedback.

CHAPTER 23

The monastery: Moments of grace

Photograph taken by author: Leaving Holy Cross Abbey, Rostrevor, Northern Ireland

The Christmas story begins with a journey; it could have started with the birth of Jesus, but there is something very important about the journey we take before an event. A journey helps set out the context and creates a narrative filled with the important people, places, and happenings that enrich and enliven the described event. This short essay was written about a journey I took shortly before Christmas 2023.

Introduction

My journey to the monastery began when I cancelled a work trip to China for health reasons. I realised I was not only sick but exhausted and in need of spiritual sustenance. Also, Christmas is a time when absences make themselves acutely felt. The trip to the monastery was my pre-Christmas time for reconnecting with God, with myself, and with those family members who have passed away that I miss so much, especially my beautiful son Fynn, who was killed in a knife crime ten years before. If I don't spend time to grieve, connect with souls, renew my spirit, love, and pray, then I get caught out at Christmas and am overwhelmed by my grief and emotions of sadness.

I began writing this on a train travelling from my home in Galway to Northern Ireland, where I would stay for three nights in a Benedictine monastery nestled in the lovely Mourne mountains. When I visit a monastery or another place that holds spiritual meaning, I like to make a 'proper journey' to get there. A proper journey for me means spending time cycling or walking, getting there with my own physical effort. This turns the journey into a pilgrimage. I like my travels to include walking, cycling, and a train or boat journey because these allow me to contemplate, process, and to feel the world passing by.

During this journey and when at the monastery, I experienced many special moments of grace, and here I will share nine of them.

Grace

Grace means two things to me:

1. An unexpected gift from God/Spirit.
2. An awakening of transcendent love.

Grace is most often experienced when we make ourselves open and receptive to the spirit. Sometimes, grace reveals itself unexpectedly;

a moment of grace can open us up and move us deeply, enabling us to receive and commune with the gift of transcendent love.

For those who don't share a spiritual faith, which was my position when younger, it is still possible to experience grace. Recognising and feeling special moments of transcendence, perhaps when immersed in sublime nature, or when witnessing something beautiful or remarkable, or touched by a deeply humane act of kindness or love. When I look back on my life, I experienced many moments of grace, the impact of which I didn't fully appreciate at the time.

Nine moments of grace

Grace 1. Café joy

The first moment of grace I experienced happened between train journeys. I travelled from my home in Galway to Dublin by train, cycled across Dublin, and found a small New York-style deli next to Connelly station, where I would leave on another train to Northern Ireland. I was hungry and ready for breakfast and ordered a fried egg sandwich. Well, this caused a bit of a stir, as the owner said to me in a bemused voice, 'Just one egg in a sandwich?' When I said yes, he looked offended, and he said, 'Can I push you to have two eggs?' I said fine. Laughter came from regular customers at another table. He then continued, 'Can I put anything else in the sandwich? Relish, cheese, lettuce?' I smiled and agreed to all. The café owner asked, 'Strong or mild cheese?' I replied strong, and sat down. The owner, after much banter with other customers, served me a breakfast baguette to remember, one that had shifted from being an egg sandwich to a delicious breakfast served with pride and love.

The grace I experienced, however, was not the fine baguette but the joy of the café, the bonhomie, the camaraderie, and being invited to become part of an engaged community. My journey had begun.

Grace 2. I was a stranger, and you welcomed me (Mathew 5.44)

The train from Dublin to Newry, travelling from Eire to Northern Ireland, follows the coast with lovely estuaries, alive with many seabirds. I unloaded my yellow bike at Newry station and had a fifteen-mile cycle to the monastery, passing over misty hills and through drizzling rain before arriving at Rostrevor, the last small town before the climb upwards to the monastery set high in the valley. Strangers welcomed me with warm hellos, spoken in their rich Northern Irish accents as I cycled past. A cyclist stopped and asked if I was alright as I struggled upward on my single-gear bike. He looked at my bike laughing and said, 'You need to get some gears for these hills!' and a woman waved from across the road when I parked my bike to pick up refreshments. A warmth passed through me as I journeyed towards the monastery. The grace I experienced was being a stranger who was made to feel welcome.

Grace 3. The laughing monk

Arriving at the monastery, I felt exhausted, having cycled uphill while still on antibiotics for a chest infection and with my bag on my back. I reflected that perhaps this was the penance part of my journey. I arrived at the small monastery shop/reception, and a monk and the receptionist were there, both smiling a warm welcome. The receptionist forgot the telephone number of the guest master, the monk whose role it was to receive visitors. The monk, in his white habit, reminded her of the number. She chuckled at her forgetfulness, and he responded with a hearty laugh. A moment of grace filled my spirit with love, and as I was welcomed with peace and joy, I felt at home already.

Grace 4. 'Truly sons are a gift from the Lord' (Psalm 127)

Grace is described in Christian terms as the unmerited love of God bestowed on us. I felt this when I attended my first prayer service at the monastery. The monks sing the psalms in plainsong, a beautiful chanting of singing and responding, and the first psalm they sang was 127. I had just been praying for my son Fynn before the service began, and these words from the psalm struck my heart:

> Truly sons are a gift from the lord
> Blessing from the fruits of the womb

This felt like my prayers were being received, a recognition, a communication from the spirit, from God, that my prayers for Fynn were heard.

Grace 5. Silent listening

In the monastery there is silence. My room is silent. I wait in the church in silence. At meal times as a guest, I was invited to eat in the monk's private enclosure. I was walked to the monastic refectory led by the guest master. I sat with another guest at a table with the monks opposite and the abbot at the top table. We wait in silence; there is a prayer of grace, and we are served food by one of the monks. A book is read to us while we eat in silence. No polite exchanges, no 'How are you?', no 'Pass the salt', just silence until we finish with a prayer and walk back to our rooms. The monastic prayer cycle begins at 6.45 am and ends at 8 pm. Prayers are said six times a day, psalms are sung, and the rest of the time at the monastery is spent in silence. The phone is off, and there is no radio in the rooms, just silence. Walking the grounds of the monastery, aside from the birdsong and other sounds of nature, silence.

The grace I experienced was that when in silence, I was able to listen; listen to my body speak, listen to my heartbeat, listen to the holy spirit, listen to God.

Grace 6. Simplicity

In the monastery, everything is paired down to simplicity. My call to book the retreat was done with the utmost simplicity, no chit-chat, no excess formalities, just a few seconds to arrange dates, arrival and leaving time. When I arrived at the monastery, the guest master monk who showed me to my room and informed me of the routine did it with utmost simplicity. At mealtimes, a monk serves the food, meals are simple, and tables are cleared. Simplicity is counter-intuitive in our busy, excessive world.

The grace I experienced was to discover again how simplicity opens a space for spirituality to awaken and come alive within me. Simplicity reminds me of the clutter I become attached to in the material world, the busyness that blocks my spiritual journey. Simplicity is an act of making a space for God, for the spirit within us to live.

Grace 7. Radical equality

At the end of my first day at the monastery, I became aware of a new freedom, the freedom from holding an identity. In our everyday lives, we have roles in our families and workplaces; we are fathers, brothers, mothers, and sisters. I am Dr Simon Western, an author, a person with a professional reputation, someone who receives projections and expectations from others ... but not in the monastery.

In the monastery, I don't speak to anyone. I don't share any information, I don't get asked anything, I am just me. I was struck by how this release from an identity enabled my shoulders to drop and my body to relax. To not have to live up to any ideas or ideals people may have about me or that I have about myself was a huge relief. I guess if you're very attached to your identity, this could also be a challenge, a threat to the self. I was not required to perform any identity. It was just me before the monks and one other guest. There were no questions, no expectations, no weight. The grace I experienced was that I could be free from the burdens and baggage that I carry each day (without realising I was carrying them) and, most importantly, to be reminded that we are all radically equal before God.

Grace 8. The stars and the natural world

I awoke before the alarm at 5.50 am, said a prayer, washed and dressed, then went outside into the dark morning, and wow! The stars shone so brightly against the dark morning sky. The plough was the clearest I had seen it in years, its tail pointing towards the north star. I didn't expect to see stars in the morning as I walked outside; my associations were that stars come out at night, and the surprise added to the beauty and joy. There were no unnatural lights as we were far from the city, and the stars shone without human interference. Seeing the wonder of the galaxy makes our world seem smaller and more fragile. I was reminded of the Earthrise picture taken from space, showing the immense beauty and the vulnerability of planet Earth. The next day, I walked through the rich greens and browns of the forest, climbing the Mourne Mountains with a friend for the afternoon. As we emerged from the forest, white clouds hugged the mountain, and mist rose from the trees as the bright sunlight warmed the day.

The grace experienced through being in and being part of nature came into my life as yet another form of prayer, another way of listening to the work of the spirit.

Grace 9. Luke 2.9 'and the brightness of God shone round about them'

My train home was cancelled due to a rail strike on Friday, which meant I had to leave the monastery on Thursday afternoon. This was both a shame and a gift. My children's school carol service was on Friday morning, and this change meant I could attend. I had been wondering about travelling home early as my children really wanted me to be there, so now I was given a gift … 'Go Simon!'

When my two children were very young, I shared with them how the sunbeams that shone down through the clouds were my son Fynn saying hello to us all from the heavens. They internalised this and would say to me, 'Look, Dad, Fynn is saying hi!' when they saw beams shining in the sky.

I packed my bag, climbed on my bike and left the monastery after lunch on a greyish afternoon. I turned onto the road from the driveway and I was literally blinded by a white light. The sun was a huge, pure white ball that lit up the grey-green valley. I don't think I have ever witnessed anything quite like it. The light was so bright that I had to shield my eyes. Fynn and God were with me …. That was truly a moment of grace.

CHAPTER 24

Seasonal awakening

Original artwork, hand-drawn by Martyna Adamska

This essay was inspired by the crop of runner beans I harvested from my garden and the process of turning these into green bean chutney. This seasonal event has been passed down to me from my parents and evokes deep emotions.

Introduction

Yesterday, I was reminded of the power that seasons have upon me and how the change in seasons has a bodily and emotional impact, stirring conscious and unconscious memories and feelings.

In pre-modern times, and in many parts of the world today, the seasons are not something to be noticed, they are life itself. Life is organised with and by the seasons. The rainfall, sunshine, heat and cold, the time for planting and harvesting, seasonal fishing and hunting and gathering are essences of how we live on this planet. The sensitive interdependencies and collaborations between humans and our non-human companions and our collective relationships with the seasons have shaped our worlds for millennia. Yet, since industrialisation and rapid urbanisation in the past century, these deep connections to life itself have been marginalised. The ever-present, relentless clock replaced seasonal rhythms, and work was organised without reference to light and darkness or warmth and cold. We became detached and alienated from nature's seasonal rhythms. Collectively, across the industrialised world, we have forgotten who we are in relation to the seasonal planet.

Environmental seasons are marked by weather changes, lunar cycles, tidal changes, and the length of days. Humans aligned with the seasons and created cultural seasonal markers. Festivals, rituals, gatherings, and celebrations mark environmental seasonal changes. These cultural seasonal markers reflect the human relationship to the environment and recognise a human need for patterns and rituals for locating ourselves in the mysteries of the planet. In a recent episode of my Edgy Ideas podcast, my guest, Liz Rivers, discussed the importance of nature in her life and her belief that workplace organisations should pay more attention to seasonal patterns. She drew on the Celtic calendar as a way of connecting our workplaces with the rhythms and cycles of the natural world. The Celtic calendar marks times in the year when the light changes. It follows the autumn, winter, spring, and summer, marking the shortest and longest days, which in turn mark the beginning and end of seasons.

Each religion has its own cultural seasonal markers (often laid over nature's seasons). The Christian calendar is filled with seasonal markers, Easter and Christmas being the main ones, but if you follow the rhythms of Christian life as closely as the monastics do, each day becomes part of a season, which becomes part of a yearly cycle, which becomes a life. Thomas Merton, the Cistercian Monk, writes about this:

> The harmonious structure of regular observances ... the monk lived by the sun and the moon and the seasons but all nature was elevated and made sacred by liturgy which gathered up all the monk's acts and all his experience, ordering and offering everything to God.[133]

He describes the monk working in the fields, making bread, tending the animals, alongside reading scripture and taking part in the liturgy and communal prayers five times each day.

> In this way not only did the monk live in the midst of nature, and the joys and beauties of the woods and mountains, but his whole life was steeped, besides, in perfect poetry and music, his life was filled with fascinating stories and images, symbols and pictures.

This description beautifully captures a world filled with meaning, a world following the seasons of nature entangled with the seasons of culture.

Secularisation has robbed us of these cultural seasonal rhythms, as industrialisation has robbed us of these environmental seasonal rhythms.

Without the anchor points of collective and communal rhythms and patterns, we become detached and separated from reality itself. We then make up our own realities, telling ourselves that we can exploit natural resources without consequence. No surprise then when an environmental crisis takes place or when post-modernism announces a post-truth world and the end of the grand narrative. What logically follows are climate disasters, conspiracy theories, widespread mental health problems, and fake news, as there are not enough reality markers to anchor us to the greater truths that transcend individual will (sorry, Nietzsche, you were wrong).

Personalising the seasons

This week is the end of the summer holidays for my children, and school starts on Friday. In my garden, the children and I harvested our crop of runner beans. For me, this is a traditional family marker of a seasonal change; the green beans are harvested, and the chutney is made.

As I walked to the shop with my dog, Peach, to buy the vinegar, onions, and sugar for the chutney, I looked across the misty, rainy Galway Bay and saw a cruise ship leaving port, perhaps the last one this summer. The cool rain and the ship sailing away seemed symbolic to me, marking the end of the summer, with autumn/fall arriving early this year. That evening, I returned to a family pattern. I listened to the BBC Proms classical concert on the radio and set about making the chutney, as my mother did every year using the beans my father grew.

The process of harvesting, cleaning, and carefully cutting the beans is a meditative process, and the spirit of my mother (who has passed away) comes to me. The smells of the boiling chutney, spicy and vinegary, sharp and sweet, return me back to my childhood home. Melancholy, love, and beauty fill the kitchen as Peach, our dog, sleeps in peace.

The old jam jars have been cleaned, then sterilised in the oven and filled with the rich, hot, spicy chutney … autumn, we welcome you! The final jar of last year's chutney has just finished, as winter heads our way; the new chutney will be ready for the feasts of Samhain, celebrated these days as Halloween.

This process of planting, growing, preparing, and cooking seasonal food gives me a link to my ancestors who passed away. The physical and emotional experience brings me closer to family and brings a deep communion with nature. I am glad the rhythms of the season are part of my life. I am thankful my family passed cultural rituals to me, and I hope the transmission of these traditions will pass on to my children.

CHAPTER 25

Everyday spirituality

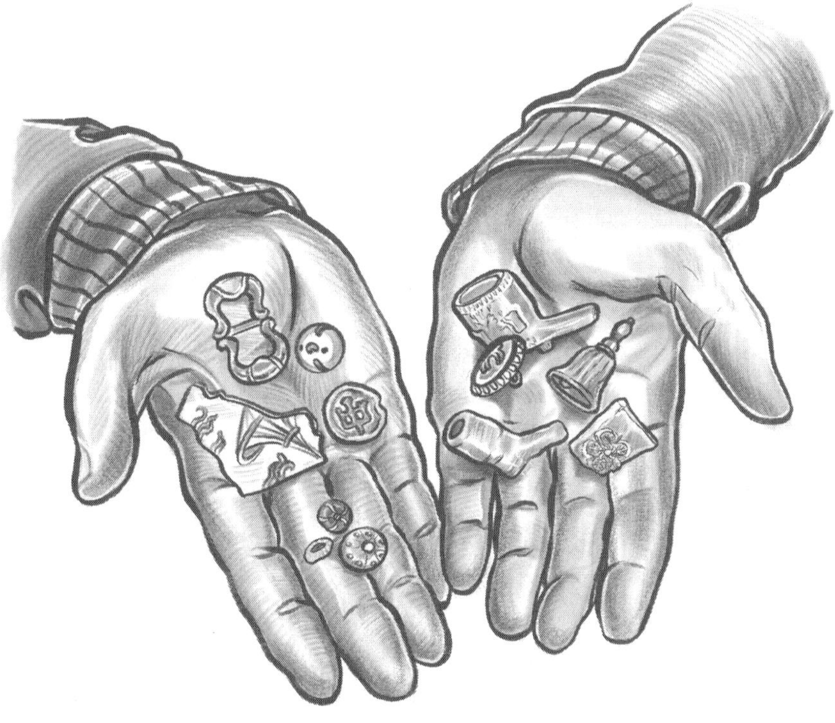

Original artwork, hand-drawn by Martyna Adamska

This essay follows a work trip to London, where I experienced the power of everyday spirituality, and reveals a deep beauty that infuses my life. I mark three composting moments in this chapter.

Composting

Composting is a learning activity I am developing, which we use on our training courses. It takes reflection to a different level, beyond the limits of our cognitive process. Composting is to allow your body to metabolise thoughts and process bodily experiences. Composting converts what is initially considered waste into rich nutrients, which become food for ideas, thoughts, and actions. Composting only works if diverse elements are involved: micro-elements go to work unseen by us, the unconscious and the body speak when given the conditions of space, time, and physical engagement with the elements around us. Our bodies and thoughts work alongside others; thoughts arise from connections with ourselves and with others: people, animals, and nature. To compost it is vital to move the body, to walk, eat, rest, and to be close to nature; even a plant in the office makes a difference. Composting produces the rich nutrients that enable ideas and souls to grow. It enables so much knowledge, that is usually wasted in our rush to get things done, to be turned into rich food for thought. Composting has magical qualities as any gardener will tell you.

Introduction

On Sunday, I travelled to London for work and arrived hungry and late. On arrival at Whitechapel Tube station in London, the graffiti was the first thing to grab my attention. There was pro-Palestine political graffiti as well as other graffiti that just made me laugh, particularly the pithy 'Nietzsche is Dead'. I found a café near my old home in London's East End, where I sat with Bangladeshi/English men and women and ordered my favourite fish curry and hot chai to drink.

Travelling to London is powerful for me, often beautiful, and always a painful experience. It was while living in Whitechapel that I heard of the violent death of my son Fynn, and I spent over a year in deep trauma, grieving, wandering the streets of East London. The shock of that time stays with me today. Whenever I visit London, I am drawn back to the East End, to where I used to live, where I cried, and where

I am embraced by my melancholy, which is reignited in the familiar cafés, streets, markets, and parks of Whitechapel, London Fields, Brick Lane, and Dalston. Alongside the grief is the pleasure of being in multicultural, vibrant, cosmopolitan London … Why are people so afraid of diversity, it's such a joy!

On Monday morning, I went for a run before breakfast, passing my old flat, a red brick factory conversion that I loved, and then headed for the water. There is something about the river Thames that always draws me. After Fynn's death, I had grieving routes that often took me to the river, stopping to light candles in churches on the way. The river offers movement, and it is one of the few places in London where you can see big skies and light. I would wander the banks of the Thames to collect fragments of pottery and coloured glass polished by the river, some of it very old. Collecting fragments from people's past lives spoke to my condition at that time; I never made sense of why, but why didn't matter … it was just something I was drawn to do and which I found strangely comforting. I have kept all the pottery/glass I collected, and perhaps one day, the fragments will become a beautiful mosaic.

On Monday morning, I met an old friend/colleague, and we caught up on work and life and planned new possibilities. I went to the office of a large humanitarian organisation I work with to meet with a senior leader. We had a buzzing and creative conversation about the radical changes needed in the humanitarian sector and how these might be manifested. These two warm and creative meetings raised my morale, which is much needed when I encounter so much disenchantment in workplaces these days.

Next, I had a third meeting with a very good friend/colleague who works for a technology company in Silicon Valley. We talked mainly about faith, social challenges, and the need for a paradigm change. We have worked together in many companies and contexts and always return to the big picture; society needs awakening, and it needs a spirit-based approach!

I entered the large East London Mosque on the way back to my hotel, seeking peace from the busy streets. I sat on the carpet, read a bit of the Koran, and enjoyed being with Muslims undergoing their prayer rituals. Islam gets a bad rap these days in many quarters, yet when you enter a mosque (as a man), there is a calm, peaceful world inside. It reminded me how important spaces and architecture are. Churches are filled with benches and tell a story of hierarchy, with everything facing the raised front of the church, the place of the priest who has greater access to God than the lay people sat below.

The mosque is more egalitarian, with no chairs, just carpet, and the only point of reference is Qibla, the direction of prayer to Mecca. The non-democratic piece is the gender-specific maleness of the mosque. Sometimes, gender division creates spaces where brotherhood and sisterhood can be experienced differently from in mixed spaces, which feminist sisters recognise. The problem in this mosque, and in much of Islam, is the space for women is restricted, and the power imbalance between men and women undermines its egalitarian ethos.

The following day, I went to St Martin-in-the-Fields church in Trafalgar Square to meet Rev Richard Carter, who offered me spiritual support when Fynn died. On two occasions, St Martin's invited me to talk about Fynn to an annual gathering of families who have suffered the bereavement of children killed through violence. Richard has become a good friend, and it was lovely to attend morning prayers in the church and go for a coffee. We recorded an Edgy Ideas podcast[134] together recently, sharing stories of grief, love, and grace. Richard knows grief close up, and we have a brotherly bond.

Composting 1

Grieving for a lost loved one, particularly the loss of your child, is a continual journey. I return to places to be with Fynn, to feel and experience him in my body and soul. It makes me very sad, but in the sadness, I find some love and solace. I believe this processing and grieving sustains my parallel life, one that is filled with the love of my family in Galway. Holding these powerful feelings together, the past and present, grief and joy, love and sadness, and dealing with the demands of work and a busy life are not easy.

Another composting reflection is how select workplace relationships become deep friendships. Also, how real places and emotional spaces can bring our souls to life. This return to place took me on the next leg of my journey.

Mount St Barnard monastery

Leaving London, I travelled to Birmingham by train to be picked up by Doug, a Church of England priest I met when I taught leadership at a theological college. We drove to Mount St Barnard Cistercian (Trappist) monastery, where I would spend the night before going to Leicester to offer a workshop for thirty-six Church of England priests on a leadership training programme.

The setting of the monastery is beautiful. I was there thirteen years ago, a few months after Fynn died. The monks begin their day at 3:30 am for prayers, and I recall sitting with them in the middle of the night, finding deep peace and weeping while the world slept. Knowing that the monks prayed for our souls as we sleep, and have been doing so for centuries, brings a transcendent peace to me. Doug and I walked and had a rich conversation about our different work, about the changing role of faith and the Church in society.

My time at the monastery was a little troubled, my emotions were stirred, memories of my last visit rose in my body, and I struggled as I had a number of work commitments that needed dealing with. I had a sleepless night and wondered if I had tried to pack too much into my schedule (something I have been working on in my psychoanalysis). Coming to the monastery requires letting go, and I hadn't given myself time to let go, for the next day, I travelled to Leicester. I accepted that my monastic visit was to be less than perfect. I prayed with the monks and fellow pilgrims. I was grateful for the beauty, the peace, and the chanting of the psalms, and I ordered my taxi early to step into a different space and prepare for my leadership workshop.

Composting 2

The monastery is a place I have found which resonates with my soul. Benedictine monasteries, with their prayer rhythms, contemplative silence, and love of work, have profoundly influenced me. The monks put a high value on manual labour; they regard work as prayer and prayer as their work. This simple insight from St Benedict was profound for me and enabled me to enjoy mundane, manual work more. I had sometimes thought I was wasting time and not prioritising the important things when gardening, tidying my office, or making bread. Surely, I had more important things to do, like writing my PhD or my latest book. The idea that work was prayer was transformational for me. Now, I try to see all my work as prayer; when stressed, I try unsuccessfully, but then I pray and try again.

Church of England leadership training

I arrived in Leicester to lead a training session for a Church of England leadership programme. Leicester is a place of ethnic diversity and a vibrant city, which always gives me a friendly welcome. I ate South Indian vegetarian dosa for lunch and felt blessed. I walked in the sun and then caught up with work meetings online and prepped for the following day.

The following morning, I arrived at the venue feeling a little anxious. Sitting in front of thirty-six priests can feel quite intimidating, and I shared this experience at the beginning of my workshop. I find that if I share my anxieties rather than try to cover them up, it has three effects. First, by naming the anxiety, it magically tends to diminish or disappear entirely, and second, I bond more easily with the group I am teaching. I think this is because sharing a vulnerability immediately creates a human connection and makes a statement that I am not pretending to be some expert hiding behind a role, I am just another person with strengths and vulnerabilities. The third impact is that by presenting my immediate experience when facing the group, it opened up a wider dialogue and reflection where priests shared how their roles, their white collars, are often intimidating to others and how they feel and respond to this. In the room, Evangelicals, liberals, and conservative-traditionalist priests were working in many different church roles. They held diverse interpretations of Christianity and the role of the Church. The leadership session I ran was very engaging, and we explored many psycho-social aspects of their leadership roles. I left tired and felt that my time in the UK had been enriching in many ways.

Composting 3

How often do we lump together groups and categorise them in a way that suits us? Christians are like this … They believe this … The Church of England is … Muslims are … French people are …. This trip reawakened me to the plurality and diversity we experience if open to it. From ethnic diversity in cosmopolitan cities to the diversity of Christian beliefs, even within a 'homogenous' group of Church of England priests.

Another theme of this trip was my engagement with different parts of the Muslim community. Before I left for this work trip, I watched an Ireland vs Pakistan cricket match with my family and enjoyed being with the boisterous Pakistani cricket supporters. Then, staying in Whitechapel and spending time with the Bangladeshi men and women in cafés, sharing their food and spending time in their place of worship, and then later in Leicester, which has a very large Muslim community. I feel very at home in these places. I am not sure if it is the difference itself I feel very at home with, or multiculturalism, or if this feeling is specific to certain cultures. I have always felt very 'at home' in the Middle East, having spent time in Eastern Turkey, Syria, Israel, and Palestine. Perhaps it's the café culture and lack of alcohol, Islamic architecture, the integration of prayer into daily life, the call to prayer, along with the vibrant markets and great food (I am a big fan of flatbreads). If I believed in past lives, I would assume one of my past lives was spent in a community like this. Reflecting on this, I also loved being in India and Nepal, and I enjoy Hindu culture as well. I pray and visit the Krishna temples in Dublin and Soho often.

Everyday spirituality

One final reflection is that a living spirituality that is part of daily life, and not just something coupled with a church on Sunday, is really important to me. This is another reason why I am drawn to some cultures more than others. I feel more at home where spirituality is collectively embraced and entangled in our lives. When spirituality becomes dogmatic, hierarchical, or fundamentalist, or when it is neatly packaged to be performed once a week, then I walk away.

Modernity has disenchanted our worlds, taken the spirit world and collapsed it into formal and hierarchical religion, or secularisation, or individualistic New Age spirituality that worships the self and lacks transcendence.

I believe a vital task for society is to re-enchant our worlds, which means bringing the transcendent back as an everyday spiritual experience. Prayer, gratitude, love, service, and work as prayer.

Part III

Weaving our futures

Introduction to Part III

There are two final chapters to the book that look towards the future. Chapter 26 sets out the paradigm change we face as we move from the modern age to the Precarious-Interdependent Age. It then invites readers to think about what it will take to transition from where we are now, to where we need to be, with the emphasis on what it means to live a good life in this new paradigm we are entering.

The final chapter, Island contemplations, concludes by weaving threads of this book together. The aim is not to integrate but to highlight fragments that illuminate some of the cultural and sociopolitical themes and to weave our human essence into these.

The chapter ends with a message of hope. Not a false hope based on flight from our troubles, or some grandiose nonsense as spouted by so many populist politicians, about returning to a golden past age. The hope I describe emerges from the soul enrichment that comes when we reconnect and celebrate our relationships and interdependencies with all things in the cosmos. Once again belonging as one of many, and as a part of the whole, on this small, fragile, and beautiful planet.

CHAPTER 26

Living well in the Precarious-Interdependent Age

I have been working with the concept of the Precarious-Interdependent Age for quite a while.[135] During the Covid-19 pandemic, I realised that Covid was not only a global viral event, but it marked a discontinuity, a break from the modern age that we have lived in for the past few centuries, and that we take as the norm. This essay attempts to clarify why it's important to a) recognise this paradigm shift, and b) to begin to think hard about what it means to live well in a Precarious-Interdependent Age.

Introduction

The P-I Age marks a paradigm shift, taking us beyond the twentieth-century age of modernity. It fundamentally changes what it means to live well together on this small, beautiful, and fragile planet that we share with our multi-species companions. To address the personal, social, and environmental challenges we face in the P-I Age means to shift mindsets from our current modernist way of thinking to a P-I way of thinking, and this isn't easy for three reasons. First, in the West, we have been conditioned to think in a particular way since the Enlightenment and industrialisation. We are entrapped (often unconsciously) in modern mindsets that see the world through linear progress, economic growth, individualism, and human power presiding over nature and each other. Second, there are many vested interests in short-termism to keep things as they are, reproducing existing powerful elites, despite knowing this is a self-destructive path for both humanity and for many of our non-human companions sharing our planet. Third, making a paradigm shift means stepping into unknown territory, taking risks, and thinking very differently, and many find this anxiety-producing and turn away, repressing the need to change while acting defensively, and sometimes aggressively, as we see in climate denial and populist nationalism.

This chapter will first define the P-I Age, discuss what caused it, and address when the P-I Age announced itself. The next section challenges the doomsayers and moves to offer some thoughts on living well in the P-I Age.

Definition of the Precarious-Interdependent Age

The P-I Age began in earnest during the late twentieth century and was crystallised into being by the Covid-19 global pandemic. The two words signify the changes we face.

Precarious: We live in a precarious age because the dominant ideology conceived by Enlightenment and modernist thinkers, which claims that science and reason would lead to a progressively more civilised, free, and stable future, is over. Social and political disruptions and repercussions are occurring in response to the environmental emergency and the rapid technological disruptions. This creates precarity that leads to devastation for some and to widespread social anxieties for others. The idea that we lived in a trajectory of progress and that each next generation would be more prosperous, healthy, and happy has disappeared into a cavernous hole. Uncertainty, instability, and polycrisis are the new norm. The foreseeable future will be precarious, creating multiple challenges and also new opportunities for us to live differently and to create new ways of being.

Interdependent: Human life on this planet has always been a life of coexistence with other human and non-human companions. Modernity separated culture and nature, setting humans above the environment, imagining we could control nature and use it as an inexhaustible resource.

The Covid pandemic revealed our global interconnectedness as never before, and the environmental emergency confirms that we are knotted together in an entanglement of interdependence that cannot be undone. Our human dependence on each other requires us to collaborate to address climate change and to adapt to new conditions, such as regulating artificial intelligence (AI). Technological advances have increased our hyper-connectivity, impacting trade, travel, and politics, and it means our dependence on each other has been amplified. There are many in retreat, building fantasy walls and dreaming of a nostalgic return to an imagined golden age of nationalism, stability, and prosperity while the rest of the world burns. Yet climate change continues to bring local and global disasters at the same time as trade wars and real wars reveal our social precarious-interdependency. We are inextricably bound together. We are interconnected and interdependent with each other, with our multi-species companions, and with the environment.

These two words are connected by a hyphen because it is together that they convey powerful meaning.

Precarious-Interdependence: We cannot separate precarity from interdependence, for they are entwined together. Interdependence is always precarious, as we have to rely upon one another. To be interdependent is to let go of being in control and let others have a say. This undermines the fantasy of being autonomous sole actors in total control of our destinies. Interdependency is resisted because it subverts this modern myth of individuality, control, and superiority. To address precarity without recognising our interdependence is to fail in our understanding. Solving problems in isolation ignores the systemic implications on the whole. One country closing its borders to migrants doesn't solve the underlying problem of what is causing migration; it increases the precarity elsewhere and turns a blind eye to other systemic problems the country faces, such as living in a demographic time bomb with an ageing population and needing more people to function as a healthy society. Precarity simply shifts to another part of the system and then returns unexpectedly. We cannot ignore that precarious challenges are systemic, not singular, their causes and remedies are interconnected and interdependent. Our lives are scaffolded,[136] we extend and embody ourselves, individually and collectively with the material world around us. Technology, machines, the built and natural environment, and relationships with humans and non-humans all scaffold us, creating the environments, contexts, and ways we live. Interdependence isn't simply a feature of us engaging with an 'other', it means that we are constantly enmeshed in our material worlds, co-creating how we live together. This scaffolding is a constantly changing process, always precarious, often incredibly creative, where the whole becomes much greater than the sum of the parts. Our interdependencies mean that we cannot address precarious problems in isolation; collaborative and connected thinking is needed.

The Precarious-Interdependent Age requires a reimagination of how to live well together on this fragile planet. Precarity is entangled with interdependence, and together, they offer us a way forward, which I will discuss later in the chapter.

What is the cause of the P-I Age?

We live in hybrid ecosystems consisting of technology, people, and the environment. These ecosystems are often treated separately, yet they are entangled and interdependent. These ecosystems are living networks, they are in rapid change mode, they are disruptive, and together, they have created the P-I Age.

Environmental disruptions

Climate change and biodiversity loss are the greatest drivers of the P-I Age, manifesting in more frequent and severe weather events; hurricanes, droughts, fires, and floods are increasingly commonplace. These environmental crises not only cause immediate destruction but also highlight the need for long-term adaptation to this new precarious reality. However great our efforts to combat climate change and biodiversity loss are now, the impacts will still be immense. How damaging it will be is the question. The devastating impacts are already being experienced in the most precarious environmental regions, and expected and unexpected consequences will visit many of us soon. Forced migrations of millions fleeing desertification and floods are predicted in the coming years. Conflicts/wars over mineral and energy resources, water shortages, and food chain disruptions are likely outcomes.

Technological transformations

The technological revolution continues to accelerate, changing how societies function and how we interact. Rapid advances in AI, quantum computing, and digital communication are radically changing all aspects of life. Economic impacts such as job losses from AI and robotics will produce winners and losers, opportunities, and challenges. How we work has already been impacted; hybrid offices, home working, mobile surveillance, and algorithmic management are only the start of changes to come. The increasing interdependencies caused by ever-greater connectivity in the NS produce opportunities for some and devastation for others. Education and health care will be delivered and consumed in new ways, positively for some, not for others. Digital divides occur, impacting old and young, rich and poor, global North and global South. Our very identities, politics, and subjectivities are impacted by the constant churn of new technologies. How we relate to others and to ourselves is increasingly mediated through technology.

Sociopolitical shifts

The sociopolitical landscape is also transforming. These changes are heavily influenced by the two disruptions above. The rapid pace of change impacts us not only in material ways but also psychologically and emotionally. At a meta-level, we already see new politics emerging. Economic connectivity and interdependences of global markets led to the rise of China as an economic-political power, and now we see a push-back via economic nationalism aligning with populist nationalism. Immigration tops the political agenda in many countries as migrants increasingly flee from wars, environmental collapse, economic depravity, and political oppression. At micro-levels, climate change impacts our mental health as we increasingly hear the 'bad news' of devastating hurricanes, fires, ice melts, and global warming. Technologies impact not only work but also subjectivities; for example, children become tethered to their parents via cell phones, which changes their experience of gaining independence and alters parent–child relations in regard to autonomy and risk. Employees carry their work around with them on laptops and cell phones, unable to escape the reach of algorithmic surveillance, and blurring work-home life with an impact on health and families.

These three disruptive forces are entangled; they are part of the Precarious-Interdependent ecosystem in which we live.

The P-I Age arrived with a pandemic

The truth of Precarious-Interdependence first announced itself loud and clear in 2008 when digital finance led to a world financial collapse. Banks and financial institutions that were credit-rated as AAA stable and secure were exposed as being completely precarious. Digital finance meant that greater connectivity and interdependencies were hardwired into the system beyond the understanding of the financial regulators. This meant that after one bank collapsed, the whole financial system was impacted with devastating speed. Further interdependencies and entanglements led to economic knock-on effects, causing a recession and millions of people to lose their homes and jobs. Yet we turned a blind eye and continued on the same path of exponential growth. Then came the pandemic.

> We live in times where the Real of nature is re-appearing in traumatic ways, undoing human omnipotent fantasies. The macro ecosystems of the climate crisis are imposing themselves, and micro-ecosystems have unleashed a viral contagion, a pandemic that is shaking the world.[137]

At the height of the Covid-19 pandemic, I wrote an academic paper identifying that the Precarious-Interdependent Age had arrived.[138] When the pandemic struck, we realised there was no outside from nature. The virus revealed just how precarious, interdependent, and connected we are. The Precarious-Interdependent Age had been crystallised into being, and could no longer be ignored.

Doomsayers, deniers, and dissonance

There are two core responses to the truth of the P-I Age:

1. *Denial and dissonance.* The first response is to revile it because it forces us to let go of the dominant ideology of modernity, which is based on an omnipotent fantasy that humans sit above nature, that

we are in control of our destinies, and we are masters of the environment. Precarious-Interdependence announces itself daily in catastrophic local climate events: extreme air pollution, wildfires, droughts, famines, and floods. Yet, we continue to turn a blind eye. Instead of acknowledging the precarity of our ecosystems and of our interdependencies, many turned to populist nationalism, conspiracy theories, and climate denial. Others turn to a dissonant response: acknowledgement and helpless helping. Many of those who accept climate change turn to greenwashing, and mainstream politicians retreat to the comforting modernist narrative that economic growth will save us.

2. *Doomsayers.* Precarity and interdependence are the master signifiers of our times. There are other acronyms trying to capture these social changes, such as VUCA and BANI.

   VUCA stands for:

   Volatility: The speed and magnitude of change.

   Uncertainty: The lack of predictability and the difficulty in forecasting future outcomes.

   Complexity: The many interconnected parts that can lead to confusion and chaos.

   Ambiguity: The unclear cause-and-effect relationships make it hard to interpret situations.

   BANI is a more recent framework that addresses some limitations of VUCA:

   Brittleness: Systems that are rigid and can break under pressure.

   Anxiety: The emotional response to instability and unpredictability.

   Non-linearity: Unpredictable and disproportionate effects of small actions.

   Incomprehensibility: Situations that are too complex to fully understand.

Both frameworks are aimed to help organisations navigate challenges in rapidly changing environments. These acronyms are descriptors that identify a more simple truth, which is that we live in precarious times. However, they do not address the other vital signifier, which is our holistic interdependence. They both focus on the negative and don't point to any way forward. There are many other doomsayers who are keen to identify the challenges and crisis but offer little in the way of what to do.

When addressing the P-I Age, we must aim to identify and acknowledge the precarity and interdependence and then think hard about what this means to live well in the P-I Age.

Living well in the P-I Age

It can be claimed that we have always lived in P-I times. In pre-modern times in Europe and today in many societies, particularly with First Nations and Indigenous peoples, the P-I Age is understood as the way the world is. Different words and languages are used, but the precarity of life alongside a holistic ontology and acceptance of interdependencies within the cosmos is a given. All of the material world and nature are alive and animated by spirits. The past, present, and future are entangled, ancestors speak, rocks speak, stars speak, they all have their own language, and they are all part of the whole. This enchanted world changed with modernity, accompanied by the secularism and rationalism that came with it.

To live well in the P-I Age today is not to attempt to return to a pre-modern age and become 'porous selves',[139] meaning we be open to the power of a spirit world, without agency over our lives. However, the modern turn that created our 'buffered selves', isolating us from the power of spirits and separating us from the environment, has left us bereft of an understanding of holism and alienated us from the living web of life, the environment, and from ourselves.

Precarious-Interdependence means engaging with the world in new ways, or perhaps, more accurately, to remember past ways of engaging and learning to integrate these into our present-day fields of knowledge, experience, and perceptions.

Our challenge is to accept that Precarious-Interdependence is our present and future reality. Our desires to be controlling and omnipotent and to remove fear and risk are futile. Our desires to constantly grow the economy, gain ever more material wealth, and seek a perverse kind of progress can only lead to a dystopian future.

To live well in the present and future means to learn to live in less stable conditions. There is no salvation story, only a new narrative of adaptive and regenerative living in a P-I Age.

Precarity means being more alive

When facing precarity, we are forced to think, to be aware, to be agile, and to become more alive. Precarity can be transformative: 'Precarity is the condition of being vulnerable to others. Unpredictable encounters transform us; we are not in control, even of ourselves'—Anna Tsing.[140]

To learn to live well with precarity means to think beyond it being simply a bad alternative to the hope of stability. This is not to diminish the devastating impact of living in precarious war or emergency crisis conditions such as an earthquake.

Yet precarity is not only a negative force. A by-product of living with precarity is this different way of being that demands liveliness and alertness. Precarity and vulnerability are partners and to live well with others means to live more vulnerably and more empathetically.

Interdependence means belonging

When living interdependently, we learn the joys of sharing, collaborating, coexisting, and, most of all, belonging to a whole. We decentre ourselves and find ourselves a microelement, connected to billions of other microelements that make up the whole, the cosmos.

Gary Snyder, poet and environmentalist, writes:

> When an ecosystem is fully functioning, all the members are present at the assembly. To speak of wilderness is to speak of wholeness. Human beings came out of that wholeness and to consider the possibility of reactivating membership in the Assembly of All Beings is in no way regressive.[141]

Snyder, like many other environmentalists and deep ecologists, believes that humans have become dissociated from nature and from place. When we lose our connection to place, to the natural environment, we lose our way, and finally, we lose ourselves. To live well in dynamic cohabitation with other humans and non-humans means to realise our interdependence, develop greater empathy, decentre ourselves, and become less controlling and more collaborative.

Humans' greatest achievements have been realised by developing their interdependence with the environment around them. Humans learnt how to scaffold their lives, utilising the context around them. They learnt to create niches in the world, embracing human and non-human others. They didn't just adapt to conditions, they co-created environments, they scaffolded what was around them to create dynamic communities and cultures which enabled them to live well in vastly diverse conditions.

'Think we must, we must think'

The challenge to think in new ways is vastly underestimated. There are many clichés used, like 'thinking outside the box', but our thinking is usually reactive, conformist, and entrapped in the social discourses that surround us. We repeat social norms and are entrapped by ways of thinking and ways of being. Thinking differently is key to living well in the P-I Age, and it takes practice and courage. Donna Haraway writes, 'Think we must. We must think. That means, simply, we must change the story; the story must change.'[142] The story we must change is the modernity story of growth, linearity, hierarchy, separatism, categorisation, scientific reductionism, efficiency, productivity, individualism, and messiah leaders. The story that we must learn to narrate together, and in many diverse ways, is the story of how to live well in the P-I Age.

Hannah Arendt wrote that 'Thinking is to train one's imagination to go visiting.'[143] To allow our thinking to be expansive, generative, and to go visiting is to embrace the vulnerability of interdependence and the aliveness of precarity. Thinking takes place not only in our minds but also in our bodies and through our extended selves. Thinking is not a solitary act of neurons connecting in the brain. Thinking is an embodied, collective, and interdependent endeavour.

Dystopian thinkers spread a growing cult of doom and despair that creates paralysis. Psychoanalysis teaches us to live with uncertainty and develop an associative way of thinking. Wilfred Bion's use of Keats' concept of 'negative capability'[144] refers to the therapist's ability to embrace uncertainty and ambiguity without the need for immediate resolution. It relates to the capacity to tolerate confusion, doubt, and complexity in the therapeutic process. Applied psychoanalysis helps develop thinking and understanding based on the ability to hold multiple perspectives, tolerate uncertainty, and process our emotional and bodily experiences.

To live well in the P-I Age is to co-create a new story and step out of the modernity trap. It requires thinking differently and living with not knowing and without retreating to old ways. It means thinking with our bodies, our extended selves, and with the other human and non-human life around us. Listening and noticing rather than reacting and doing.

To live well in the P-I Age is to come alive, to re-enchant ourselves, and to rediscover the animated world we separated ourselves from. The task is to embrace precarity, to reduce its worst impact, to regenerate where we can, and to take joy from belonging and interdependence.

To live well means to collaborate and to live closer to the edge, to become more vulnerable and, at the same time, more resilient, creative, and strong. Precarious-Interdependence is not only a warning of things to come, it is an opportunity and a teacher, telling us to become more interconnected with our spirit and discover the deep grounding joy of belonging to the whole.

CHAPTER 27

Island contemplations

Photograph taken by author on the Aran Islands, Ireland 2024

I began writing this final chapter while waiting to catch the ferry to Inis Oírr, the smallest of the three Aran Islands, positioned in the expanse of Galway Bay, Ireland, at the very edge of Europe. These islands hang delicately between the slate-grey sky and the vast black-blue Atlantic Ocean, with nothing between them and the American continent far, far away.

I have been visiting the Aran Islands since the 1980s and they hold a special place in my heart. On a clear day, I can see them from the beach near my home, where I walk my dog, and when on the islands, I look back and see the mainland where I live. This creates an embodied reflexivity; the act of looking out, travelling to the islands, and looking back creates both a physical and a contemplative experience. The physical journey manifests itself into a personal pilgrimage, not to visit a shrine or holy place, but to visit a special soul place within myself. The journey crossing the sea, the raw nature of the Aran Islands, and the solitary time to walk and think release a multitude of associations and memories. I experience a sharpened sense of noticing all that is in me and around me. Feelings, including melancholy, awe, connectedness, calmness, and engagement enrich me. I am travelling to the Aran Islands to write this ending chapter because where better to contemplate weaving our futures than on a personal pilgrimage to a wild and beautiful place?

It is November 2024; the weather is cold, dry, and overcast. Cloud-filled skies are full of movement, creating a changing dark-light canopy above me. Large waves crash into the rocks on one side of the island, and the sea is peaceful and calm on the other. Perhaps it is a metaphor for the world we live in today. As I write, the American presidential election has just delivered a stunning victory to a man and a movement who say hateful things, threaten vulnerable people, talk of America first, show scant regard for global solidarity, and are climate change deniers. The world feels in a precarious place. US politics are not an anomaly, but a magnified version of trends in Europe and Asia, where authoritarianism and nationalism are on the rise. Wars with terrible consequences take place in Ukraine, the Middle East, Sudan, and other regions. This weekend a 'Soul at Work' retreat event I had planned in Spain was cancelled due to flooding which destroyed villages, killing more than 200 people. A sign of the climate events which are happening with increasing frequency. The word polycrisis captures the attention as

AI and technological change bring further opportunities and disruptions. These worrying events unfold like the waves crashing into the rocks, and yet much of the world carries on in a largely peaceful and calm way, walking on the other side. We live in strange times. Antonio Gramsci, the Italian philosopher and political theorist, famously wrote: '*The old is dying and the new cannot be born: in this interregnum a great variety of morbid symptoms appear.*'[145]

This statement appears in his *Prison Notebooks*, written during his incarceration under Mussolini's fascist regime. It encapsulates his analysis of periods of social transition, where the established order is breaking down, and there is a gap, an interregnum, as a new order has not yet emerged to replace it. It feels like we are in one of those times, and the challenges we face are the morbid symptoms appearing. Gramsci also wrote of the 'pessimism of the intellect, optimism of the will', meaning that we must use our intellect to address the challenges and face up to reality, however pessimistic, while avoiding paralysing cynicism or fleeing into blind hope and idealism.

This book has aimed for this balance, to dig deep into events, and to offer a particular analysis that looks awry at them while avoiding 'helpless helping' and 'the happiness imperative'. These chapters also point to a different reality than Gramsci was writing about. We are not in-between two periods of modern history waiting for a socialist revolution, or some other form of a bright new democratic and egalitarian future. We are facing a paradigm change which demands we mobilise the optimism of the collective soul, which opens us up to relearn from the distant past and to learn anew how to live well in, and how to re-enchant our lives in a P-I Age.

This book has presented events, cultural themes, and personal experiences as an entanglement. This final chapter will weave fragments of this entanglement together, to sense-make and synthesise where possible, before turning my gaze to the future.

Weaving fragments

I weave fragments together in a non-linear way as there is no unifying story to be told, no over-arching explanation, and no dive into a happy ending. However, there are glimpses of subjective truth, beneath-the-surface insights, and connections that may lead to revelations, and there is the optimism of the soul.

Weaving themes:

- Inner theatre and the external world
- Ethics and meaning
- Ecosystems and critical thinking
- Conscious and unconscious dynamics
- Soul work—re-enchantment
- Culture wars, diversity, populism
- Technology and networks
- Institutions and organisations

Inner theatre and the external world

The book begins with a chapter tracing my work history, asking what authored the author, revealing how different work experiences shaped my inner world. This learnt experience is then applied to my life and work, playing a small part in shaping the world around me.

The inner and outer worlds are entangled, 'the baker makes the bread and the bread makes the baker'. Throughout the book, I try to engage with how my subjectivity, feelings, thoughts, and emotions are data that can help me understand and potentially influence the world around me. We all have inner theatres, with scripts, stories, and dramas taking place within us. This cannot be reduced to the psychology of a behavioural stimulus-response, it is much more nuanced and participative. We are constantly in the process of making each other; this applies to humans and in the non-human world. Sympoiesis means to make with, and as Donna Haraway writes, 'nothing makes itself'.

This relationality has been long undervalued in modernity's reductionist scientific worldview. I explore these themes in the 'Therapy culture' section. We don't just receive experiences like blank sheets; we are already filled with perceptions, thoughts, and feelings inscribed into us from relationships, culture, and nature around us. We carry wounded-selves and celebrated-selves, seeking others like us, and can become enlivened or entrapped in dysfunctional lives. This applies to individuals and whole societies. What emerges in the politics of today comes largely from the libidinal economy, that is, how our emotions, unconscious fears, and anxieties are played back to us by political forces. We are forever seeking to fulfil our desires, and yet these desires are entangled between conscious and unconscious pulls. Our desires are always in relation to important figures in our lives and to wider cultural norms and demands. The big Other's voice is never far away, and it appears throughout this book.

Ethics and meaning

The sections on war and the environment specifically address the challenge of taking an ethical stance in a complex world. I draw on my Quaker faith to invite readers to ask themselves, 'What canst thou say?' drawing on George Fox's question that challenges us to look deep within and listen to what our spirit—the inner light—is saying to us. I make an argument that ethics come from how we make meaning, and this has to be contextualised and understood with an eye to history and our social and cultural histories and biases. As we face increasing precarity through more environmental crises, human conflicts, AI, and technology disruptions, digging deep to gain meaning and develop our ethical selves is a vital task for each and all of us.

Ecosystems and critical thinking

The book refers to ecosystem thinking a lot, as it enables us to see beyond linear cause and effect and helps us take account of multiple and often contradictory influences. Ecosystems fundamentally describe how we live, the Covid chapter shares how technology, people, and the environment are entangled in complementary and hybrid ecosystems. Our task is to embrace this relational way of being and to craft new ways of living more collaboratively alongside our humans and non-human companions on this planet.

Not all systemic thinking is put to good use. A warning comes in the chapter on the Ukrainian war, revealing how systemic thinking can become distorted and used to explain away anything we wish. People say, 'well, it's systemic', as if this annuls the ethics and critical thinking required to understand and make choices. Similarly, the words 'it's complex' can infer a giving up on thinking, producing paralysis. Staying with the trouble, thinking with others, and thinking harder are a more responsible path. Ecosystem thinking, therefore, must be accompanied by critical theory and ethics, which means asking ourselves where is power held, how it is being used, and for what purpose? Are the choices we are making working for the common good and for the planet? In the Digital age section of the book, the chapter on NIPI—networks, identity, power, and influence—offers a practical framework to use when working in organisations. NIPI frames how we can look differently at organisational and social dynamics, moving away from mechanistic organisational frameworks that dominate contemporary thinking. If we can radically shift our thinking, engage with organisations and society as ecosystems, and apply critical thinking to our work, the potential space of transformation opens.

Unconscious dynamics

The theme of the unconscious appears like a recurrent dream floating through this book. I am intrigued by how when I offer insights as an executive coach and organisational consultant they are so well received, and yet paradoxically the dogmatic requirement for empirical data and reductionist numbers remains stubbornly dominant in organisational life. Tapping into the unconscious desires and defences in organisational and social life is an essential part of an ecosystemic approach, not to replace empirical data, but to fill the gap as data alone is never enough.

Working with the unconscious not only offers a different lens to supplement hyper-rational approaches, but it does something much more important. It brings the human back into human resources and decentres messiah leaders and hierarchical approaches. To engage with the unconscious is to acknowledge that 'we are not masters in our own house' to cite Freud. Modernity is infused with individualism, hierarchy, and control. The essence of this approach is to claim that God is dead and that we are masters of ourselves, that we can be masters of others (slavery and hierarchy), and that we are definitely masters of nature. If we engage with our unconscious seriously, we have to acknowledge a lack of control, a vulnerability. As discussed in the chapter on desire, even our individual desires are never ours alone. However, the paradox is that by accepting this lack of control, the insights we develop can liberate us from dysfunctional patterns and traps, giving us more influence and choices over our lives. Working with the unconscious is often misunderstood as a dive into personal depth psychology. Yet our unconscious is relational, it is always shaped in relation to others, to individuals and groups we identify with, to landscapes and places we associate with, and to ghosts of the past that live within us. Acknowledging the unconscious brings a different lens to how we think and how we live, below are five insights:

1. *Emotional and embodied beings*: Our bodies hold unconscious emotions when we cannot think of them consciously, for instance, our bodies feel anxious when we haven't worked out why. We are emotional and embodied beings, not just rational thinking machines.
2. *Relational beings*: Our unconscious dynamics and inner theatres always take place in relation to others, both human and non-human.
3. *Vulnerability*: Working with the unconscious demands that we accept being vulnerable and not being totally in control. This opens a space for relational development and emancipatory insights.
4. *Curiosity*: We cannot work with the unconscious without developing curiosity about ourselves and others. This means tolerating not-knowing, which opens a space for creativity and learning something new.
5. *Lack*: We are always lacking something, we never have the full picture nor can we experience total fulfilment. There is always something unsaid, something in the unconscious that is not yet present to us. An appreciation of lack has two impacts. First, it keeps us humble, accepting we don't know everything! Second, lack points to the real, that is, what is missing/lacking is usually a clue as to what really matters, what is most important to us.

Soul work and re-enchantment

Soul work, spirituality, religion, faith, God, and transcendence are forbidden territory in most workplaces and in much of modern secular society. 'God is Dead!' As discussed in the chapter on the wounded- and celebrated-self, Eastern practices of yoga, mindfulness, and other

New Age spiritualities can be offered in workplaces to de-stress and improve well-being, yet these are used instrumentally, in other words to optimise employee performance. Throughout these chapters, particularly in the Re-enchanting our Worlds section, I share my own experience of how everyday spirituality and moments of grace bring me closer to the eternal love that binds us together within the cosmos. We recently designed a 'Soul at Work' retreat at the Eco-Leadership Institute, focusing on soul, ecology, and creativity in the workplace. Soul work has to be done alongside ecosystemic and critical thinking, and when it is left out, the lack undermines the whole project. Spirituality offers a plurality of personal experiences; for some, a secular human spirit informs their work, others feel spiritual but not religious, and others are part of a religious faith tradition. In all cases, our souls have to be engaged if radical change is going to take place.

Modernity disenchanted the world, taking away the spirit life of animals, plants, micro-organisms, forests, rocks, rivers, and the unseen spirit/energy of the material world, including the spirits of our ancestors. We cannot return to pre-modern mindsets and ways of living, nor would we choose to. Yet Indigenous peoples lead the way in how they retain relational ontologies[146] through dynamic cultures which integrate relational values and processes within the modern context in which they live today. Indigenous, African, and First Nations ways of knowing, being, and relating to the world can teach Western societies much about the interconnectedness of all things. They can teach us how spirituality, relationality, and land-centred ways of being can transform our engagement with an animated world that is crying out for us to remember this reality. The world around us is animated and infused with spirit, and the only way we can re-engage with this is to undertake deep soul work to rediscover and find new ways to live in greater harmony and balance with all entities and to recognise our place as humans in the cosmos.

Culture wars, diversity, populism

The chapters focusing on culture and politics aim to shine a light on the dominant themes that have had such an outsized impact on society in the past decade. Culture wars, woke, diversity, and identity issues have led to gains by some, and also created divisions that have been amplified by populist and nationalist politics, and by liberals who lean towards splitting and soft forms of authoritarianism. What I try to show in these chapters is that diversity issues are really important, that plurality and acceptance of difference are central to a healthy society, and yet a more nuanced approach to understanding the polarising splits and hatred is required. The radical position is to engage in dialogue and to hold a mirror to ourselves and to own our projections and our acting-out behaviours. The psychoanalytic concept of how we take unconscious 'pleasure in our displeasure' is vital here. Complaining about the aggressor while enjoying our victim status, or our grandiose self-righteousness, simply means the cycle of hatred is perpetuated.

Technology and networks

As I review these chapters on technology and networks, it becomes so much clearer how technological change is so interrelated with environmental and social change. The technological revolution since digitalisation has been profound, impacting all aspects of life. The NS amplifies our interdependencies and interconnectedness in ways we are forever trying to keep up with. The sudden explosion in AI demands a NIPI response (networks, identity, power, and influence): how will AI impact our ecosystems and networks, our workplaces and social spaces, our relationships and identities? When AI betters some forms of human intelligence, what does this do to us? Who has the power to regulate or not to regulate AI so it can be used for the good of all? What checks and balances are there, and how will AI influence the wider world? As technology continues its unstoppable advance, asking NIPI questions of networks, identity, power, and influence will be essential. These chapters also ask important questions about our presence and absence and how we navigate virtual and physical spaces and manage fast-changing and fluid border regimes. The disruptive society requires adaptive responses; it also requires anchored spaces and contact with the land, with nature to provide places of containment for us to think and thrive.

Institutions and organisations

Three chapters focus on institutions. In what authored the author I discuss the total institutions/asylum I worked in as a psychiatric nurse and how modern institutions and organisations can also create very conformist cultures. I then address the monarchy following the death of Queen Elizabeth II and how establishment institutions create dependency and hierarchical cultures. The demise of respect for institutions such as the monarchy and the Church leaves a gap, which is either filled with narcissistic individualism and collective anxiety, or with new forms of solidarity that lead to supportive interdependency cultures. Monasteries are perhaps the longest-established institutions in the West, and my experience of spending time in monastic settings has been so very powerful. Monasteries transcend modernity and offer counter-cultural spaces like no other. The Benedictine monks follow a rule and take vows of stability, celibacy, and obedience, which turn the values of the secular world upside down. What is extraordinary about these monasteries is the paradoxical freedom and transcendent love that I experience in them.

In Chapter 22, I discuss organisations as the lifeblood of society as they are vital in all aspects of our lives. Our challenge is to reimagine organisations, to change current perceptions of organisations as being formal structures and buildings that operate with hierarchies like efficient machines. Only when we see them more clearly, as animated webs of life, as living ecosystems that are constantly adapting, will we harness organisational power to work for the common good as networks of desire.

Weaving our futures

This beautiful island is a good place to weave the threads of this book into a final reflection.

The precarious edge

Walking the island this morning, I am literally on a precarious edge. Such a small island, three by two kilometres with a population of 300, I wonder how long the population can survive here? There is a water shortage, and the Blasket Islands south of here remind us of the precarity as they became uninhabited in 1953, largely due to a diminishing elderly population and weather conditions. Yet there is a resilience here, a steadfastness both in the people and in the rocks and nature itself.

Being here makes me feel edgy and alive. As I walked by the wild sea yesterday, it awakened me. Precarious edges on cliff walks take your breath away. The precariousness I feel here is a good template for how we might live in a P-I Age. The precarity is not of such magnitude that it is directly life-threatening or creates suffering, like in some parts of the world. Perhaps the opposite, this 'moderate precarity' creates the liveliness that can resurrect the spirit. Yet there are real dangers in the immediate and long term. Immediate dangers from a wild sea that takes lives from experienced fishermen, volatile weather patterns and longer-term dangers from the weather changes have an unknown impact on the Gulf Stream in which these islands sit. Precarity will increase across the globe, and while we must embrace it, we should not romanticise it either. As I took the small ferry across the sea, I thought of those fleeing wars, political oppression, and economic devastation, who risk their lives on the small boats in the Mediterranean and English Channel. Our future work is to take responsibility and act in all ways possible to mitigate against the worst impacts of climate, conflict, and economic precarity. This means long-term and short-term collaboration between fellow humans and between humans and the web of life that sustains us all.

Alongside precarity, resilience and regeneration are always present. When I first visited the islands in the 1980s, they were starkly different, an almost pre-modern, peasant-style living took place here. Now the harbour has been upgraded, and cows no longer need to be lowered from cargo boats into the sea and pulled behind the curragh rowing boats to the beach. Regular ferries mean tourism, which has brought hotels, guest houses, food outlets, bicycle hire, and tours in the summer. The internet brings the world to the Aran Islands, for better or worse, bridging borders that once made these places so isolated. These islands have survived much, including a potato famine, relying on a closeness and relationship to the land and sea inspired by a storytelling and music tradition and a closeness to the ancestors.

Interdependencies

These islands reveal how interdependencies acutely manifest, where humans and nature have lived here in entangled existences for more than 4,000 years. Prehistoric burial chambers and spectacular hill forts from 2500 BC remain on the islands. The hand-built curraghs, small fishing boats made of wood, canvas, and tar, rowed with two or four or six men, are still in use, alongside modern fishing boats. The relationship between the sea and land is everything here. The islands are magically woven with webs of hand-built dry stone walls, standing against the winds. They create small fields, micro-climates sheltered from the wind to grow potatoes, and meadows for cows to graze. The biodiversity and the flowers in spring time are exceptional as seaweed is the main fertiliser.

In some parts, the limestone pavements were covered with sand and seaweed to create the soil in which to sustain a family and grow vegetables. In the past flotsam and shipwrecks provided wood and other resources to use and build with.

These islands have always attracted writers and contemplative souls. Irish writer, playwright, and poet John Millington Synge spent time here, which greatly influenced his work. I marvel at the beehive monastic huts and churches dating from the fifth century that reveal how spirituality thrived in these isolated places for millennia. Human life on the islands is never separate from the mainland, the interdependencies have always been present. Flour, sugar, and porter (beer) were some of the basics that were imported by curragh in the past. Today, the tourists, the daily delivery of supplies, the newspapers, the electricity provision, water when needed, all enhance what was previously a far greater precarity of existence. People leave and people arrive here, and there are connections across the globe. Emigration has meant that close and distant relatives are found in Manchester, London, Boston, and Sydney, creating an international community web.

The interdependency with the environment remains alive, the farming and fishing continue, if diminished. The winds and the rain, the sun and the storms continue to lash the islands and provide mesmerising light. Today, I walked before breakfast and met a seal pup sleeping peacefully on the beach, another moment of grace.

The future

The future we all face is unpredictable; what is known is that precarity and interdependence will underpin it. The journey we embrace demands a deep and radical faith in each other and in the natural world. I am reminded of the ancient monastic practice, deeply rooted in Celtic Christianity of Peregrinatio (from the Latin word for 'pilgrimage' or 'journey'). This spiritual practice transcended the concept of a structured pilgrimage to a holy site like Jerusalem or Rome. Instead, it called for complete surrender to divine guidance, leaving home and familiar surroundings to embrace the unknown. It is said Irish monks sailed from shores with no oars, with the aim of radical surrender, having faith that God and the winds would guide the pilgrims to where they needed to be. There is something about recovering a sense of Peregrinatio, to sense our way forward step by step, following our collective soul guides.

Our challenge is to decentre humanity and, in doing so, to find our place once again. To locate ourselves closer to the land and discover where we fit into the ecosystems of contemporary society, and within the webs of life that we share on this planet.

It is time to embrace edge living, not to keep fighting to be at the top of a hierarchical order. Economic growth will not save us, and nor will military domination. Leadership from the edge delivers change that can go viral, and the multitude of small changes will lead to greater sustainable changes in our ecosystems.

The planet has much to teach us humans. We have much to learn from plants, animals, fungi, and viruses. New science is revealing interconnectivity, resilience, and adaptive patterns across species, and we must join this journey of discovery.

Contemplative thinking

A new/old form of thinking is required for the P-I Age, one that embraces and learns the connectivity of all things from Indigenous peoples and weaves this with our modern insights and knowledge. A contemplative thinking that allows our souls to become part of the thought process is required. An embodied thinking that listens to our bodies and to the places we inhabit, the land, sea, and air around us. Perhaps the greatest need is to develop and relearn a way of thinking-with-others, with other humans and non-humans, with nature and technology, to fully listen to and learn with our ecosystems. AI must not be allowed to further diminish or erode our capacity to think. My hope is that AI and digitalisation awaken us, and stimulate a return to contemplation, a counter-cultural movement to contrast with the quick fix of Chat GPT. AI and technology will then become part of an ecosystem of thinking. It is our choice how it influences these ecosystems.

Mutuality and 'cosmozens'

'Mutuality in our ecosystems'. This phrase is a necessary working ethic for all citizens of the planet. We require a consciousness-raising, a soul-inspired transformation that places mutuality at the heart of our diverse and interconnected worlds.

I have been thinking a lot about citizenship during the writing of this book, thinking about the importance of individual and collective engagement and our responsibilities as citizens. Yet reflecting on this I realise that citizenship is not the right term, it's yet another trap of language. We take for granted ideas and terms that entrap us in modernity mindsets. The word citizen refers to those living in a city, creating a boundary and separation between city dwellers and the land, between urban living and the web of life that sustains us.

Three major discoveries were said to have undermined our human centricity and our omnipotent grandiosity. Copernicus dethroned man from the centre of the universe, proving that the Earth was not the centre of the cosmos, we were just another planet circling the sun. Darwin undid the narrative that humans were divine and came from God via the Garden of Eden, showing how evolution took place and our emergence from the animal kingdom. Freud, who pioneered psychoanalysis, showed how our conscious will was subjected to our unconscious desires, and we were not 'masters in our own house'. These three profound discoveries should have humbled the human-centric dominant narrative. Yet history shows that we weren't humbled, we merely rewrote the narrative, switching faith from the divine to a new faith in our scientific brilliance, and followed the Enlightenment path, striving for infinite progress through the domination of nature and of human nature.

A new story is urgently required that truly decentres humans and helps us find our place in the universe. A story where we are not subjects of a monarch nor citizens of a political order. Bruno Latour in *Down to Earth: Politics in the New Climatic Regime*,[147] shares his vision of humans as 'Earthbound' or 'Terrestrials' acknowledging the Earth's significance as a shared home deserving care and reverence. It is time we adopted our true status as cosmozens and tell a new story that embeds humans in the land, that finds our place in the wider cosmos. Humans are diverse people who have uniquely learnt to adapt and coexist in all types of environment, from deserts to the Arctic Circle, from huge cosmopolitan cities, to edge living, gathering, hunting communities. We already know how to adapt, and how to live precariously and interdependently with our human and non-human companions in the vast cosmos that give us life.

To be a cosmozen is to partake in mutuality with all beings and all life around us. This means acting with solidarity, thinking with our bodies and souls, and working towards a good society and the well-being of the planet. When we raise our consciousness and acknowledge our place as one small part of the cosmos, re-enchantment follows. When re-enchantment takes place, we recover our dignity and recognise the dignity of all. We rediscover our soul place in human society and in the wider ecosystems that sustain us all on this fragile and beautiful planet called Earth. This is our future.

Afterword, July 2025

I am sitting outside a café in the warm sunshine in Manchester, UK, undertaking the final edits of this book. The morning news links the sunshine to skin cancer and climate change and advises sun cream and shade. I mourn the loss of our innocence, of a time when a sunny day was a gift, just simply a day to be enjoyed. The news these days is brutally repetitive, narrating the horrors of human conflicts and human-made 'natural' disasters: wars, bombings, floods, heatwaves, followed by anti-immigrant stories and revealing how the political and economic global order is rapidly in transition. The Precarious-Interdependent Age I discuss earlier is not an imaginary future state, it is unmistakably present. The world is precarious, and like it or not, we are interdependently connected to the environment and to each other .... There is no outside of nature, and no idealised nation state that can shut out the rest of the world and climate change. Our shared task is to learn to live together on this fragile planet, and the chapters in this book, while written over the past seven years, remain acutely relevant to that task.

To be in Manchester is fitting, as it's the birthplace of the Industrial Revolution which produced the modern and disruptive times we live in. Manchester retains many factories, mills, the ship canals and other waterways that powered us towards the urban and modern cultures

Photograph taken by author, statue of Emily Pankhurst, Manchester, UK

that have been both emancipatory and enslaving. Two statues caught my attention here, one of Frederich Engels who wrote *The Conditions of the Working Class* based on his observations and research on the terrible working conditions in Manchester's factories, which later informed his work on the communist manifesto with Marx. The other statue is Emily Pankhurst in St Peters Square, the famous suffragette, with the inscription 'deeds not words' to accompany her. Two emancipatory thinkers and activists who were pioneers and criticised the power structures that inflicted oppression and cruelty on so many. I hope this book follows their emancipatory lead.

This book wrote itself in many ways, and is an example of how parts come together to form an interdependent whole. Essays written in the moment, in response to events and experiences spoke to each other, and became entangled. Personal stories, social and political stories, and spiritual stories woven into a strong fabric that hopefully provides the reader with rich material to work with. Each reader will bring their own experiences to this book, and will identify with different aspects weaving their own narratives from the stories shared.

My hope is that these chapters spark a reaction, provoke emotions and empathy, and create a different kind of space for new thinking to take place. Critical and emancipatory thinking, looking awry at what is before us, escaping deeply embedded modernist mindsets, embracing small moments of grace in our daily lives, and experiencing a new sense of connectivity and belonging. Each small step taken helps us move a little closer to living a 'good life', and creating the 'good society'.

Notes

Introduction

1. Western, S. (2020). Covid-19: an intrusion of the real, the unconscious unleashes its truth. *Journal of Social Work Practice*, *34*(4): 445–451. https://doi.org/10.1080/02650533.2020.1842725

Chapter 1

2. Menzies Lyth, I. (1960). A case study in the functioning of social systems as a defence against anxiety. *Human Relations*, *13*: 95–121.
3. This is not to paint the stereotypical gendered picture of female nurses as caring angels, which draws on the essentialist rhetoric that women are naturally more humane and emotionally literate leaders than men. Scandals of cruel leadership in 'caring' institutions such as hospitals, children's homes, monasteries, and convents reveal that caring or harsh leadership behaviour is less gender specific, and more closely linked to perverse organisational cultures.
4. Puwar, N. (2004). *Space Invaders: Race, Gender and Bodies out of Place*. Oxford: Berg.
5. Obholzer, A., & Roberts, V. Z. (Eds.) (1994). *The Unconscious at Work*. London: Routledge.

6. Goffman, E. (1961). *Asylums: Essays on the Social Situation of Mental Patients and Other Inmates.* New York: Doubleday.
7. Western, S. (2014). Autonomist leadership in leaderless movements: Anarchists leading the way. *Ephemera: Theory & Politics in Organization, 14*(4): 673–698.
8. Western, S. (2010). Eco-leadership: Towards the development of a new paradigm. In: B. Redekop (Ed.), *Leadership for Environmental Sustainability.* New York: Routledge.

Chapter 2

9. Sandford, A. (2020, April 2). Coronavirus: Half of humanity on lockdown in 90 countries. *Euronews.* https://www.euronews.com/2020/04/02/coronavirus-in-europe-spain-s-death-toll-hits-10-000-after-record-950-new-deaths-in-24-hou (last accessed 21 April 2024).
10. Carroll, R. (2020, October 19). Ireland to impose 5km travel limit in strict new Covid lockdown. *The Guardian.* https://www.theguardian.com/world/2020/oct/19/ireland-to-impose-5km-travel-limit-in-strict-new-covid-lockdown (last accessed 27 November 2025).

Chapter 3

11. Taylor, F. W. (1947). *The Principles of Scientific Management.* New York: Harper.
12. Badiou, A. (2007). *Being and Event.* London: A&C Black.
13. McLaverty-Robinson, A. (2014, December 15). Alain Badiou: The Event an A to Z of theory. *Ceasefire Magazine.* https://ceasefiremagazine.co.uk/alain-badiou-event/ (last accessed 27 November 2025).
14. Miller, J.-A. (2011). *Lacan's Later Teaching,* Lacanian Ink21 [Online]. www.lacan.com/frameXXI2.htm (last accessed 15 November 2025).
15. Western, S. (2023). Covid: An intrusion of the real. In: H. Brunning & O. Khaleelee (Eds.), *The Covid Trail: Psychoanalytic Explorations* (pp. 139–156). Bicester, UK: Phoenix.
16. Gramsci, A. (1971). *Selections from the Prison Notebooks.* New York: International Publishers, 1989.

Chapter 5

17. Religious Society of Friends. (2013). *Quaker Faith and Practice: The Book of Christian Discipline of the Yearly Meeting of the Religious Society*

of Friends (Quakers) in Britain (5th edn). Britain: Yearly Meeting of the Religious Society of Friends.

18. Religious Society of Friends. (2013). *Quaker Faith and Practice: The Book of Christian Discipline of the Yearly Meeting of the Religious Society of Friends (Quakers) in Britain* (5th edn). Britain: Yearly Meeting of the Religious Society of Friends.

Chapter 6

19. Bryant, M. (2022, September 17). Tea in the cold and a visit from the King: The people waiting all night to see the Queen. *The Guardian*. 17 April 2024.
20. Stavrakakis, Y. (2007). *The Lacanian Left*. Edinburgh, UK: Edinburgh University Press.
21. For a comparative view of a state funeral ritual, see the documentary film about Stalin's death, *State Funeral* by Sergio Loznitsa.
22. Gapper, J. (2022, September 16). The King's problems with pens break the royal spell. *Financial Times*. https://www.ft.com/content/a012fd35-d737-47a0-977a-edaabf0e1a35 (last accessed 27 November 2025).
23. Piketty, T. (2014). *Capital in the Twenty-first Century*. Cambridge, MA: Harvard University Press.
24. Armstrong, D. (2018). *Organization in the Mind: Psychoanalysis, Group Relations and Organizational Consultancy*. Abingdon, UK: Routledge.
25. Winnicott, D. W. (Ed.) (1971). *Playing and Reality*. London: Tavistock.

Chapter 7

26. Stavrakakis, Y. (2007). *The Lacanian Left*. Edinburgh, UK: Edinburgh University Press.
27. See Chapter 12.
28. The term libidinal is used in psychoanalysis to refer to the unconscious, bodily, and emotional energies that drive our behaviours.
29. Corbyn was later excluded from the Labour Party following claims of antisemitism. This was heavily disputed but it highlights how the politics of binary splitting play out.
30. Kentish, B. (2017, July 22). Tory MP and father of six Jacob Rees-Mogg says he has never changed a nappy. *The Independent*. https://www.independent.co.uk/news/uk/politics/jacob-reesmogg-never-changed-a-nappy-lbc-nigel-farage-nanny-conservatives-a7854791.html (last accessed 27 November 2025).

Chapter 8

31. Western, S. (2019). *Leadership: A Critical Text*. London: Sage.
32. Casey, C. (1995). *Work, Self and Society after Industrialisation*. London: Routledge.
33. Freud, S. (1924). Mourning and melancholia. *The Psychoanalytic Review (1913–1957), 11*: 77.

Chapter 9

34. Taylor, C. (2009). *A Secular Age*. Cambridge, Massachusetts, and London, England: Harvard University Press.
35. Alter, C., Haynes, S., & Worland, J. (2019). Greta Thunberg: Time person of the year. *Time Magazine*. https://time.com/person-of-the-year-2019-greta-thunberg/ (last accessed 31 October 2020).
36. McLuhan, M., & Fiore, Q. (1967). *The Medium Is the Massage: An Inventory of Effects*. New York: Bantam.
37. Alter, C., Haynes, S., & Worland, J. (2019). Greta Thunberg: Time person of the year. *Time Magazine*. https://time.com/person-of-the-year-2019-greta-thunberg/ (last accessed 31 October 2020).
38. Moore, S. (2019, October 1). Greta Thunberg's defiance upsets the patriarchy—and it's wonderful. *The Guardian*. https://www.theguardian.com/commentisfree/2019/oct/01/greta-thunbergs-defiance-upsets-the-patriarchy-and-its-wonderful (last accessed 31 October 2020).
39. Shrimsley R. (2020) Why middle aged men hate Greta. *Financial Times*. https://ft.com/content/843e1fa4-ea26-11e9-85f4-d00e5018f061 (last accessed 31 October 2020).
40. Alter, C., Haynes, S., & Worland, J. (2019). Greta Thunberg: Time person of the year. *Time Magazine*. https://time.com/person-of-the-year-2019-greta-thunberg/ (last accessed 31 October 2020).
41. Meyer, R. (2019, September 23). Why Greta makes adults uncomfortable. *The Atlantic*. https://www.theatlantic.com/science/archive/2019/09/why-greta-wins/598612/ (last accessed 31 October 2020).
42. I am aware of the debate about colonialist mindsets and 'white saviours' which I have empathy with. The point I am making here is that Greta amplifies these voices that get little attention at climate conferences, recognising also that the need to hear their voices directly is paramount.

43. O'Toole, F. (2019, September 28). Greta Thunberg is a prophet, preacher, rulebreaker, avenging angel. *The Irish Times*. https://www.irishtimes.com/opinion/fintan-o-toole-greta-thunberg-is-a-prophet-preacher-rulebreaker-avenging-angel-1.4030064 (last accessed 27 Nov- ember 2025).
44. Alter, C., Haynes, S., & Worland, J. (2019). Greta Thunberg: Time person of the year. *Time Magazine*. https://time.com/person-of-the-year-2019-greta-thunberg/ (last accessed 31 October 2020).
45. Petter, O. (2019, November 7). Margaret Atwood says Greta Thunburg is the 'Joan of Arc' of environmentalism. *Independent*. https://www.independent.co.uk/life-style/margaret-atwood-greta-thunberg-joan-of-arc-environmentalism-climate-change-a9188841.html (last accessed 27 November 2025).
46. Rourke, A. (2019, September 2). Greta Thunberg responds to Asperger's critics: 'It's a superpower.' *The Guardian*. https://www.theguardian.com/environment/2019/sep/02/greta-thunberg-responds-to-aspergers-critics-its-a-superpower#:~:text=And%20then%20you%20know%20you,different%20as%20a%20%E2%80%9Csuperpower%E2%80%9D (last accessed 27 November 2025).
47. O'Toole, F. (2019, September 28). Greta Thunberg is a prophet, preacher, rulebreaker, avenging angel. *The Irish Times*. https://www.irishtimes.com/opinion/fintan-o-toole-greta-thunberg-is-a-prophet-preacher-rule-breaker-avenging-angel-1.4030064 (last accessed 27 November 2025).
48. Taylor, C. (2009). *A Secular Age*. Cambridge, MA: Harvard University Press.
49. Melucci, A. (1989). *Nomads of the Present: Social Movements and Individual Needs in Contemporary Society*. London: Hutchinson.
50. Watch Greta Thunberg's climate speech in Bristol - as it happened. (2020, 28 February). *The Guardian*. https://www.theguardian.com/environment/2020/feb/28/watch-greta-thunbergs-climate-speech-in-bristol-live (last accessed 27 November 2025).
51. Western, S. (2014). Autonomist leadership in leaderless movements: Anarchists leading the way. *Ephemera: Theory & Politics in Organization, 14*(4): 673–698.

Chapter 10

52. Czachor, E. M. (2022, November 9). 'Florida is where woke goes to die,' Gov. Ron DeSantis says after reelection victory. *CBS News*. https://www.cbsnews.com/news/ron-desantis-florida-where-woke-goes-to-die-midterm-election-win/ (last accessed 27 November 2025).

53. Wingate, S. (2022, July 29). Rishi Sunak vows to tackle 'woke nonsense' and 'left-wing agitators'. *The Independent.* https://independent.co.uk/news/uk/rishi-sunak-liz-truss-british-conservative-party-english-b2134501.html (last accessed 27 November 2025).
54. Hatterstone, S. (2022, August 15). Dear Liz Truss: I'm woke, not business-minded and a leftwinger. Am I not your type of Jew? *The Guardian.* https://www.theguardian.com/commentisfree/2022/aug/15/liz-truss-woke-jew-jewish-community
55. Lee, B. (2020, December 6). Congresswoman Barbara Lee: Resisting the rise of hatred in the era of Trump. *Essence.* https://www.essence.com/news/congresswoman-barbara-lee-rise-hate-crimes-trump-presidency/ (last accessed 27 November 2025).
56. Ghazail, R., & Shennan, R. (2021, April 27). What does woke mean? Definition of woke culture in 2024—and what critics mean by 'woke police'. *National World.* https://www.nationalworld.com/whats-on/arts-and-entertainment/what-does-woke-mean-definition-woke-culture-2024-3215758 (last accessed 27 November 2025).
57. This is called surplus enjoyment, or *plus-de-jouir* in Lacanian psychoanalysis.

Chapter 11

58. Festinger, L. (1957). *A Theory of Cognitive Dissonance.* Redwood City, CA: Stanford University Press eBooks. https://doi.org/10.1515/9781503620766
59. Li, P. P. (2012). Toward an integrative framework of indigenous research: The geocentric implications of yin-yang balance. *Asia Pacific Journal of Management, 29*: 849–872.
60. Festinger, L. (1957). *A Theory of Cognitive Dissonance.* Redwood City, CA: Stanford University Press eBooks. https://www.degruyterbrill.com/document/doi/10.1515/9781503620766/html
61. Foucault, M. (2023). Discipline and punish. In: *Social Theory Re-wired* (pp. 291–299). London: Routledge.
62. Bauman, Z. (2013). *Liquid Modernity.* Great Britain: John Wiley.
63. Dale, D. (2024, June 6). Fact-check: Donald Trump makes false claim about babies and abortion. *CNN.* https://edition.cnn.com/2024/06/06/politics/fact-check-donald-trump-abortion-babies-executed/index.htm (last accessed 2 November 2024).
64. TERF = trans-exclusionary radical feminist, a derogatory term used to identify those viewed as hostile to transgender people.
65. Rohr, R. (2024, July 29). A reign of peace and harmony. Center for Action and Contemplation. https://cac.org/daily-meditations/a-reign-of-peace-and-harmony/ (last accessed 23 February 2026).

Chapter 12

66. Western S. (2012). *Coaching and Mentoring: A Critical Text.* London: Sage.
67. Cobb, K. (2005). *The Blackwell Guide to Theology and Popular Culture.* Oxford, UK: Blackwell.
68. Stavrakakis, Y. (2007). *The Lacanian Left.* Edinburgh, UK: Edinburgh University Press.
69. Moscowitz, E. (2001). *In Therapy We Trust: America's Obsession with Self-Fulfillment.* Baltimore, MD: Johns Hopkins University Press.
70. Bright, A. (2009). Here, now. *The Point*, 1.
71. Wilber, K. (2017). *The Religion of Tomorrow: A Vision for the Future of the Great Traditions—More Inclusive, More Comprehensive, More Complete.* Boulder, CO: Shambhala.
72. Heelas, P. (1996). *The New Age Movement: The Celebration of the Self and the Sacralization of Modernity.* Oxford, UK: Blackwell.
73. Western, S. (2012). *Coaching and Mentoring: A Critical Text.* London: Sage.
74. Heelas, P. (1996). *The New Age Movement: The Celebration of the Self and the Sacralization of Modernity.* Oxford, UK: Blackwell.
75. Furedi, F. (2013). *Therapy Culture: Cultivating Vulnerability in an Uncertain Age.* London: Routledge.
76. Rogers, C. (1951). *Client-centered Therapy: Its Current Practice, Implications and Theory.* London: Constable.
77. Maslow, A. (1968). *Toward a Psychology of Being.* New York: Van Nostrand.
78. Berardi, F. (2009). *The Soul at Work: From Alienation to Autonomy.* Semiotext(e).
79. Duggan, K. (2024, August 19). Joe Biden can expect rapturous welcome at Democratic National Convention. *The Irish Times.* https://www.irishtimes.com/world/us/2024/08/18/biden-may-defeat-trump-twice-first-by-running-against-him-and-then-by-not/ (last accessed 27 November 2025).
80. Berardi, F. (2009). *The Soul at Work: From Alienation to Autonomy.* Semiotext(e).
81. Lasch, C. (1979). *The Culture of Narcissism: American Life in an Age of Diminishing Expectations.* New York: W. W. Norton.
82. Fitzpatrick, M. (2000). *The Tyranny of Health: Doctors and the Regulation of Lifestyle.* London: Routledge.
83. McGowan, T. (2013). *Enjoying What We Don't Have: The Political Project of Psychoanalysis.* Lincoln, NE: University of Nebraska Press.

84. Giddens, A. (1991). *Modernity and Self Identity: Self and Society in the Late Modern Age*. Cambridge: Polity.

Chapter 13

85. Debord, G. (1967). *The Society of the Spectacle*. Binghampton, NY: PM Press, 2024.
86. Lacan, J. (2009). *My Teaching*. London: Verso.
87. Donne, J. (n.d.). No Man Is an Island. *Poetry.com*. https://www.poetry.com/poem/22559/no-man-is-an-island (last accessed 2 November 2024).

Chapter 14

88. https://niamhswanton.com/ (last accessed 27 November 2025).
89. Mann, B. (2022, October 25). 4 U.S. companies will pay $26 billion to settle claims they fueled the opioid crisis. *NPR*. https://www.npr.org/2022/02/25/1082901958/opioid-settlement-johnson-26-billion (last accessed 27 November 2025).
90. U.S. Department of Justice. (2020, October 21). Opioid manufacturer Purdue Pharma pleads guilty to fraud and kickback conspiracies. https://www.justice.gov/archives/opa/pr/opioid-manufacturer-purdue-pharma-pleads-guilty-fraud-and-kickback-conspiracies (last accessed 27 November 2025).
91. Okunade, I. (2023, November 24). Green lies: The most infamous greenwashing examples revealed. *Green Hive*. https://www.greenhive.io/blog/greenwashing-examples#:~:text=the%20Competition%20Bureau.-,Innocent%20Drinks,the%20worst%20plastic%20polluters%20globally (last accessed 27 November 2025).
92. Western, S. (2025). From salvation aid to eco-mutualist aid the psychosocial dynamics of INGOs and humanitarianism. *Socio-Analysis, 26*: 52–75.

Chapter 15

93. Berardi, F. (2009). *The Soul at Work: From Alienation to Autonomy*. Semiotext(e).
94. Stavrakakis, Y. (2008). *The Lacanian Left*. Edinburgh, UK: Edinburgh University Press.
95. See Chapter 6.
96. McGowan, T. (2012). *The End of Dissatisfaction?: Jacques Lacan and the Emerging Society of Enjoyment*. Albany, NY: State University of New York Press.

97. McGowan, T. (2012). *The End of Dissatisfaction?: Jacques Lacan and the Emerging Society of Enjoyment*. Albany, NY: State University of New York Press.
98. Berardi, F. (2009). *The Soul at Work: From Alienation to Autonomy*. Semiotext(e).
99. McGowan, T. (2012). *The End of Dissatisfaction?: Jacques Lacan and the Emerging Society of Enjoyment*. Albany, NY: State University of New York Press.
100. Stavrakakis, Y. (2008). *The Lacanian Left*. Edinburgh, UK: Edinburgh University Press.
101. Furedi, F. (2003). *Therapy Culture: Cultivating Vulnerability in an Uncertain Age*. London: Routledge.
    Berardi, F. (2009). *The Soul at Work: From Alienation to Autonomy*. Semiotext(e).
102. Ehrenreich, B. (2009). *Bright-sided: How the Relentless Promotion of Positive Thinking has Undermined America*. New York: Metropolitan Books

Chapter 16

103. INEOS. (n.d.). No human is limited campaign. *INCH Magazine*. https://www.ineos.com/inch-magazine/articles/eliud-kipchoge/no-human-is-limited-campaign/ (last accessed 2 November 2024).
104. Freud, S. (1917a). A difficulty in the path of psycho-analysis. In: *The Standard Edition of the Complete Psychological Works of Sigmund Freud* (Vol. 17, pp. 139–144). London: Hogarth.
105. Freud, S. (1915c). Instincts and their vicissitudes. *Standard Edition, 14*: 109–140. London: Hogarth.
106. Sartre, J.-P. (1946). *Existentialism Is a Humanism*. P. Mairet (Trans.). New York: Philosophical Library.

Chapter 17

107. Haraway, D. J. (2016). *Staying with the Trouble: Making Kin in the Chthulucene*. Durham, NC: Duke University Press.
108. Crenshaw, K. (1989). *Demarginalizing the Intersection of Race and Sex: A Black Feminist Critique of Antidiscrimination Doctrine, Feminist Theory, and Antiracist Politics*. University of Chicago Legal Forum, 1989, 139–167.
109. Coaston, J. (2019, May 20). The intersectionality wars. *Vox*. https://www.vox.com/the-highlight/2019/5/20/18542843/intersectionality-conservatism-law-race-gender-discrimination (last accessed 2 November 2024).

110. Jones, O. (2020). *Chavs: The Demonization of the Working Class*. New York: Verso.
111. Haraway, D. J. (2016). *Staying with the Trouble: Making Kin in the Chthulucene*. Durham, NC: Duke University Press.
112. Bion, W. R. (1961). Experiences in groups. *Journal of the American Psychoanalytic Association*, *4*: 887–909.

Chapter 18

113. Puwar, N. (2004). *Space Invaders: Race, Gender and Bodies Out of Place*. New York: Berg.
114. Winston Churchill cited in Vallance, E. (1979). *Women in the House*. London: Athlone; in Puwar, 2004, p. 13.
115. Fanon, F. (2008). *Black Skin, White Masks*. C. L. Markmann (Trans.). New York: Grove.
116. Anderson, A. (2022, March 7). In their place: the heavy burden of being black in a white space. *The Guardian*. https://www.theguardian.com/commentisfree/2022/mar/07/being-black-in-white-spaces-racism (last accessed 23 February 2026).

Chapter 19

117. Castells, M. (2000). *The Rise of the Network Society, The Information Age: Economy, Society and Culture, I*. Oxford: Blackwell.
118. Turkle, S. (2011). *Alone Together: Why We Expect More from Technology and Less from Each Other*. New York: Basic Books.

Chapter 20

119. Nail, T. (2016). *Theory of the Border*. Oxford: Oxford University Press.
120. Nail, T. (2016). *Theory of the Border*. Oxford: Oxford University Press.
121. Osuna, J. J. O. (2022). Populism and borders: Tools for constructing 'the people' and legitimizing exclusion. *Journal of Borderlands Studies*, *39*(2): 203–226. https://doi.org/10.1080/08865655.2022.2085140.
122. Rogin, A. (2018, November 3). Trump hails 'beautiful' barbed wire on southern border in Montana rally speech, slams Tester over VA Secretary saga. *ABC News*. https://abcnews.go.com/Politics/trump-hails-beautiful-barbed-wire-southern-border-montana/story?id=58937747 (last accessed 27 November 2025).
123. Nail, T. (2016). *Theory of the Border*. Oxford: Oxford University Press.

Chapter 21

124. Drew, C., & Philipps, D. (2015, June 16). As stress drives off drone operators, Air Force must cut flights. *The New York Times.* https://www.nytimes.com/2015/06/17/us/as-stress-drives-off-drone-operators-air-force-must-cut-flights.html (last accessed 27 November 2025).
125. Boffey, D. (2023, August 7). 'Like playing a computer game': On the frontline with one of Ukraine's deadliest drone pilots. *The Guardian.* https://www.theguardian.com/world/2023/aug/07/like-playing-a-computer-game-on-the-frontline-with-one-of-ukraines-deadliest-drone-pilots (last accessed 23 February 2026).

Chapter 22

126. Western, S. (2019). *Leadership: A Critical Text.* 3rd edition. London: Sage
127. Armstrong, D. (2018). *Organization in the Mind: Psychoanalysis, Group Relations and Organizational Consultancy.* London: Routledge.
128. Castells, M. (2001). *The Internet Galaxy: Reflections on the Internet, Business, and Society.* Oxford: Oxford University Press.
129. Castells, M. (2001). *The Internet Galaxy: Reflections on the Internet, Business, and Society.* Oxford: Oxford University Press.
130. Foucault, M. (1980). *Power/Knowledge: Selected Interviews and Other Writings, 1972–77.* C. Gordon (Ed.). London: Harvester.
131. Ricoeur, P. (1992). *Oneself as Another.* Chicago, IL: University of Chicago Press.
132. Western, S. (2014). Autonomist leadership in leaderless movements: Anarchists leading the way. *Ephemera: Theory & Politics in Organization, 14*(4): 673–698.

Chapter 24

133. Merton, T. (1993). *The Waters of Siloe.* Orlando, FL: Harcourt Brace Jovanovich.

Chapter 25

134. https://simonwestern.substack.com/p/the-city-is-my-monastery (last accessed 27 November 2025).

Chapter 26

135. Western, S. (2020). Covid-19: An intrusion of the real the unconscious unleashes its truth. *Journal of Social Work Practice, 34*(4): 445–451.
136. Osborne, T., & Rose, N. (2024). Against posthumanism: Notes towards an ethopolitics of personhood. *Theory, Culture & Society, 41*(1): 3–21. https://doi.org/10.1177/02632764231178472
137. Western, S. (2020). Covid-19: An intrusion of the real the unconscious unleashes its truth. *Journal of Social Work Practice, 34*(4): 445–451.
138. Western, S. (2020). Covid-19: An intrusion of the real the unconscious unleashes its truth. *Journal of Social Work Practice, 34*(4): 445–451.
139. Taylor, C. (2004). *Modern Social Imaginaries*. Durham, NC: Duke University Press.
140. Tsing, A. L. (2015). *The Mushroom at the End of the World: On the Possibility of Life in Capitalist Ruins*. Princeton, NJ: Princeton University Press.
141. Snyder, G. (1990). *The Practice of the Wild*. New York: North Point.
142. Haraway, D. J. (2016). *Staying with the Trouble: Making Kin in the Chthulucene*. Durham, NC: Duke University Press.
143. Arendt, H. (1978). *The Life of the Mind*. San Diego, CA: Harcourt Brace Jovanovich.
144. Bion, W. R. (1961). Experiences in groups. *Journal of the American Psychoanalytic Association, 4*: 887–909.

Chapter 27

145. Gramsci, A. (1971). *Selections from the Prison Notebooks*. Q. Hoare & G. Nowell-Smith (Eds. & Trans.). London: Lawrence Wishart.
146. McMahon, M. (2025). Roar of relational peoples. *AlterNative: An International Journal of Indigenous Peoples, 21*(1): 178–187. https://journals.sagepub.com/doi/10.1177/11771801241310310
147. Latour, B. (2018). *Down to Earth: Politics in the New Climatic Regime*. Hoboken, NJ: John Wiley & Sons.

Index